Managing Mental Illness
After COVID-19 Infection

Managing Mental Illness After COVID-19 Infection

Edited by Stephanie A. Collier, MD, MPH

Contents

List of Contributors

Carmen Black
Department of Psychiatry
Yale School of Medicine
New Haven
CT, USA

Mallory Bryant
Department of Medicine
Vanderbilt University Medical Center
Nashville
TN, USA

Stephanie A. Collier
Harvard Medical School
Boston, MA, 02115 and McLean Hospital
Belmont
MA, 02478, USA

Drew Cumming
Department of Psychiatry
Massachusetts General Hospital
Boston
MA, USA

Virmarie Diaz Fernandez
Concert Health
Orange Park
FL, USA

Maria C. Duggan
Critical Illness, Brain Dysfunction and
Survivorship Center
Vanderbilt University Medical Center
Nashville
TN, 37232, USA

Joshua D. Feder
Department of Psychiatry
University of California at San Diego
School of Medicine
La Jolla
CA, USA

Gregory Fricchione
Department of Psychiatry
Massachusetts General Hospital
Boston
MA, USA

Susan Hatters Friedman
Department of Psychiatry
Case Western Reserve University
Cleveland
OH, 44106, USA

Jacob Holzer
Department of Psychiatry
Harvard Medical School
Boston
MA, USA

Jennifer Hulme
Department of Family and
Community Medicine
University of Toronto
Toronto
ON, M5G 1V7 Canada

Mara Kailin
The University of Denver
Counseling Psychology Program
Morgridge College of Education
Denver
CO, USA

Chris Kenedi
Duke University Medical Center
Durham
NC, USA

Helen Lavretsy
Hope Therapy Center/UCLA Medical
School Integrative Psychiatry
Burbank
CA, 91502, USA

Sarah Nguyen
Department of Psychiatry
University of California Los Angeles
Los Angeles
USA

Hanadi A. Oughli
Department of Psychiatry
University of California Los Angeles
Los Angeles
USA

Dale E. Panzer
Department of Psychiatry
Drexel University School of Medicine
Philadelphia
PA, USA

Cynthia Peng
Department of Psychiatry
Brigham and Women's Hospital
Boston
MA, USA

Alison Rembisz
Department of Psychiatry
Harvard South Shore
Brockton
MA, USA

Talya Shahal
Veterans Administration Boston
Healthcare System
Harvard Medical School
Boston
MA, 02132, USA

Megan Shedd
Department of Psychiatry
University Hospitals/Case Western
Reserve University
Cleveland
OH, USA

Stacey Simmons
Department of Psychiatry
University of California Los Angeles
Los Angeles, 90095, USA

Ryan L. Ta
Division of Geriatric Medicine
Vanderbilt University Medical Center
Nashville
TN, USA

Ana Trueba
Department of Psychology
McLean Hospital
Harvard Medical School
Belmont
MA, USA

Department of Psychology
Universidad San Francisco de Quito
Quito, Ecuador

List of Abbreviations

Chapter 1

post-traumatic stress disorder (PTSD)
Inter-Agency Standing Committee (IASC)
mental health and psychosocial support (MHPSS)
psychological first aid (PFA)
World Health Organization (WHO)

Chapter 2

Equal Employment Opportunity Commission (EEOC)
exposure and response prevention (ERP) [Table 2.1]
intensive care unit (ICU)
magnetic resonance imaging (MRI)
Montreal Cognitive Assessment (MoCA)
Occupational Safety and Health Administration (OSHA)
polymerase chain reaction (PCR)
positron emission tomography (PET)
post-traumatic stress disorder (PTSD)
St. Louis University Mental Status Examination (SLUMS)

Chapter 3

acceptance and commitment therapy (ACT)
central nervous system (CNS)
cognitive behavioral therapy (CBT)
Emergency Use Authorizations (EUA)
Food and Drug Administration (FDA)
magnetic resonance imaging (MRI)

mind-body therapies (MBT)

mindfulness-based stress reduction (MBSR) [Figure 3.1]

mindfulness-based cognitive therapy (MBCT) [Figure 3.1]

mindfulness-based relapse prevention (MBRP) [Figure 3.1]

N-Acetylcysteine (NAC)

National Institute of Health (NIH)

post-traumatic stress disorder (PTSD)

problem solving therapy (PST)

religion and spirituality (R/S)

ribonucleic acid (RNA) viruses

severe acute respiratory syndrome coronavirus 2 (SARS-CoV-2)

Sudarshan Kriya Yoga (SKY)

transcranial magnetic stimulation (TMS)

Whole Health System Approach (HEALTH)

Chapter 4

acute respiratory distress syndrome (ARDS)

Age-Friendly Health Systems (AFHS)

Confusion Assessment Method (CAM)

Critical Illness, Brain Dysfunction, and Survivorship (CIBS) Center

Differentiate Aging and Dementia (AD8)

Food and Drug Administration (FDA)

General Anxiety Disorder-7 (GAD-7)

Hospital Elder Life Program (HELP)

Institute for Healthcare Improvement (IHI)

intensive care unit (ICU)

Montreal Cognitive Assessment (MoCA)

Pain, Agitation, Delirium, Immobility, and Sleep (PADIS) guidelines

Patient Health Questionnaire-9 (PHQ-9)

post-intensive care syndrome (PICS)

post-traumatic stress disorder (PTSD)

Primary Care PTSD Screen for DSM-5 (PC-PTSD-5)

Chapter 5

acceptance and commitment therapy (ACT)

cognitive behavioral therapy (CBT)

electroconvulsive therapy (ECT)

major depressive disorder (MDD)
mindfulness-based cognitive therapy (MBCT)
Patient Health Questionnaire-2 (PHQ-2)
primary care physician (PCP)
serotonin-norepinephrine reuptake inhibitors (SNRIs)
selective serotonin reuptake inhibitors (SSRIs)
severe acute respiratory syndrome coronavirus 2 (SARS-CoV-2)
transcranial magnetic stimulation (TMS)

Chapter 6

acceptance and commitment therapy (ACT)
cognitive behavioral therapy (CBT)
entromedial prefrontal cortex (VMPFc) [Figure 6.1]
exposure and response prevention (ERP)
generalized anxiety disorder (GAD)
obsessive-compulsive disorder (OCD)
orbitofrontal cortex (OFC) [and Figure 6.1]
periaqueductal gray (PAG) [Figure 6.1]
post-traumatic stress disorder (PTSD)
prefrontal cortex (PFC)
selective serotonin reuptake inhibitors (SSRI)
ventral tegmental area (VTA) [Figure 6.1]

Chapter 7

adverse childhood experiences (ACE)
neuroleptic malignant syndrome (NMS)
phencyclidine (PCP)
post-traumatic stress disorder (PTSD)

Chapter 8

adenosine triphosphate (ATP)
angiotensin-converting enzyme-2 (ACE2)
aspirin (ASA)
beats per minute (bpm)
CC chemokine receptor 5 (CCR5)
chronic fatigue syndrome (CFS)

Centers for Disease Control and Prevention (CDC)
Coenzyme Q10 (CoQ10)
cognitive behavioral therapy (CBT)
Epstein-Barr virus (EBV)
G-protein coupled receptors (GPCRs)
graded exercise therapy (GET)
high-efficiency particulate air (HEPA)
human herpes virus 6 (HHV-6)
human herpes virus 7 (HHV-7)
human immunodeficiency virus (HIV)
hyperbaric oxygen therapy (HBOT)
hyperbaric oxygen therapy for Long COVID syndrome (HOT-LoCO)
Janus kinase (JAK) inhibitor
mast cell activation syndrome (MCAS)
minimum efficiency reporting value (MERV)
monoclonal antibodies (mABs)
multisystem inflammatory syndrome in children (MIS-C)
myalgic encephalomyelitis (ME)
myalgic encephalomyelitis, or chronic fatigue syndrome (ME/CFS)
N-acetylcysteine (NAC)
National Public Radio (NPR)
nicotinamide adenine dinucleotide (NAD+)
nicotinic acetylcholine receptors (nAChRs)
nitric oxide (NO)
obsessive-compulsive disorder (OCD)
polymerase chain reaction (PCR) test
post-exertional malaise (PEM)
postural orthostatic tachycardia syndrome (POTS)
randomized controlled trial (RCTs)
rheumatoid arthritis (RA)
ribonucleic acid (RNA)
selective serotonin reuptake inhibitors (SSRIs)
severe acute respiratory syndrome coronavirus 2 (SARS-CoV-2)
therapies for Long COVID (TLC)
transcranial direct current stimulation (tDCS)
transcutaneous vagus nerve stimulation (tVNS)
UHN Emergency Department (ED)
University Health Network (UHN) News
vascular endothelial growth factor (VEGF)
World Health Organization (WHO)

Chapter 9

5-hydroxyindoleacetic acid (5-HIAA)
acute respiratory distress syndrome (ARDS)
Centers for Disease Control and Prevention (CDC)
cerebrospinal fluid (CSF)
chronic obstructive pulmonary disease (COPD)
Diagnostic and Statistical Manual (DSM)
electrocardiogram (EKG or ECG)
Food and Drug Administration (FDA)
Edinburgh Postnatal Depression Scale (EPDS)
human chorionic gonadotropin (hCG)
intensive care unit (ICU)
intramuscular (IM)
intravenous (IV)
neonatal intensive care unit (NICU)
Patient Health Questionairre-9 (PHQ-9)
post-traumatic stress disorder (PTSD)
selective serotonin reuptake inhibitors (SSRIs)
traumatic brain injury (TBI)
urinary tract infection (UTI)
World Health Organization (WHO)

Chapter 10

American Academy of Physical Medicine and Rehabilitation (AAPM&R)
American College of Obstetrics and Gynecologists (ACOG)
attention deficit hyperactivity disorder (ADHD)
Center for Disease Control and Prevention (CDC)
cognitive behavioral therapy (CBT)
Edinburgh Postnatal Depression Scale (EPDS)
emergency room (ER)
gastrointestinal (GI)
human chorionic gonadotropin (hCG)
intensive care unit (ICU)
Maternal COVID-19-related Prenatal Exposure (MOM-COPE)
messenger ribonucleic acid (mRNA)
neonatal intensive care unit (NICU)
Patient Health Questionairre-9 (PHQ-9)

postural orthostatic tachycardia syndrome (POTS)
respiratory syncytial virus (RSV)
selective serotonin reuptake inhibitors (SSRIs)
World Health Organization (WHO)

Chapter 11

American Academy of Physical Medicine and Rehabilitation (AAPM&R)
anorexia nervosa (AN)
attention deficit hyperactivity disorder (ADHD)
Centers for Disease Control (CDC)
central nervous system (CNS)
child-parent psychotherapy (CPP)
cognitive behavioral therapy (CBT)
DIR-Floortime (Developmental, Individual-differences, and Relationship-based model)
Diagnostic and Statistical Manual of Mental Disorders, Fifth Edition, Text
    Revision (DSM-5TR)
electroconvulsive therapy (ECT)
gastrointestinal (GI)
generalized anxiety disorder (GAD)
Hungry, Angry, Lonely, Tired (HALT mnemonic)
irritable bowel syndrome (IBS)
obsessive-compulsive disorder (OCD)
parent-child interaction therapy (PCIT)
Patient-Reported Outcomes Measurement Information System (PROMIS measures)
Pediatric Symptom Checklist-17 (PSC-17)
post-traumatic stress disorder (PTSD)
postural orthostatic tachycardia syndrome (POTS)
respiratory syncytial virus (RSV)
serotonin-specific reuptake inhibitor (SSRI)
trauma-focused cognitive behavioral therapy (TF-CBT)

Chapter 12

generalized anxiety disorder (GAD)
major depressive disorder (MDD)
obsessive-compulsive disorder (OCD)
polycystic ovary syndrome (PCOS)
serotonin-norepinephrine reuptake inhibitors (SNRIs)
selective serotonin reuptake inhibitors (SSRIs)
tricyclic antidepressants (TCAs)

1

Introduction

Stephanie A. Collier

Harvard Medical School, Boston, MA, 02115 and McLean Hospital, Belmont, MA, 02478, USA

Every few years, our communities face trials that test our collective spirit and resilience. It could be dealing with the aftermath of a hurricane or flood, or the heartbreak of losing someone close to us. These situations push us to our limits. Lately, we have found ourselves in the grips of an entirely different beast – a pandemic that has changed how we live every day. As variants of COVID-19 circulate across the globe, they challenge not only our physical health but also our mental well-being. For some, the virus has been a direct catalyst for mental illness.

Understanding the link between an infection and its mental health effects is tricky. The brain is a complex organ with approximately 100 billion nerve cells (neurons) weaving a network of 100 trillion connections. It is within this dense network that we are beginning to understand many of the factors affecting the presentation of disease. How does an infection that leads to fever, cough, and difficulty breathing cause mental disorders? More importantly, how can we harness the latest body of research to improve mental health outcomes?

Year after year, healthcare professionals across disciplines – doctors, nurses, and therapists – are expanding our toolkit for treating the mental health consequences of this virus. Treating mental illness requires more than just a pill. Healthcare professionals are listening to your experiences to find the best treatments for you.

What Are the Effects of COVID-19 on Mental Health?

The reach of COVID-19 extends far beyond its immediate physical toll, touching various aspects of mental health. You have likely seen how infection can lead to drastically different physical symptoms in people around you. In terms of mental health,

COVID-19 infection can cause or contribute to virtually every psychiatric disorder. Some people may experience anxiety or depression as a result of infection. Others develop post-traumatic stress disorder (PTSD) following a traumatic experience, like a stay in the intensive care unit. Others struggle with the physical effects of the virus, such as fatigue and ongoing difficulties breathing, which affect their mood and motivation.

The line between a "normal" response to stress and a "pathological" one is often blurred. Diagnostic criteria, or how we make a diagnosis based on a person's symptoms, also change over time. What classifies as a mental disorder varies across cultures. This is important, as clinicians can cause harm when applying a diagnostic label that does not fit a person's explanatory model of their symptoms. While this book organizes chapters around common psychiatric diagnoses, we acknowledge the diverse experiences of our readers. Symptoms do not always fit neatly into diagnostic categories.

The downstream effects of COVID-19 infection on a person's mental health can be life-changing, even if they do not culminate in a full-blown psychiatric illness. Yet, interventions can significantly alleviate distress. Recall the early pandemic days: the paradox of social isolation at a time when connection was most needed led to a spike in loneliness, particularly among older adults and people living with disabilities. While not "sick" in the traditional sense, their distress was sky-high – and certain actions may have reduced their distress.

Many of us have experienced grief and loss, often multiple losses, as the virus devastated our communities. Grief is the most natural response to a significant loss, and *it does not require treatment*. However, we can still bear witness and support those in the throes of mourning – this book aims to guide you in that process.

Addressing mental illness in the era of COVID-19 requires us to consider both psychological and social dimensions. The pandemic's disruption has ushered in economic turmoil for countless individuals, who may now be facing job insecurity and financial hardships. We cannot think about interventions and treatment without recognizing barriers of care around the globe.

In spite of numerous efforts and campaigns, mental illness remains feared and stigmatized. Discrimination in the face of the pandemic prevented those struggling with mental distress from receiving the help and support they needed. Psychiatric complications from COVID-19 have left many people shunned, shackled, and struggling to regain functioning.

Navigating Community Resources

Patients frequently ask me where to find support. This book aims to be practical, with chapters providing additional resources. In addition to trying out different interventions and treatments, I encourage readers to connect with mental health professionals. I understand that navigating community resources can be daunting, and it is influenced by geographical and logistical factors. Here is a primer on finding the right level of care:

- Outpatient clinics
  - Provide medical care and monitoring following COVID-19 infection
  - Appointments are usually in-person but may be remote
- Telemedicine and telepsychiatry
  - Deliver clinical and mental healthcare from a patient's home
  - Are often more practical for the patient
- Integrated care
  - A team approach involving primary care clinicians, behavioral health clinicians, and oftentimes social workers
- Rehabilitation centers
  - Improve both cognitive and physical effects of the virus
  - Include physical therapy, occupational therapy, and other rehabilitative services
- Home health services
  - Provide rehabilitation and care in a person's home
- Community support groups
  - Allow people to connect with others to share experiences
  - Helpful for learning about coping strategies

Key Messages in Managing Mental Illnesses Due to COVID-19

In the maze of today's information overload, pinpointing trustworthy information can be challenging. Thankfully, for medicine and public health, there are a number of organizations that you can trust. For people interested in addressing the mental health effects of COVID-19 infection, the World Health Organization (WHO) is a good starting point. The WHO provides key messages on the management of mental illnesses, including guides for specific groups, such as children and older adults.

The Inter-Agency Standing Committee (IASC), which is composed of United Nations agencies and other humanitarian organizations, also provides excellent briefings on key mental health and psychosocial support (MHPSS) to prevent and treat mental illnesses in the wake of COVID-19 (IASC 2020, pp. 2–7). The IASC bases their guidance on a pyramid of interventions that starts with the essentials – access to food, shelter, and healthcare – and builds up to specialized support by mental health specialists. For those involved in prioritizing mental health resources, this multilayered COVID-19 response strategy includes:

1) **Securing the basics**: Ensuring everyone has access to essential needs such as food, shelter, and healthcare, and feels safe in their environment.
2) **Building support systems**: Strengthening the networks that bind us, be it through family and community supports.
3) **Cultivating community resilience**: Empowering community members to support each other's well-being, essentially training them to be the first line of psychological support.
4) **Providing specialized care**: Recognizing and addressing the needs of those with more complex mental health challenges, ensuring they have access to the expert care they require.

Psychological First Aid (PFA)

While psychological first aid (PFA) is not a new concept, its application has never been more critical. The World Health Organization, and many other organizations, champion PFA as a frontline psychosocial support – one simple enough that anyone can learn, yet robust enough to make a difference in the immediate aftermath of trauma (World Health Organization, World Trauma Foundation and World Vision International 2011). The essence of PFA is active listening, but it is more than just hearing the accounts and distress of someone in crisis. It is about validating experiences without judgment, offering a stabilizing presence during upheaval.

PFA's utility has expanded amid COVID-19, requiring innovative delivery methods. You can deliver it *via* telehealth platforms, ensuring continuity of care while adhering to infection control protocols. It is also able to address the unique stressors of the pandemic head-on, such as the challenges of living in lockdown and quarantine, the effects of prolonged isolation, anxiety about viral exposure, and the sorrow of losing loved ones.

One of PFA's core functions is informational: demystifying COVID-19 to reduce fear and counteract misinformation. Moreover, PFA empowers individuals by tapping into their strengths and local support systems for better coping. It also connects them with essential services, ranging from medical and mental health services to financial and food assistance.

Purpose of this Book

This book explores how COVID-19 impacts mental health, moving beyond the neurological effects to consider the full scope of mental illness. It examines the complex mix of environment, genetics, social support, existing medical conditions, and pandemic-induced stress affecting mental health and resilience.

A person's mental state can influence all body systems. For example, social isolation can weaken the immune system and reduce resistance to infections. Enhancing social connections, even during isolation, can mitigate loneliness while lowering the risk of anxiety and depression.

Interventions are easier said than done. Coming up with creative solutions takes time and effort, and most people in the depths of sickness do not want a list of to-dos (or should-dos). This book acknowledges that the path to wellness is not one-size-fits-all. What we offer are evidence-based strategies that can work consistently. We provide tips on how to manage challenging emotions, avoid maladaptive coping, and promote healthy lifestyles.

How to Use this Book

Assembled here is knowledge gathered from various medical specialties – psychiatry, psychology, emergency medicine, and geriatric medicine. Our authors have expertise in integrative therapies, forensics, mind-body medicine, and working with special populations (children, adolescents, older adults, and women in the peripartum period). Each chapter is based on the most up-to-date knowledge at the time of writing. Whether you are dealing with mood swings or anxiety, this book distills research into actionable advice, with the goal of transforming suffering into manageable states.

There is no right way to use this book. You can read it from beginning to end, or you can skip to the chapter that is most relevant to your symptoms. Each chapter can act as a stand-alone chapter to guide you and your loved ones through one of the mental illnesses caused by, or exacerbated by, COVID-19 infection.

We've studied the virus and its aftermath for a few years. We now have a better sense of what works, and what does not work, to improve mental illness and psychological distress. In this book we explore common symptoms during and after infection, medication treatments and alternative therapies, psychotherapy, and social interventions. The authors understand that most people do not receive treatment in specialized clinics for post-COVID-19 symptoms, and treatments for mental illnesses are not always available due to cost, stigma, and access. Where possible, we highlight low-cost and easily available interventions proven to make a difference. We want to use our experiences and knowledge to help you find meaningful improvement in your post-COVID-19 journey.

References

Inter-Agency Standing Committee (2020). Addressing Mental Health and Psychosocial Aspects of COVID-19 Outbreak. Version 1.5. *IASC Reference Group on MHPSS in Emergency Settings.*

World Health Organization, War Trauma Foundation and World Vision International (2011). *Psychological First Aid: Guide for Field Workers.* Geneva: World Health Organization. https://iris.who.int/bitstream/handle/10665/44615/9789241548205_eng.pdf?sequence=1 (accessed 13 Aug 2024).

2

Mental Illnesses Associated with COVID-19 Infection

Jacob Holzer[1], Dale E. Panzer[2], and Ana Trueba[3,4]

[1] *Department of Psychiatry, Harvard Medical School, Boston, MA, 02115, USA*
[2] *Department of Psychiatry, Drexel University School of Medicine, Philadelphia, PA, 19102, USA*
[3] *Department of Psychology, McLean Hospital, Harvard Medical School, Belmont, MA, 02478, USA*
[4] *Department of Psychology, Universidad San Francisco de Quito, Quito, 170901, Ecuador*

Introduction

COVID-19, or coronavirus disease 2019, is the disease caused by the virus SARS-CoV-2. It can be highly contagious, spreads rapidly, and causes respiratory and other symptoms. The clinical picture of COVID-19 varies widely. Patients can experience an array of symptoms, ranging from none to severe multisystem impairment, potentially leading to death. Some individuals may develop a chronic post-COVID-19 condition called Long COVID.

The virus is spread through droplets and particles through the air, primarily by breathing. It lands on the eyes, nose, or mouth, and lingers on surfaces. Certain patient groups are at higher risk for severe infections, including the elderly, people who are immunocompromised, and those with underlying medical conditions.

Antibodies, proteins that are part of the immune system to fight infections, can be detected through a test, indicating a positive infection, a history of an infection, or prior vaccination. However, antibody levels may diminish over time. It is known that the virus causing COVID-19 undergoes modifications, resulting in variants with changing levels of contagiousness and severity of illness (Centers for Disease Control and Prevention. 2023).

The onset of COVID-19 started in December 2019 when a cluster of patients in China developed an atypical pneumonia-like illness. By January 2020, the virus appeared in the northwest part of the US and then spread across the country (Centers for Disease Control and Prevention. 2023). Since the introduction of COVID-19 into the US and around the world, extensive research has been conducted. This research has significantly enhanced our understanding of the virus, its clinical impact, and interventions for preventing infection and reducing illness severity. There are two key interventions widely available in the US. One is the vaccine and booster series produced by various pharmaceutical companies. Vaccines have undergone modifications over time to match variations in the virus. Additionally, antiviral medications, such as nirmatrelvir/ritonavir (brand name Paxlovid), are taken once symptomatic infection has started.

COVID-19 infection is associated with psychiatric and neurological symptoms in some patients, and the COVID-19 infection can directly impact the brain due to inflammation (Siow et al. 2021). Brain tissue inflammation, called encephalitis, can cause cognitive symptoms – confusion, problems focusing attention, and memory difficulties (Komaroff 2023). An encephalopathy (general term for altered brain function) can develop due to various factors, including inflammation, low oxygen, effect of drugs and toxins, or metabolic (body chemistry) problems (Ellul et al. 2020). COVID-19 can also affect the brain autonomic system, which can cause problems with a person's blood pressure and heart rate. In addition, the COVID-19 virus can cause damage to the linings of blood vessels and increase the risk of blood clotting, which can lead to strokes (Nannoni et al. 2021) and heart attacks. Psychiatric disorders can occur as part of the COVID-19 infection including depression, anxiety, and psychosis. Patients with more severe COVID-19 infections have an increased risk of cognitive decline later. COVID-19-related ongoing low-grade brain inflammation can lead to chronic symptoms, including pain, fatigue, and cognitive difficulty including difficulty concentrating and recalling information.

This chapter will review the different facets of COVID-19 infection on an individual's mental health. We will describe how COVID-19 infection may worsen preexisting psychiatric conditions and discuss the neurobiology of COVID-19. We will consider its impact on the brain and how it results in problems with mood, thinking, behavior, cognition, and memory. We will review the psychological impact of COVID-19 including stress on affected individuals and their family members. Finally, we will provide examples on how patients and families can interact with physicians and healthcare clinicians around their mental health issues related to COVID-19 infection. We will first present three cases based on our clinical experience working with COVID-19 patients. The first two cases are of patients seen early in the pandemic before the availability of vaccines and antiviral treatment. The third case involves a patient seen more recently. We changed all patient identifiers to protect patient privacy.

Clinical Cases

Mr. Johnson is a 38-year-old man working full-time in law enforcement. He was seen for psychiatric consultation following a complex lengthy hospital course in the intensive care unit (ICU) after COVID-19 infection. Before his infection, he was in excellent physical health, athletic, and physically active. Although he had experienced a few periods of mild depression throughout his life, his depression had responded well to individual supportive therapy without medications. His infection happened early in the pandemic and pre-dated the availability of vaccines and antiviral medication. His early hospital course was marked by complications, including severe lung problems. This resulted in low blood oxygen levels that required sedation and placement on a ventilator. During his hospitalization, he developed organ failure, blood clots, and blood bacterial infections (known as sepsis). He slowly improved physically, and when his breathing ability had improved, he was removed from the ventilator. When I first saw him, he was in the ICU, awake but in a severely confused state (called delirium). Over a lengthy hospital course of approximately two to three months, he steadily improved. However, he continued to have muscle weakness, residual mild confusion, and complaints of difficulty concentrating and remembering. He was also severely depressed. He was able to discuss aspects of his hospital course (although much of it was a blur due to the sedation and confusion), and it became clear that he felt very traumatized by his experience. He told me he felt severely depressed and anxious, had difficulty sleeping, and intermittently felt hopeless. He would misinterpret things he saw and heard in his room, although he denied experiencing formed hallucinations. He had passive thoughts about whether life was worth living, but he denied active suicidal thoughts or plans. He was fully oriented when I saw him, but he had difficulty with bedside tests of more complex attention tasks (such as sustained attention and the ability to shift between competing tasks) and recall. He was treated with a combination of a serotonin-reuptake inhibitor antidepressant, a low dose of sedating antipsychotic medication as needed, used for acute anxiety and confusion, and a low dose of a sedative-hypnotic medication for sleep. He also received bedside supportive counseling. When I saw him after a few weeks, he reported about a 50% improvement in his level of depression and anxiety and told me that he believed he was able to cope better. Additionally, his sleep had improved, and he no longer experienced confusion. However, he shared significant worries with me that included worries about his ability to work at his previous job, his home life and relationships, and his ability to engage in athletic activities.

Mr. Brown is an 81-year-old man who was admitted to rehabilitation following a complex course at a general hospital. He was generally in good health, but he had a history of mild cognitive difficulties and mild depression. He was initially admitted to the hospital in acute respiratory distress, sleepy, and confused. Evaluation in the emergency room showed a low blood oxygen level, numerous abnormalities on laboratory testing, and acute confusion. He was close to respiratory arrest. He was diagnosed with severe COVID-19 infection. He was intubated and admitted to the ICU. Following a lengthy hospital course with several complications including kidney failure, infections, and skin breakdown, he was felt to be stabilizing and sent to a rehabilitation setting for continued medical care and rehab. When evaluated psychiatrically, he had a tracheostomy (surgically placed airway in front of the base of the neck to help with breathing) and was on a ventilator. When I saw him, he was awake, but not in any distress. He was unable to talk but could nod/gesture and would "mouth" responses. He was also able to write out answers. His writing was illegible and nonsensical – he replied to questions with lines and squiggles. Based on his responses, he was clearly confused and unable to provide any meaningful history. He was distracted, and at times he would not respond to questions. He made errors when tested with basic yes/no questions testing comprehension. The nurses noted that he would get frustrated and agitated at times. He was treated with a low dose of a second-generation antipsychotic medication, which can sometimes help with acute confusion and agitation. Over his hospital course, he appeared to settle down in terms of frustration and agitation, but he remained in a confused state during his three-month stay in the hospital.

Mrs. Cooper is a 52-year-old woman who came to my psychiatry clinic with concerns about her thinking. She told me she had a long history of depression. She had previously been treated with antidepressant medications and individual therapy. Based on her history and symptoms, she appeared to have "double depression." This involves a long history of persistent low-level depression, along with periods of more severe depression, the latter responding to antidepressant medications. She identified that she had always felt somewhat depressed. When I saw her, she reported mild depression and a number of stressful issues in her life that could be contributing to her depression. She also mentioned to me that she was struggling with thinking, concentration, and focusing her attention. She thought her symptoms may be consistent with "brain fog." She told me these symptoms were not new, especially during times when she felt stressed, such as after a breakup and when work became stressful. She also reported sensitivity to noisy and busy environments, struggling more with her memory and attention in certain settings. She was up to date with her COVID-19 vaccinations and boosters. Last year, she was infected with COVID-19 and had a cough. She took a home test that was faintly positive, and a confirmation polymerase chain reaction (PCR) test was positive. She thinks she had a low-grade fever during that time but did not have other symptoms. She completed a course of nirmatrelvir/ritonavir. She reported no change in her mood symptoms since the infection, although she felt she had more difficulty with concentration and focusing her attention since the COVID-19 infection. Despite her symptoms, she continued to work, and functioned well (although she told me she felt a bit slower at work and struggled more with complex tasks).

Impact on Preexisting Conditions

The limited medical research on the impact of COVID-19 on people with preexisting mental health conditions highlights the diverse ways the infection can affect people. Many find it scary, given the potential for severe illness or death, with numerous unknowns – from asymptomatic cases to critical illness requiring life support. Additionally, there is the added stress of loneliness, isolation, and uncertainty related to home testing, as negative test results aren't always 100% accurate.

In Canada, a research study revealed a higher risk of anxiety, depression, and poor family functioning during the initial quarantine for the COVID-19 pandemic, especially among young parents with limited household income or preexisting psychiatric conditions (Hwang et al. 2022). Early pandemic data indicated a negative impact on mental health, with variables such as preexisting psychiatric conditions, female gender, and prior trauma exposure associated with increased psychological symptoms that, in some cases, persisted as restrictions lessened (Plomecka et al. 2021). In a study of military veterans, preexisting psychiatric conditions, being single, pandemic-related social restrictions, and financial stress were all linked to persistent loneliness (Na et al. 2022).

In the UK, a large study examining preexisting psychiatric conditions found a negative impact on mental health during the pandemic. Individuals with psychiatric conditions noted a transition to the highest levels of symptoms, with anxiety being the most affected mental health condition. Women and older adults were more affected compared to their baseline (Hampshire et al. 2022). Another large study addressing preexisting mental health conditions suggested that people with such conditions were more vulnerable and were likely to suffer greater psychological effects due to the pandemic. In general, people with preexisting psychiatric conditions experienced more psychological distress and anxiety during the early phase of the pandemic, with adverse impacts on specific conditions like eating disorders and obsessive-compulsive disorders. External factors such as unemployment, work stress, and financial stress were related to higher levels of distress in people with mood disorders (Carvalho et al. 2022). In another large Canadian study of the pandemic's impact, patients without a psychiatric history showed positive anxiety and depression symptoms when surveyed, while those with preexisting psychiatric conditions reported worsening anxiety, depression, and suicidal ideation. More severe psychological impact was associated with several variables, including female gender, younger age, low income, poor coping skills, multiple psychiatric conditions, previous trauma exposure, worsening physical health, and poor family relationships (Robillard et al. 2021).

When we explore the impact of COVID-19 on individuals with more severe psychiatric conditions, those requiring in-patient psychiatric hospitalizations face heightened risks of illness and death. The research sheds light on a significant need for transfers to medical units, bringing with it an associated upswing in the risk of acute confusion and delirium. Factors such as advanced age, the presence of an organic mental disorder, acute confusion, and severe respiratory illness stand out as contributors to an increased risk of death (Dobre et al. 2023). Furthermore, the medical literature underscores an alarming surge in suicidal ideation and attempts during the course of the COVID-19 pandemic (Yan et al. 2023).

No one would find it shocking that the pandemic took a toll on the mental well-being of healthcare workers. A survey looking at the experiences of healthcare workers highlighted that those with psychiatric diagnoses reported a heightened perception of negative impacts on their symptoms. This, in turn, correlated with more severe psychiatric outcomes and increased stress stemming from the need to avoid physical contact with others (MacKenzie et al. 2021). Throughout the pandemic, the research spotlight also turned toward the pervasive issue of burnout among practicing physicians and surgeons (Alkhamees et al. 2023).

Neurobiology of COVID-19

COVID-19 can infect the brain. This can lead to many symptoms ranging from headaches, a loss of sense of smell and taste (Najt et al. 2021), or brain fog. It can also lead to more serious (but less frequent) neurological complications like strokes and seizures. COVID-19 infection can also affect your thinking, which we will review in more detail below. In general, following infection people can be slower in their thinking and less accurate in reporting details. They can also struggle with complex tasks involving planning and reasoning.

There are several ways that COVID-19 can affect the brain. It can impact blood vessels, disrupting blood flow and potentially reducing the delivery of oxygen to the brain, which may lead to blockages and increase the risk of stroke. Additionally, COVID-19 can cause inflammation, which damages both blood vessels and brain tissue, further compromising brain health (Marshall 2023). Autopsy studies have shown that the COVID-19 virus can penetrate the brain, although we are still learning about the consequences of viral infection on the brain (Stein et al. 2022). We do know that combining anti-inflammatory drugs (like steroids) with antiviral drugs (like remdesivir) is more effective at reducing neurological complications than using either medication alone.

COVID-19 infection can alter brain functioning, resulting in symptoms such as depression, anxiety, brain fog, memory difficulties, and fatigue. The virus is thought to enter the brain by different routes, including the nasal passages, the respiratory tract, and to a lesser extent, through the eyes. Brain fog is thought to result from the immune response and inflammation. People experiencing brain fog may have difficulty with memory, attention, concentration, or decision-making. They may feel confused at times or struggle with their usual activities. Research has shown that, although it is not common for the virus to invade the brain, even mild COVID19 cases can negatively impact the brain (Kumar et al. 2023). As outlined above, inflammation appears to be a common pathway. We think that chronic inflammation also leads to the symptoms associated with Long COVID. Reports suggest that the immune system can go into overdrive (Ricks 2020), attacking the body's own organs, tissues, and blood vessels rather than targeting foreign invaders. Studies have shown changes in brain size (volume atrophy) and brain cell connections in Long COVID (Van Beusekom 2023). Long COVID can result in both neurological and neuropsychiatric symptoms, including cognitive decline, mood symptoms, tremors, and even seizures (Ducharme 2023).

COVID-19 infection can also damage the brain indirectly through its effects on other parts of the body. High fevers, low oxygen levels, and organ failure–which can lead to toxin buildup–can all contribute to the inflammation's impact on the brain. Additionally, reduced blood flow and an increased risk of clotting can result in serious complications like delirium, coma, and even death. Research from the U.K. has shown that COVID-19 infection can lead to a decrease in brain volume, particularly in regions related to taste, smell, and memory (Douaud et al. 2022).

Post-COVID-19 Psychiatric and Neuropsychiatric Disorders

There are important variables to consider in the association of mental health issues and COVID-19 (Vindegaard and Benros 2020). One key factor is the impact of stress, including social isolation, loneliness, disruption of daily routines, and uncertainty about the future. Another significant concern is the potential worsening of preexisting mental health conditions. In addition, there is a risk of developing new post-COVID psychiatric and neuropsychiatric conditions.

The incidence of specific symptoms varies greatly, although studies have shown that neuropsychiatric symptoms are more common in patients after the resolution of early COVID-19 medical symptoms (Efstathiou et al. 2022). There is also a growing belief that the severity of the initial infection may be linked to a higher likelihood of developing long-term neuropsychiatric symptoms, particularly if the initial phase of the illness involved reduced oxygen or blood flow to the brain. While the introduction of vaccines and antiviral treatment has decreased the frequency and severity of these conditions in many patients, many others remain at risk. Psychiatric symptoms can occur during the active, acute phase of COVID-19 infection or persist long-term. We describe the most common ones below. Table 2.1 highlights key clinical concepts or "pearls" related to specific conditions.

Table 2.1 Clinical diagnoses and pearls for COVID-19-related mental disorders.

Diagnosis/Condition	Clinical Pearls
Anxiety	• Various types (generalized anxiety, panic disorder, social anxiety) • Treatment includes therapy and medications. • Limit caffeine and alcohol. • Relaxation techniques • Identify triggers, coping skills, and supports.
Bipolar disorder	• Can include intense excitement or happiness, irritability, aggression, increased activity, elated or expansive mood, and increased energy • Characterized by episodes of depression and mania (or hypomania, a milder form of mania without significant impact on functioning) • Treatment includes mood stabilizers and therapy.
Brain fog	• Treated with cognitive rehabilitation, focus on physical activity/exercise, good nutrition, and sleep hygiene. • Medications may be indicated.
Depression	• Common symptoms include low mood, fatigue, and changes in sleep and appetite. • Ask about suicidal thoughts and develop a safety plan. • Treatment includes therapy, medications, increasing physical activity, optimizing nutrition, and improving sleep.
Insomnia	• Causes of disrupted sleep include medical, neurological, and psychiatric conditions, poor sleep hygiene, and substances including caffeine. • Treated with CBT and medication. • Exercise and relaxation techniques are helpful.
Obsessive-compulsive disorder (OCD)	• Characterized by intrusive thoughts (obsessions) and repetitive behaviors (compulsions) • Exposure and response prevention (ERP) is a primary form of therapy. • Medications are often used in conjunction with therapy.

Post-traumatic stress disorder (PTSD)	<ul><li>Characterized by trauma-related intrusive thoughts, flashbacks, hypersensitivity to sounds, and symptoms triggered by a stimulus</li><li>Treated with trauma-focused therapy and medications</li></ul>
Schizophrenia, psychosis	<ul><li>Can experience hallucinations, delusions, and disorganized thinking</li><li>Treatment includes antipsychotic medications.</li><li>Supportive therapy and community integration are important.</li></ul>
Suicidality	<ul><li>A psychiatric emergency</li><li>Treatment may include developing a safety plan, therapy and medications.</li><li>Treatment often involves family</li><li>May require psychiatric hospitalization</li></ul>

Mood and Anxiety Symptoms

COVID-19 infection may trigger a mood episode through a combination of psychosocial factors, such as social isolation and disrupted sleep patterns, as well as biological factors, including the direct effects of the viral infection on the brain and the indirect effects of inflammation. People with mood disorders may experience symptoms such as dysphoria, irritability, or severe depression. They may struggle with sleep, appetite, and energy. Others may have racing thoughts. While less common than depression, the onset of mania may also occur in the context of COVID-19 infection. Mania is characterized by irritability, aggression, increased activity, elated or expansive mood, and increased energy. There does not appear to be a direct correlation between the severity of the COVID-19 illness and the onset of mania (Del Casale et al. 2022). However, studies have shown a small but significant increase in the prevalence of depression and anxiety associated with COVID-19 compared to rates observed before the pandemic (Klaser et al. 2021).

Post-traumatic Stress Disorder (PTSD)

Survivors of severe COVID-19, in particular those who required intubation or ICU care, may develop symptoms of post-traumatic stress disorder (PTSD). People with PTSD may experience unwanted or intrusive memories, avoiding situations that trigger those memories – places like hospitals or clinical environments. They may also startle easily and battle bouts of depressed mood and anxiety. These changes in mood, thinking, sleep, and functioning can overlap with COVID-19 symptoms that are not directly related to PTSD.

Insomnia and Sleep Disruption

Sleep problems commonly occur in people infected with COVID-19. Numerous factors contribute to difficulty sleeping, including stress, pain and discomfort, changes in routine, and worries. Depression, confusion, hallucinations, and suspiciousness and paranoia can also disrupt sleep.

Psychosis

Psychosis is characterized by a loss of contact with reality, with symptoms including delusions, hallucinations, incoherent speech, and agitation. While instances of psychosis due to COVID-19 infection are rare compared to anxiety and mood changes, when psychosis does occur, it may be related to direct effects of the virus on the brain.

Neuropsychiatric Symptoms

Neuropsychiatric symptoms may also result from the direct brain effects of the infection. These include difficulties with thinking including experiencing "brain fog," fatigue, mood and sleep changes, headaches, dizziness, balance problems, vertigo, psychosis (as described above), and nerve pain (called neuropathy). Neuropsychiatric symptoms are common and can persist after infection. It appears individuals experience a particularly high rate of insomnia, fatigue, cognitive symptoms and anxiety in the months after COVID-19 infection (Badenoch et al. 2022).

Suicide

There is an association between a higher risk of suicide and Long COVID (Yan et al. 2023). As reviewed, Long COVID can encompass a number of symptoms, including depression, anxiety, PTSD, sleep disruption, fatigue, pain, and difficulties with thinking and memory. Some research reports have specifically found an association between Long COVID, cognitive symptoms, and suicide risk (Sher 2023).

Cognition

Brain fog is not a medical condition, but rather a general term used to describe various difficulties with thinking and memory in the setting of a number of medical conditions and situations (Benisek and Ratini 2023). This term includes problems with concentration, attention, memory, and organization. As described in the clinical case above, a person may experience sensitivity or increased difficulty concentrating and functioning in a noisy, busy environment. They may experience slowed thinking, or they might feel fuzzy or confused. They may struggle to find the right word, or they might have difficulty with decision-making and multitasking. Brain fog can occur in a number of conditions and situations, such as pregnancy, neurological conditions such as multiple sclerosis, as a result of certain medications, in some cancers and cancer treatments, in menopause, in chronic fatigue syndrome, in depression, and when people experience sleep disruptions (Sheikh 2023). In addition, brain fog can develop in association with COVID-19 infection. Symptoms of brain fog can occur early in the course of the infection, or they may persist for a longer period in Long COVID.

If you are concerned about Long COVID cognitive changes, your clinician may consider using simple screening tools, which take about 15 minutes. The Montreal Cognitive Assessment (MoCA) and St. Louis University Mental Status Examination (SLUMS) are the most commonly used screens for cognitive impairment, although they may not pick up many people with Long COVID, who have slowed reaction times, for example. However, if these screening tests show impairment, at least the clinician is alerted to investigate your complaints further. Screening tests are important in that cognitive impairments related to COVID-19 can persist beyond the "acute" infectious period and persist for months after, and these tests can monitor impairment over time (Vasile et al. 2023).

The American Medical Association wrote an excellent review of practical approaches to understanding brain fog and cognitive difficulties in COVID-19 (Berg 2023). A few highlights from this review:

1) Formal neurocognitive evaluation is important.
2) Vaccines and antiviral treatment can lower the risk of Long COVID and brain fog.
3) Identify areas you are struggling with and come up with a plan to manage those areas. This may include avoiding multitasking or taking notes and writing out plans.
4) Get a good night's sleep, eat a healthy diet, stay hydrated, and avoid alcohol.
5) Exercise your body and mind, and reduce stress levels.
6) Try to avoid getting COVID-19 again.

How does infection lead to changes in thinking? There are both direct and indirect mechanisms at play here. The virus directly infects brain tissue, but it is also the indirect effects, including brain tissue inflammation and various neurochemicals, proteins, etc. released in this process that affect thinking and memory. Low oxygen levels (hypoxemia) also affect brain tissue, as do infection-induced changes in the tiny blood vessels of the brain. There is also a "revving up" of the central nervous system (called sympathetic excitation). Finally, metabolic problems (such as problems regulating blood sugar, the production of "free radicals," and neurotransmitter changes in specific regions of the brain) can result in injury and affect thinking. Unfortunately, brain imaging (such as magnetic resonance imaging [MRI] and positron emission tomography [PET] scans) does not add much in terms of diagnostic value. COVID-19 infection can be associated with persistent imaging findings, but these are not specific to COVID-19 and are often not clinically useful. Research has shown that COVID-19 contributes to cognitive decline by damaging important brain regions associated with cognition and emotional regulation (Li et al. 2023).

Situational Stress and Psychological Impact

A common experience during the COVID-19 pandemic involved situational stress and adjustment, particularly during the earlier part of the pandemic before vaccines and treatments. People struggled with the increasing rate of sickness and death throughout the nation, quarantines and social distancing, concerns about the spread of infection, and restrictions and closures involving work and schools. Many people experienced isolation and loneliness as a result. In our clinics, we commonly treated patients who experienced these added stressors in addition to the clinical issues they were already dealing with. Although the pandemic no longer fits the definition of a public health emergency, and the associated situational stress and adjustments have lessened, they have not resolved (World Health Organization 2024).

There were a number of situational stressors during the pandemic, many of which still exist to some extent (Pfefferbaum and North 2020). One concern was the increasing worry about physical and mental health and vulnerability, in addition to worry about family members' health, in particular related to the risk of severe illness. During the pandemic, there was a significant disruption in services, particularly around healthcare – keeping appointments, going to the emergency room, getting tests, etc. Particularly during the earlier part of the pandemic, routine appointments and healthcare were delayed or postponed due to concern about spreading COVID-19. This resulted in an increase in sickness and death from other illnesses. Delays and cancellations occurred with routine health screenings and elective procedures at a time when clinical management of COVID-19 became a priority. A potentially positive outcome during the pandemic was the higher rates of use of telemedicine services, which allowed greater accessibility to healthcare for some. Unfortunately, it also led to delays in some clinical services (such as physical exams) and restrictions for patients without access to computers. There were also the financial stressors, as many people lost their jobs during the pandemic. The concerns outlined above – such as worry about personal health and the health of loved ones, disruptions in services (including heightened precautions and stress associated with emergency room and outpatient appointments), reliance on computers and telemedicine, social precautions like distancing and wearing masks, and increased financial stress related to employment gaps and layoffs – collectively affected the emotional state of many, resulting in worry, anxiety, sleep disruption, poor mood, and difficulty concentrating.

Impact on Significant Others

Although vaccines and antiviral treatment have made a significant difference in reducing the caregiver burden due to COVID-19, the effects of infection extended far beyond the infected. Particularly during the early stages of the pandemic, loved ones were oftentimes isolated in an intensive care setting. For many, not being able to spend time with their loved one during their illness became a traumatic experience, particularly in those who lost their loved ones to COVID-19. For many, physical isolation complicated their grieving process.

Family members also had to adapt to sharing a household with an infected person. This resulted in restrictions, such as isolation and/or wearing masks at home. The uncertainty that came with COVID-19 infection also added to the stress on the infected person and their family members, which contributed to fear and anxiety, particularly if the infected person was older or had multiple medical problems. The financial stressors described above also extended to family members, either through job loss or an inability to work due to infection. The disruption in education, with school closures and distance learning, had financial effects as well. Many adults had to stay home to be with their children during school closures and disruptions. There were also disparities in the quality of distance learning, as many families could not afford or obtain the technology needed.

Medical-legal Aspects of COVID-19

Several medical-legal questions have arisen related to COVID-19 infection and persistent neuropsychiatric symptoms. In this section we will review these medical-legal issues, exploring three medico-legal cases to illustrate some important points.

The severity of acute medical illness is generally considered a risk factor for ongoing symptoms. Failure to recognize or treat acute illness, coupled with a lack of recognition of Long COVID, may correlate with an uptick in medical malpractice claims over time – though this area is relatively new and complicated (Bilotta et al. 2020; Hall et al. 2022). Another important area of the law being seen is COVID-19-related disability litigation. Long COVID is generally covered by the Americans with Disabilities Act and regulated by the Equal Employment Opportunity Commission (EEOC). An important resource for disability related to COVID-19 can be found at the U.S. Dept. of Health and Human Services (U.S. Department of Health and Human Services 2021). Evidence shows that Long COVID cognitive changes include impairment in memory, global cognition, visual-spatial coordination, planning (executive function), attention, and concentration (Serrano-Castro et al. 2022). Comprehensive neuropsychiatric assessment is necessary in these cases since other conditions may mimic these cognitive changes. Cognitive testing can provide objective evidence about the merits of such disability claims, including the screening cognitive tests outlined above.

Mr. Jones was in his early 40s when his attorney asked about an assessment for possible Long COVID cognitive changes. He had a graduate degree and had effectively worked as a software programmer. He had a high fever and associated confusion, fatigue, muscle aches, and general malaise when he tested positive for COVID-19 using a home test. His primary care physician confirmed this with laboratory testing and managed his symptoms without hospitalization.

Within 10 days, he had significant symptom resolution and tried to return to work 14 days after his initial infection. He noticed that he had become forgetful and had difficulty maintaining focus and concentration. However, he hoped that resuming his normal routine would help him regain his previous baseline cognitive functioning. Unlike before, when he exceeded expectations, he made uncharacteristic mistakes at work. Since he knew his job well, he was able to work longer hours to address the issues, but soon, his supervisor gave him feedback that he was inefficient in completing tasks.

This led him to obtain a psychiatric evaluation. The MoCA showed difficulty with attention, recall of information, and planning (executive function) with a score in the mild to moderate impaired range. An MRI of the brain excluded early dementia, brain tumors, or infectious changes. As he worked longer hours to accommodate for his difficulty thinking, his stress and fatigue heightened and made it even more difficult to concentrate at work. Reluctantly, he recognized he needed time off to address these issues.

After a three-month timeframe of short-term disability and denial of long-term disability, a medical-legal evaluation was performed. He scored in the mild impaired range on the MoCA, which was abnormal for someone of his age and intelligence. Other cognitive tests provided further support for his ongoing limitations. A thorough review of his medical and treatment records showed no evidence of other potential causes of cognitive impairment, such as dementia, delirium, low sodium, vitamin deficiency, and anemia. He did not have other visual, motor, or sensory symptoms that could be seen in another neurological disorder. While he functioned adequately at home, he was unable to perform the higher-level cognitive tasks of a software programmer, and his long-term disability was eventually approved. This allowed him time to work with a psychiatrist, and he started medications to improve his focus, attention, and energy. He benefited from psychotherapy to manage the anxiety and despondency due to his difficulties with thinking, and which had led him to have significant worry about his future and ability to provide for his family. A vocational specialist identified specific cognitive limitations and offered him compensatory strategies.

With the benefit of further treatment, he could return to work after six months of long-term disability and resume being an effective employee. While not all individuals who report cognitive difficulty following COVID-19 infection are disabled, some need time for Long COVID to improve or resolve before resuming their full job duties.

It is also common for workers to claim disability due to the intensity and severity of their anxiety and depressive symptoms in the aftermath of COVID-19 infection. Some workers attribute contracting COVID-19 to exposure at work and are fearful of returning to the workplace. Anxiety can interfere with cognition and, when severe, limit a person's capacity to leave their home (called agoraphobia) and return to work on a reliable basis. Anxiety can also lead to heightened social inhibition or make it challenging to negotiate interactions with a supervisor, coworker, or customer. Some individuals with significant depression have difficulty getting out of bed each day and, therefore, are unable to report to a place of work consistently. Depression can also adversely impact cognition, making it more difficult to accomplish work tasks.

Many of these symptoms existed for Mrs. Andrews, a 28-year-old woman who had lost her job after missing time at work. She worked in the food service industry in the kitchen of a hospital cafeteria and as a cashier. She was hospitalized for three days with COVID-19 symptoms, and at one point, there was a discussion that she might require a ventilator for oxygen support. Nevertheless, she did well and appeared medically fully recovered within two weeks of infection. However, she remained fearful of returning to work as it was still the height of the pandemic, and she had known people infected more than once with COVID-19. The first time she tried to return to work, she had a full-blown panic attack with an increased heart rate, shortness of breath, and a sense of loss of control. She could not get out of her car to enter the hospital. Her worries about infection preoccupied her for most of the day and eventually kept her from leaving her home. When seen for a medical-legal evaluation, her examiner found her anxiety to be far outside the normal range of emotional reaction to COVID-19 infection. She was told she could not be expected to regularly or reliably work at a hospital cafeteria in the height of the pandemic. She decided to work with a psychiatrist to find medication to help with her anxiety, and she additionally met with a therapist for cognitive behavioral therapy. After a few months of treatment, she felt ready to return to work.

A high incidence of preexisting psychiatric illness complicates mental health-related COVID-19 disability claims. When the insured has a preexisting anxiety or depressive disorder, it must be determined whether symptoms are a result of Long COVID or part of their longstanding illness. Likewise, understanding evidence of preexisting cognitive decline is necessary to determine the extent to which Long COVID cognitive concerns are directly attributable to infection. These complex matters require a comprehensive assessment that includes reviewing pertinent past medical records and sometimes interviewing others for direct observations and/or reviewing employment records. Evaluation by a neuropsychiatrist familiar with medical-legal issues is often necessary to prove or disprove these cases when a dispute exists between the insured and the insurer. In cases where individuals are found to be physically or cognitively impaired, vocational specialists may identify strategies to help them improve their functioning at work.

Mr. Smith is a 62-year-old man with a long history of depression, who was seen for medical-legal evaluation 13 months after he contracted COVID-19. He had experienced a typical course of early illness with two to three days of symptoms followed by fatigue for a few weeks. He stated that he had been depressed ever since the infection. He explained that contracting COVID-19 had shown him his vulnerability, and he became worried about dying. He had regrets about relationships and choices in his life and feared he would die without remedying them. He continued to work as a carpenter, but work had become increasingly difficult because of his depression. Many days, he did not want to get out of bed, and he started to call in sick to work. He also had diabetes for which he took insulin, and he attributed his COVID-19 infection to a worsening of his blood sugars and need for more insulin, though no doctor told him this was the case. He indicated he lost confidence in himself since his COVID-19 infection and now had an ongoing sense of physical weakness and fatigue. As evidence of this, he stated that he worked out less frequently at the gym and for shorter amounts of time. He also stated that he was more lackluster and less involved in activities he had once enjoyed, like fishing, traveling, and spending time with friends. The medical-legal evaluation found no evidence of a connection between contracting COVID-19 and his reports of worsening depression and fatigue. Rather, the evaluation found that his emotional and physical complaints were more likely part of the natural course of his longstanding recurrent depressive disorder that he had misattributed to COVID-19 infection. He was not found to have a COVID-19-related disability.

Another common medical-legal concern is the issue of mandated employee vaccination. This complex area has been addressed in part through guidelines put out by the Occupational Safety and Health Administration (OSHA) (OSHA 2021). Many hospitals require employees to be vaccinated for COVID-19, or they may risk losing their jobs. This can cause emotional and tense employee-employer discussions related to concerns about the potential harmful effects of vaccines versus medical guidance. Often, it is difficult for an employer to find an alternative position to accommodate the employee, especially for clinicians who provide direct patient care. Employees may claim discrimination under such circumstances. Employees with preexisting illnesses, such as heart or lung disease, may fear COVID-19 vaccination despite reassurance from the medical community. There is also an argument that mandated vaccinations can violate an individual's religious beliefs. The proof is challenging in these cases and may require evidence that religious beliefs led to caution about exposure to illnesses before COVID-19. Neuropsychiatrists are often involved when undue emotional distress is claimed against an employer, such as losing one's job following vaccine refusal.

How to Talk with Clinicians About COVID-19 and Mental Health

There are several important points to consider when talking with your doctor and other clinicians about your mental health. Although it can be a difficult conversation, it helps to be open and honest about what you are experiencing. Try to mention all your symptoms, even if you're unsure whether they are related to the infection. It is also helpful to clarify how long you have had these symptoms and describe what they were like at their peak. Be sure to let your clinician know if any symptoms have interfered with your daily activities. If your symptoms are not improving over time, your doctor may suggest next steps, such as a referral to physical or occupational therapy. Additionally, it is often helpful to write out a detailed timeline of your symptoms, including when they started and when they peaked. Bringing a significant other or close friend to your appointment can also be helpful, as they can provide additional information and offer support during the appointment.

Your doctor or clinician can help you, not only in terms of treatment, but also in understanding your longer-term prognosis. There are a few questions you can expect. They will ask you about your previous psychiatric history and assess your mood, sleep, appetite, energy level, concentration, level of interest in things, and whether you are experiencing hopelessness. As anxiety is extremely common with infection, they may ask whether you have had excessive worries or panic. If you experienced hallucinations or confusion at any point during or after infection, bring this up, as this can help your doctor differentiate mood changes or anxiety from delirium. If you are currently experiencing thoughts of harming yourself or others, this is considered a psychiatric emergency. Let your clinician know right away, or call 911.

For many, the stress of COVID-19 infection, or the infection itself, can lead to a person's first encounter discussing their mental health with a clinician. Here are some questions that can start the discussion:

- Could my symptoms be related to the brain effects of COVID-19?
- What specific evaluations and treatment options are available for my condition?
- Why am I taking this medication/What is the benefit of this medication?
- How long should I take this medication, and at what dose?
- What are the side effects of the medication?
- What nonmedication interventions do you recommend?
- What coping strategies work?
- How can I reduce my stress level? Are there relaxation exercises I can do?
- Do you recommend individual or group therapy?
- If so, what kind of therapy do you recommend?

Many clinical settings now offer a hybrid model of care, combining both in-person and remote telemedicine visits. As clinical evaluation and management processes evolve over time, insurance coverage and clinic policies may also change. In some cases, patients who have been treated by telemedicine may be required to visit the office periodically, for example, to receive controlled prescribed medications.

A Sample Dialogue

Here is a sample dialogue to help you feel more comfortable discussing your mental health with clinicians.

PATIENT   I've been experiencing anxiety and physical symptoms since I had COVID-19. My heart is beating quickly, and I feel short of breath. I am confused because my doctors say there is nothing wrong with my heart and lungs. I've taken some notes about what I'm going through, including tracking my anxiety levels, physical symptoms, and sleep. Can I share these notes with you? What do you think about these symptoms? Are they normal?

CLINICIAN   It's great that you have been monitoring your symptoms–this helps me a lot. The sensation of your heart beating quickly and shortness of breath may be due to anxiety or a medical cause. Your symptoms could be due to panic attacks or an increase in anxiety symptoms following COVID-19 infection.

PATIENT   I'm worried because I read that my mental health issues could be related to the effects of COVID-19 on the brain. How do we find out if that's the case, and how can we treat this?

CLINICIAN   Let us explore your symptoms further to rule out other medical explanations. If we determine that your symptoms are due to anxiety, we can explore both medication and psychotherapy. Cognitive behavioral therapy is one approach that can help challenge negative thoughts contributing to your anxiety. Other helpful strategies might include exposure therapy, stress management, mindfulness, and meditation.

PATIENT   If we decide that I need medication, how much will it improve my anxiety? How do we find the right dose for me? What are the side effects?

CLINICIAN   I am glad you are asking these questions. We will go over all these details if we decide to start a medication. I will explain the benefits of the medication, when and how to take it, its potential side effects, and any precautions – like avoiding alcohol. Let me know how you're feeling with the medication at our next appointment.

PATIENT   My family wants to be involved in my care and can provide additional information. How can I best involve them? Could they come to my appointments?

CLINICIAN   I'm so glad you have a supportive family. As long you consent, they can be part of our discussions. They can provide helpful information about your condition and help me understand how best to support you.

PATIENT   I want to know more about in-person versus telehealth visits. How do telehealth visits work, and what are the policies related to your practice?

CLINICIAN   We offer a hybrid model, so we can be flexible about seeing you in person or remotely, depending on your preferences and needs. In-person visits have advantages, like adding structure to your day and encouraging you to leave the house and confront your fears.

PATIENT   Will the clinic continue to offer telehealth indefinitely? Are telehealth visits covered by insurance?

CLINICIAN   I am glad you asked these questions. While we aim to keep telehealth as an option, clinic policies and insurance coverage may change, requiring periodic or in-person visits. I will keep you informed if any changes occur.

Augmenting a Person's Social Networks for Support

For people struggling with depression and anxiety, the pandemic normalized and perpetuated social avoidance and isolation. In addition, the pandemic increased people's use of social media, which is related to higher anxiety symptoms (Parlak Sert and Başkale 2023) and a higher likelihood of developing depression (Primack et al. 2021). Furthermore, many people lost social connections when they switched to working remotely. In-person jobs provide a built-in social network that many people rely on.

If you are feeling more isolated and have less social support, changing your social habits and expanding your social network might be tough. You can start cultivating a more expansive social life by setting a small, realistic weekly goal. Consider goals such as reconnecting with friends you have not talked to in a while, joining a social club, or participating in activities like a yoga class. This way, you not only enhance your social connections but also incorporate active and mindful activities. In general, joining a social club or a class – whether it is focused on exercise, art, cooking, or any other interest – can be an effective way to start to increase your social network. These settings offer ongoing opportunities for social interaction without the need for you to organize or plan the activities. Furthermore, if the idea of being socially active feels overwhelming, clubs and classes allow you to socialize more passively.

Once you have picked a goal, try to break it down into smaller goals each day, especially if you find yourself procrastinating. For instance, if your goal is to join a yoga class, maybe today's task is simply searching online for yoga studios nearby and selecting a couple to contact. The next day, you could make those calls, visit the yoga studio, or buy a yoga mat. If your goal is to reconnect with an old friend, if calling feels daunting, start with a text or email instead. If you sense ambivalence toward your goal and feel tempted to avoid it, remind yourself of the reasons why you value cultivating relationships and feeling connected to others.

Conclusion

The onset and spread of COVID-19 have profoundly impacted people's lives. A growing body of research suggests that the virus affects the brain through various mechanisms, leading to adverse effects on mental health. This includes potentially worsening preexisting psychiatric conditions and causing the development of new ones due to the virus's impact on the brain. COVID-19 has also imposed significant psychological distress on both patients and their families, adversely affecting quality of life by causing feelings of isolation, financial stress, and job loss. Given these challenges, it is important for patients and their families to be aware of these factors and maintain open communication with doctors and healthcare clinicians.

Learning Points

- The early experience with COVID-19 involved a highly contagious virus: from asymptomatic cases to severe illness and even death, the virus's impact was notably variable.
- COVID-19 infection may result in depression, anxiety, and suicidal thinking.
- COVID-19 virus can directly affect brain functioning through different mechanisms. These include affecting blood vessels and blood flow, and causing brain inflammation.
- Symptoms of Long COVID include brain fog, memory difficulties, and fatigue.
- Cognitive problems related to COVID-19 infection include problems with concentration, attention, memory, and organization.

References

Alkhamees, A.A., Aljohani, M.S., Kalani, S. et al. (2023). Physician's burnout during the COVID-19 pandemic: a systematic review and meta-analysis. *International Journal of Environmental Research and Public Health* 20 (5): 4598. https://doi.org/10.3390/ijerph20054598.

Badenoch, J.B., Rengasamy, E.R., Watson, C. et al. (2022). Persistent neuropsychiatric symptoms after COVID-19: a systematic review and meta-analysis. *Brain Communications* 4 (1): https://doi.org/10.1093/braincomms/fcab297.

Benisek, A. and Ratini, M. (2023). COVID-19 and your brain: what you should know. *WebMD*. https://www.webmd.com/covid/covid-19-your-brain (accessed 15 July 2023).

Berg, S. (2023). What doctors wish patients knew about long COVID-19 brain fog. *AMA*. https://www.ama-assn.org/delivering-care/public-health/what-doctors-wish-patients-knew-about-long-covid-19-brain-fog (accessed 15 July 2023).

Bilotta, C., Zerbo, S., Perrone, G. et al. (2020). The medico-legal implications in medical malpractice claims during Covid-19 pandemic: increase or trend reversal? *The Medico-Legal Journal* 88 (1_suppl): 35–37. https://doi.org/10.1177/0025817220926925.

Carvalho, S., Coelho, C.G., Kluwe-Schiavon, B. et al. (2022). The acute impact of the early stages of COVID-19 pandemic in people with pre-existing psychiatric disorders: a systematic review. [review]. *International Journal of Environmental Research & Public Health [Electronic Resource]*. 19 (9): https://doi.org/10.3390/ijerph19095140.

Del Casale, A., Modesti, M.N., Rapisarda, L. et al. (2022). Clinical aspects of manic episodes after SARS-CoV-2 contagion or COVID-19. *Frontiers in Psychiatry.* https://doi.org/10.3389/fpsyt.2022.926084.

Dobre, D., Schwan, R., Jansen, C. et al. (2023). Clinical features and outcomes of COVID-19 patients hospitalized for psychiatric disorders: a French multi-centered prospective observational study. [article]. *Psychological Medicine* 53 (2): 342–350. https://doi.org/10.1017/S0033291721001537.

Douaud, G., Lee, S., Alfaro-Almagro, F. et al. (2022). SARS-CoV-2 is associated with changes in brain structure in UK biobank. *Nature* 604: 697–707. http://doi.org/10.1038/s41586-022-04569-5.

Ducharme, J. (2023). Scientists are just beginning to understand Covid-19's effect on the brain. *Time.* https://Time.Com/6294762/How-Covid-19-Affects-Brain-Memory (accessed 15 July 2023).

Efstathiou, V., Stefanou, M.I., Demetriou, M. et al. (2022). Long COVID and neuropsychiatric manifestations (review). *Experimental and Therapeutic Medicine* 23 (5): 363. https://doi.org/10.3892/etm.2022.11290.

Ellul, M.A., Benjamin, L., Singh, B. et al. (2020). Neurological associations of COVID-19. *The Lancet Neurology* 19 (9): 767–783. http://doi.org/10.1016/S1474-4422(20)30221-0.

Hall, R.C.W., Durns, T.A., Iannuzzi, G. et al. (2022). Post-COVID syndrome: symptoms, treatments, and forensic implications. *American Academy of Psychiatry and the Law Newsletter* 47 (3).

Hampshire, A., Trender, W., Grant, J.E. et al. (2022). Item-level analysis of mental health symptom trajectories during the COVID-19 pandemic in the UK:

associations with age, sex and pre-existing psychiatric conditions. *Comprehensive Psychiatry* 114: 152298. https://doi.org/10.1016/j.comppsych.2022.152298.

Hwang, P., Ipekian, L., Jaiswal, N. et al. (2022). Family functioning and mental wellbeing impairment during initial quarantining for the COVID-19 pandemic: a study of Canadian families. *Current Psychology* 1–13. http://dx.doi.org/10.1007/s12144-021-02689-1.

Klaser, K., Thompson, E.J., Nguyen, L.H. et al. (2021). Anxiety and depression symptoms after COVID-19 infection: results from the COVID symptom study app. *Journal of Neurology, Neurosurgery, and Psychiatry* 92 (12): 1254–1258. https://doi.org/10.1136/jnnp-2021-327565.

Komaroff, A.L. (2023). Does COVID-19 damage the brain? http://www.health.harvard.edu/mind-and-mood/does-covid-19-damage-the-brain (accessed 15 July 2023).

Kumar, P.R., Shilpa, B., and Jha, R.K. (2023). Brain disorders: impact of mild SARS-CoV-2 may shrink several parts of the brain. *Neuroscience and Biobehavioral Reviews* 149: 105150. https://doi.org/10.1016/j.neubiorev.2023.105150.

Li, Z., Zhang, Z., Zhang, Z. et al. (2023). Cognitive impairment after long COVID-19: current evidence and perspectives. *Frontiers in Neurology* 14: 1239182. https://doi.org/10.3389/fneur.2023.1239182.

MacKenzie, M., Daviskiba, S., Dow, M. et al. (2021). The impact of the coronavirus disease 2019 (COVID-19) pandemic on healthcare workers with pre-existing psychiatric conditions. *Psychiatric Quarterly* 92 (3): 1011–1020. https://doi.org/10.1007/s11126-020-09870-y.

Marshall, M. (2023). How covid-19 affects the brain. *New Scientist (1971)* 257 (3424): 14–15. https://doi.org/10.1016/S0262-4079(23)00189-6.

Na, P.J., Straus, E., Tsai, J. et al. (2022). Loneliness in U.S. military veterans during the COVID-19 pandemic: a nationally representative, prospective cohort study. *Journal of Psychiatric Research* 151: 546–553. https://doi.org/10.1016/j.jpsychires.2022.05.042.

Najt, P., Richards, H.L., and Fortune, D.G. (2021). Brain imaging in patients with COVID-19: a systemic review. *Brain, Behavior, and Immunity-Health.* https://doi.org/10.1016/j.bbih.2021.100290.

Nannoni, S., de Groot, R., Bell, S., and Markus, H.S. (2021). Stroke in COVID-19: a systemic review and meta-analysis. *International Journal of Stroke* 16 (2): 137–149. https://doi.org/10.1177/1747493020972922.

Occupational Safety and Health Administration (OSHA) (2021). Workers' Rights under the COVID-19 vaccination and testing ETS. http://www.osha.gov/sites/default/files/publications/OSHA4159.pdf (accessed 15 July 2023).

Parlak Sert, H. and Başkale, H. (2023). Students' increased time spent on social media, and their level of coronavirus anxiety during the pandemic, predict increased social media addiction. *Health Information and Libraries Journal* 40 (3): 262–274. https://doi.org/10.1111/hir.12448.

Pfefferbaum, B. and North, C.S. (2020). Mental health and the Covid-19 pandemic. *New England Journal of Medicine* 383 (6): 510–512. https://doi.org/10.1056/NEJMp2008017.

Plomecka, M., Gobbi, S., Neckels, R. et al. (2021). Factors associated with psychological disturbances during the COVID-19 pandemic: multicountry online study. *JMIR Mental Health* 8 (8): e28736. https://doi.org/10.2196/28736.

Primack, B.A., Shensa, A., Sidani, J.E. et al. (2021). Temporal associations between social media use and depression. *American Journal of Preventive Medicine* 60 (2): 179–188. https://doi.org/10.1016/j.amepre.2020.09.014.

Ricks, C. (2020). Controlling inflammation in COVID-19 patients may lessen severity of the novel coronavirus. *UC News*. https://www.uc.edu/news/articles/n20933513/why-does-covid-19-send-the-bodys-immune-system-into-overdrive.html#:~:text=Price%20says%20nervous%20system%20inflammation,these%20patients%2C%E2%80%9D%20explains%20Price (accessed 15 July 2023).

Robillard, R., Daros, A.R., Phillips, J.L. et al. (2021). Emerging new psychiatric symptoms and the worsening of pre-existing mental disorders during the COVID-19 pandemic: a Canadian multisite study; nouveaux symptomes psychiatriques emergents et deterioration des troubles mentaux preexistants durant la pandemie de la COVID-19: une etude canadienne multisite. *Canadian Journal of Psychiatry. Revue Canadienne de Psychiatrie* 66 (9): 815–826. https://doi.org/10.1177/0706743720986786.

Serrano-Castro, P.J., Garzón-Maldonado, F.J., Casado-Naranjo, I. et al. (2022). The cognitive and psychiatric subacute impairment in severe Covid-19. *Scientific Reports* 12: 3563. http://doi.org/10.1038/s41598-022-07559-9.

Sheikh, Z. (2023). Reasons you may have brain fog. http://www.webmd.com/brain/ss/slideshow-brain-fog (accessed 15 July 2023).

Sher, L. (2023). Long COVID and the risk of suicide. *General Hospital Psychiatry* 80: 66–67. https://doi.org/10.1016/j.genhosppsych.2022.12.001.

Siow, I., Lee, K.S., Zhang, J.J.Y. et al. (2021). Encephalitis as a neurological complication of COVID-19: a systematic review and meta-analysis of incidence, outcomes, and predictors. *European Journal of Neurology* 28 (10): 3491–3502. https://doi.org/10.1111/ene.14913.

Stein, S.R., Ramelli, S.C., Grazioli, A. et al. (2022). SARS-CoV-2 infection and persistence in the human body and brain at autopsy. *Nature* 612: 758–763. http://doi.org/10.1038/s41586-022-05542-y.

U.S. Department of Health and Human Services (2021). Guidance on "Long COVID" as a disability under the ADA, Section 504, and Section 1557. http://www.hhs.gov/civil-rights/for-providers/civil-rights-covid19/guidance-long-covid-disability/index.html (accessed 15 July 2023).

Van Beusekom, M.V. (2023). Studies add to picture of how COVID can affect the brain long term. Center for Infectious Disease Research and Policy, U. Minnesota. https://www.cidrap.umn.edu/covid-19/studies-add-picture-how-covid-can-affect-brain-long-term (accessed 15 July 2023).

Vasile, M.C., Vasile, C.I., Arbune, A.A. et al. (2023). Cognitive dysfunction in hospitalized patient with moderate-to-severe COVID-19: a 1-year prospective observational study. *Journal of Multidisciplinary Healthcare* 16: 3367–3378. https://doi.org/10.2147/JMDH.S432969.

Vindegaard, N. and Benros, M.E. (2020). COVID-19 pandemic and mental health consequences: systematic review of the current evidence. *Brain, Behavior, and Immunity* 89: 531–542. https://doi.org/10.1016/j.bbi.2020.05.048.

World Health Organization (2024). Coronavirius Disease (COVID-19) pandemic. https://www.who.int/europe/emergencies/situations/covid-19 (accessed 15 July 2024).

Yan, Y., Hou, J., Li, Q., and Yu, N.X. (2023). Suicide before and during the COVID-19 pandemic: a systematic review with meta-analysis. *International Journal of Environmental Research and Public Health* 20 (4): 3346. https://doi.org/10.3390/ijerph20043346.

3

Management of Neuropsychiatric Symptoms Related to COVID-19: An Integrative Approach

Hanadi A. Oughli[1], Sarah Nguyen[1], Stacey Simmons[2], and Helen Lavretsky[1]

[1] Department of Psychiatry, University of California Los Angeles, Los Angeles, 90095, USA
[2] Hope Therapy Center/UCLA Medical School Integrative Psychiatry, Burbank, CA, 91502, USA

John, a 45-year-old History Professor, experienced COVID-19 for the first time after attending a week-long conference in New York, interacting with people from various parts of the world. Upon returning, he began showing signs of fatigue, myalgias, sore throat, cough, fever, and poor appetite. A rapid antigen test confirmed a COVID-19 infection, prompting John to quarantine in a separate room away from his family.

During the first few days, John felt alone and isolated, experienced brain fog, and struggled with concentration. He had trouble keeping up with his teaching responsibilities, leading to feelings of depressed mood and anxiety. Opting against medications or supplements for his neurologic and psychiatric symptoms, John investigated alternative and integrative approaches to treatment. He found an online resource that provided breathing exercises for anxiety and engaged in mindfulness-based practices to boost resilience and tolerance during quarantine.

Once out of quarantine, John returned to his daily routine but noticed lingering intense fatigue and difficulty completing simple household chores, a departure from his baseline of 7-mi runs. Collaborating with a trainer, he gradually increased his endurance and activity level, starting with gentle walking and controlled breathing exercises, progressing to light household and gardening activities. As his tolerance improved, John embraced moderate-intensity exercises like brisk walking and resistance exercises. In addition, he chose to use supplements for brain health that included vitamins B complex, vitamin D3, and gingko biloba. To help with energy, he took American Ginseng and Ashwagandha. He used Valerian root capsules to manage his anxiety symptoms and insomnia. Eventually, he added acupuncture and Chinese herbs to rebalance his symptoms of anxiety and insomnia, as well as occasional headaches. After he experienced initial improvement in anxiety and sleep, his psychiatrist recommended a trial of memantine for his memory problems. Nine months after the onset of symptoms, he was able to work again. He also returned to his pre-COVID-19 exercise regimen, including daily 7-mi runs.

Introduction

Coronaviruses, a group of single-stranded ribonucleic acid viruses (RNA viruses), can cause mild upper respiratory tract infections in individuals with intact immune systems. Notably, they possess neuroinvasive capabilities and have been detected in the brain, spinal cord, and cerebrospinal fluid of individuals with seizures and inflammatory brain disorders.

As our understanding of COVID-19 evolves, it becomes clear that it is a complex, multi-organ disease with a broad spectrum of long-term effects, including neurologic and psychiatric symptoms. The neurological complications associated with COVID-19 are believed to stem, at least in part, from an exaggerated inflammatory response leading to neuroinflammation and neurochemical changes. These complications are observed in both adults and children. Surprisingly, there are currently no approved treatments specifically for the neuropsychiatric symptoms associated with COVID-19.

The Food and Drug Administration (FDA) has issued Emergency Use Authorizations (EUA) for various drug therapies, despite lacking FDA approval. This highlights the urgency in addressing the neuropsychiatric impact of COVID-19. There is a pressing need to develop a comprehensive and integrated approach to treat patients experiencing neuropsychiatric symptoms like depression, anxiety, and post-traumatic stress disorder (PTSD) in the context of COVID-19.

In this chapter, we explore treatments from the perspective of integrative medicine for those impacted by COVID-19. Advocating for a holistic approach, we recommend a multi-disciplinary integrative strategy that addresses the diverse needs of the rapidly growing population of COVID-19 survivors.

Evidence for Brain Injury and Underlying Mechanisms of COVID-19 Infection

How Does COVID-19 Affect the Brain?

In the complex landscape of COVID-19, the involvement of the central nervous system (CNS) is an increasingly reported aspect and is associated with changes in brain blood vessels and inflammation and glial changes. Brain imaging sometimes helps us identify structural changes in the brain and identify the neurologic and psychiatric symptoms associated with COVID-19. Brain imaging studies show disruption to brain integrity that last for up to three months after a COVID-19 infection, suggesting long-term neurological consequences. Structural magnetic resonance imaging (MRI) plays a crucial role in detecting damage to subcortical and deep white matter structures, as well as the corpus callosum due to COVID-19.

In one study, changes in the brains of 785 participants of the UK Biobank who tested positive for a COVID-19 infection and completed two imaging scans over a four-month period showed significant long-term effects, including a decrease in brain size, which is correlated with cognitive decline (Douaud et al. 2022). This suggests a degenerative process resulting from the neuroinflammatory events associated with SARS-CoV-2 infection. Hypometabolism, characterized by decreased brain glucose consumption, in the post-illness stage of COVID-19 also involves several brain regions, including the olfactory gyrus, right temporal lobe, as well as other limbic regions, like the amygdala and the hippocampus. Hypometabolism has also been associated with greater executive dysfunction and inattention in COVID-19 patients. Collectively, these results propose that COVID-19 can have lasting negative effects on cognition, especially in terms of attention and executive function (Kas et al. 2021).

Clinical Management of COVID-19 Neuropsychiatric Symptoms: An Integrative Approach

The treatment of patients with neuropsychiatric symptoms of COVID-19 presents a considerable challenge. The complexity of the underlying mechanisms, leading to longer-term complications and neuropsychiatric symptoms in COVID-19 patients, has made it challenging to establish pharmacological guidelines or standard protocols. Currently, no approved treatments specifically target the neuropsychiatric symptoms related to COVID-19 infection. Consequently, a balanced integrative approach that combines pharmacotherapy, psychotherapy, and complementary medicine, stands as a promising avenue for improving clinical symptoms.

As COVID-19 infection can lead to changes in thinking, behavior, and physical strength, a comprehensive treatment approach involves specialists across various specialties. Treatment can involve care by clinicians working in a variety of different medical fields, including primary care/internal medicine, cardiology, pulmonology, neurology, rheumatology, infectious disease, and psychiatry. The efficacy of a multidisciplinary approach lies in its integration, and this has led to the establishment of COVID-19 clinics nationwide, with more than 66 clinics to date.

COVID-19 clinics often adopt an inclusive approach, offering a full spectrum of diagnostic, treatment, and support services. This entails creating centralized resources that streamline access to multiple specialties, standardizing assessments and care. Such integration also allows for the longitudinal identification of clinical patterns, contributing valuable insights to ongoing research efforts aimed at understanding the complications of COVID-19.

In the following section, we will focus on pharmacotherapy, dietary supplements, mind-body interventions, and the role of spirituality in addressing the cognitive and mental health concerns experienced by individuals navigating the aftermath of COVID-19. Several medications have been proposed to treat COVID-19 neuropsychiatric symptoms. However, to date, no pharmacologic guidelines or standard protocols exist for managing these symptoms. Nevertheless, the US Department of Veterans Affairs has advocated for a "Whole Health System Approach (HEALTH)" (U.S. Department of Veterans Affairs 2022).This approach places significant emphasis on cultivating overall body and mind well-being, not only by regulating lifestyle factors like diet and sleep, but also by addressing the stress induced by COVID-19 and its resulting disabilities.

Pharmacotherapy and Dietary Supplements

Medications to Treat COVID-19

The preferred treatments for COVID-19 infections include antiviral agents, such as nirmatrelvir-ritonavir (Paxlovid) and remdesivir, which have minimal psychiatric side effects. On the other hand, glucocorticoids, such as dexamethasone, are used in hospitalized patients with severe COVID-19 and are associated with various psychiatric symptoms like depression, euphoria, insomnia, psychosis, and personality changes.

People taking medications to treat depression, anxiety, PTSD, and other mental illnesses can generally continue their treatment without modifications, with a few exceptions. Paxlovid can decrease (bupropion) or increase (desvenlafaxine, trazodone) certain antidepressants. Its use is also contraindicated in patients taking certain antipsychotics and mood stabilizers. For more on drug interactions, see Chapter 12.

Treating Brain Fog

One of the most debilitating psychiatric symptoms of COVID-19 infection is "brain fog," which generally refers to an inability to focus, with poor concentration and a lack of mental clarity. Chapter 8 will go into more detail about treatment options. Although we cannot recommend any supplements at this time, we understand that people with brain fog are often willing to try almost anything. Clinicians may also turn to off-label prescribing in an attempt to target the underlying mechanisms of Long COVID. Memantine is thought to reduce oxidative stress and inflammation in the brain, potentially reducing virulence. There are data from one trial in older adults with depression and cognitive impairment that show improvement in brain and cognitive function with memantine compared to placebo (Laird et al. 2019; Lavretsky et al. 2020).

Clinicians may also favor adaptogens (e.g. Rhodiola, Eleutherococcus, and Schisandra, Ashwagandha, and Ginseng) (Karosanidze et al. 2022), as studies indicate they may help people experiencing chronic fatigue and brain fog (Karosanidze et al. 2022). Other agents, like the combination of N-Acetylcysteine (NAC) and guanfacine, showed positive results in 8 out of 12 patients in one small study (Fesharaki-Zadeh et al. 2022). Participants reported improvement in their memory, organizational skills, and ability to multi-task with this combination. Both guanfacine and NAC reduce inflammation in the brain. It appears that guanfacine protects specific brain areas from psychological stress, whereas NAC protects the brain by elevating antioxidant levels and decreasing calcium overload.

Boosting Immunity

Oral supplements like zinc, ascorbic acid (vitamin C), and vitamins B complex and vitamin D seem to play a role in reducing the severity and duration of COVID-19 infections by boosting the immune response (Michos and Cainzos-Achirica 2021). Vitamin D potentially affects the balance between anti-inflammatory and pro-inflammatory proteins, whereas zinc is essential for maintaining immune health. Zinc deficiency is associated with upper and lower respiratory tract infections, especially in older adults, and can reduce the duration and severity of common cold symptoms. Vitamin C, known for its powerful antioxidant properties, has potential anticancer and antiatherosclerosis properties. Additionally, it can boost immunity and modulate immune mechanisms in the body.

The evidence supporting the use of supplements as a treatment for COVID-19 is somewhat limited. A recent study examining the role of vitamin C in the treatment of COVID-19 illness showed that its use was safe and associated with reduced hospital mortality (Olczak-Pruc et al. 2022). However, a research team evaluating the effects of high-dose zinc gluconate, vitamin C, and their combination found no significant differences in reducing the duration of COVID-19 symptoms when compared to usual care alone (Thomas et al. 2021). The study was stopped early due to poor results, and the National Institute of Health (NIH) COVID-19 Treatment Guidelines Panel states that there is limited evidence to recommend either for or against the use of these supplements for treating COVID-19 patients (Tosato et al. 2022; Olczak-Pruc et al. 2022). It is important to note that, by law, dietary supplements cannot be marketed as a treatment or prevention option for COVID-19. Despite the surge in the sales of dietary supplements marketed for immune health post COVID-19, we do not recommend taking zinc gluconate or vitamin C as treatment for COVID-19.

Mind-body Therapies (MBTs)

Mind-body therapies (MBTs) can be beneficial in individuals with mental health disorders, as they enhance resilience. These techniques focus on improving a person's physical, emotional, intellectual, and spiritual well-being. These skills may continue to provide long-term benefits through self-regulation with continued practice, which is of particular interest given the implications of inflammatory mechanisms of COVID-19 and the subsequent and potential long-term complications. Individuals can consider starting MBTs alone, or integrating them with pharmacological approaches.

MBTs can be divided into mindfulness exercises and meditative practices. Mindful movement exercises that integrate conscious breathing practices with mindful movement include yoga, Tai Chi, and Qigong. Meditative practices that do not include movement are made up of progressive relaxation, mindfulness, meditation, and acceptance therapies such as mindfulness-based stress reduction therapy (MBSR) and mindfulness-based cognitive therapy (MBCT). MBTs are associated with a lower risk of side effects compared to pharmacological treatment and more invasive approaches, such as transcranial magnetic stimulation (TMS), and incorporate the belief that wellness is a state of balance among the spiritual, physical, and emotional selves.

The mechanisms through which meditative therapies affect resilience and improve mental health may differ depending on the type or component of meditative therapy being used. In Figure 3.1, we present a model outlining the hypothesized mechanisms by which MBTs may bolster resilience against mental illness and alleviate psychiatric symptoms. In practical terms, mindfulness interventions play a role in reducing cognitive and emotional reactivity, rumination, and worry, often serving as mediators for the positive impact of mindfulness practice on mental health. Moreover, studies have explored the effects of mindfulness meditation on immune function, revealing potential influences on specific markers of inflammation, biological aging, and a reduction in the activity of pro-inflammatory proteins.

Many studies have highlighted the potential impact of MBTs on immune functions in patients with mental health disorders like depression or anxiety. This extends to patients with conditions such as fibromyalgia, cancer, and more recently, those recovering from COVID-19 (Yang et al. 2022). MBTs including

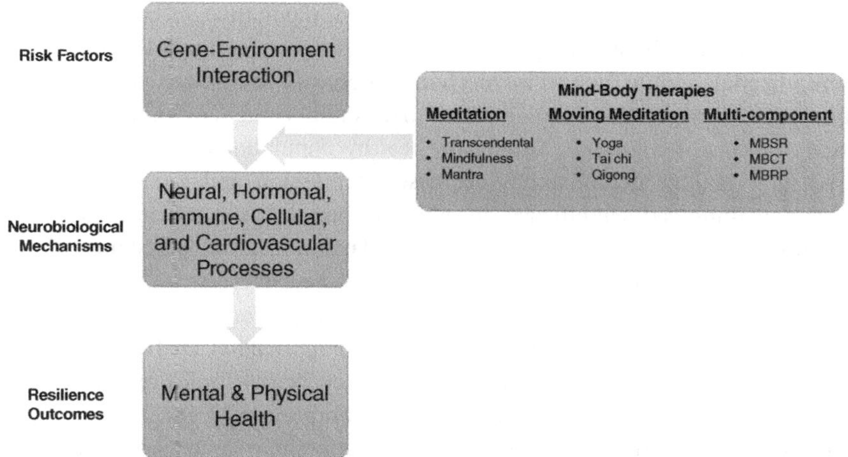

Figure 3.1 The mechanisms by which mind-body therapies enhance resilience to neuropsychiatric symptoms.

meditation, yoga, Tai Chi, and Qigong showed the strongest evidence in two recent reviews examining integrative approaches in treating older adults with PTSD, anxiety, depression, and neurocognitive disorders (Nguyen and Lavretsky 2020; Nguyen et al. 2022). Furthermore, breathing-based MBTs can help patients with COVID-19 manage cardiac and pulmonary injuries. Incorporating MBTs into a person's treatment may reduce the chronic health burden associated with COVID-19 and reduce inflammation.

Meditation

Mindfulness meditation practice brings about changes in brain regions significant enough to show up on neuroimaging studies. Meditation affects areas involved in processing self-relevant information (precuneus); self-regulation, focused problem-solving and adaptive behavior (anterior cingulate gyrus); interoception (insula), and reorienting attention (angular gyrus). The long-term practice of meditation may lead to increased "brain fitness" through increased training, and it may account for the self-regulatory abilities observed in meditators.

Yoga

Yoga is a physical discipline, which includes asanas (postures), pranayama (breathing techniques), and dhyana (meditation). The physical and cognitive benefits associated with yoga are due to mechanisms including pranayama and activation of the parasympathetic nervous system, meditative, or contemplative practices, increased body perception, and enlargement of certain brain areas such as the amygdala. While the precise mechanisms are still being clarified, the learning aspect of yoga practice may contribute to the enhancement or improvement of various aspects of cognition. Studies on healthy populations undergoing yoga-based interventions demonstrates decreased depression and anxiety, reduced stress, and improved self-efficacy. In addition, breath-based practices, such as yogic-breathing, confer benefits for cardiovascular and respiratory systems, allowing better oxygenation of the blood and brain.

A recent study looked at the role of Sudarshan Kriya Yoga (SKY) in oxidative stress and immune response and how this can be applied to COVID-19 patients (Zope et al. 2021). SKY is an advanced controlled cyclic rhythmic breathing technique found to improve stress, depression, insomnia, and PTSD. This review supported prior research showing that yogic practices may decrease sympathetic overactivity, escalate parasympathetic activity, and serve as an important therapeutic intervention to improve PTSD and other anxiety severity. Further, a recent trial showed the positive impact of daily online yoga lessons for 140 community-dwelling older adult women in mitigating fears of COVID-19, reducing anxiety, and promoting resilience and overall well-being (Pandya 2021).

Addressing COVID-19-Related Fatigue

Pacing

Pacing is an effective management strategy for addressing the post-exertional malaise and brain fog seen in patients with COVID-19. It aims to avoid overexertion by balancing rest with activities. For more on pacing, see Chapter 8. Although levels of physical activity improved in a "structured pacing protocol" in one small study (Parker et al. 2023), this protocol was based on increasing levels of exercise, similar to graded exercise, and should generally be avoided in people with COVID-19 post-exertional malaise to prevent symptom exacerbation.

Aromatherapy

Incorporating aromatherapy, specifically the inhalation of essential oils, proves beneficial in addressing fatigue and enhancing energy levels during the recovery phase from COVID-19, particularly among women (Hawkins et al. 2022). The exact mechanism of action of essential oils is unclear, although researchers hypothesize that essential oils enter the bloodstream through the respiratory system and activate the limbic system, affecting emotions and behavior.

Religion and Spirituality and Their Role in Neuropsychiatric Care

Over the past 30 years, researchers have examined the impact of religion and spirituality (R/S) on overall health and well-being. Investigators in many fields such as medicine, psychology, psychotherapy, nursing, social work, palliative care, and psychiatry have found positive correlations between improved health, wellness, beliefs, and behaviors associated with R/S. Regardless of the discipline investigating the importance of R/S, it is patients' ability to make or find meaning in the face of suffering that creates positive outcomes.

Spirituality is defined as a dynamic and intrinsic aspect of human behavior and attention through which people seek ultimate meaning, purpose, and transcendence. Meanwhile, religion involves an organized entity with rituals and practices that focuses on a higher power. Through the practices, beliefs, values, and traditions of R/S people experience and confront mortality and deep meaning. As a result, people can live out their beliefs in relationship to their self, family, community, society, nature, and the significant or sacred (Del Castillo 2021). You may or may not choose to engage in existential questions with your healthcare clinician. However, dealing with any health crisis, especially one that brings the possibility of death or chronic disability, is naturally laden with profound philosophical questions and dread. Through engagement with the beliefs and practices of any number of deeply held traditions, patients and their families are given a lens through which to confront mortality and make meaning of their experience in that confrontation. All human beings require meaning to enjoy good quality of life. Confronting an illness like COVID-19 can challenge all the ways that people traditionally make meaning.

Strongly held beliefs, including those associated with a spiritual dimension of healthcare, are linked to reduced anxiety around death, pain, and disability. A particular faith does not have a monopoly on well-being. All strongly held belief systems, including atheism (Weber et al. 2012), are associated with improved quality of life in the face of illness and mortality. When a patient believes in a higher power or greater meaning, the futility of suffering is often mitigated. In comparison, negative associations with R/S beliefs, such as a belief in being punished, or losing faith due to one's own suffering or that of a loved one, unsurprisingly lead to negative outcomes (Weber et al. 2012). Patients who believe that their illness is a form of punishment from God may suffer greater emotional and psychological dysregulation than their nonbelieving counterparts.

Psychiatrists and psychologists share many aspects of caring for patients with their peers in the realm of spiritual care. We all address the loss of meaning, existential anxieties, and the fear of the unknown. Rabbis, priests, pastors, imams, and lay ministers of all faiths and practices – even those who attend to people's spiritual needs in unconventional ways – can meet these needs through prayer, ritual, or related interventions. We often address interlocking needs, and studies have shown that patients fare much better when their care team acknowledges the spiritual dimension of their lives (Haslam et al. 2021; Koenig 2009). When physicians and psychotherapists overlook how patients are making meaning of their illness, these patients often perceive the medical profession as cold and uncaring. While psychologists do not engage in prayer with their patients, it is well within their scope to suggest practices like mindfulness meditation, or to inquire about their patients' religious or spiritual affiliations.

Biopsychosocial Model of Treatment

Providing psychotherapy to patients dealing with COVID-19 symptoms mirrors the challenges encountered in supporting patients with chronic illnesses. The emotional distress experienced by these patients resembles the struggles of those recently diagnosed with conditions marked by inconsistent or idiopathic presentations, such as multiple sclerosis, Lyme disease, or chronic fatigue syndrome/myalgic encephalomyelitis. When patients receive any of these diagnoses, reaching out to a psychiatrist or psychotherapist can be beneficial.

Navigating the complexity of symptoms and illnesses can be challenging for these patients. A lot of us place our trust in science and medicine, assuming that physicians and their respective medical specialties understand most ailments and have mastered their treatments. It can be disheartening when the proposed treatments are experimental, or physicians are in the process of conducting research to gain a deeper understanding of the patient's illness. Additionally, there is a common misconception among us regarding the relationship between illness and translational research. Many believe that identifying an illness and finding a treatment or cure are more closely connected than they actually are.

George Engel's (1977) biopsychosocial model challenges the idea of science being a pure antidote to our patients' medical, psychiatric, and psychological struggles. Engel proposed that to facilitate a patient's recovery from any illness, regardless of its origin, we must consider the biological, psychological, and social factors in the patient's life. Treating someone for narcolepsy without knowing they work nights or have a new baby at home would result in poor outcomes and neglect the context of the patient's experience. As mental health professionals, we treat people who are suffering, not just a disease process. Patients suffering with COVID-19 symptoms often face a unique set of challenges, including the potential for social isolation. It becomes imperative to introduce interventions that offer deeper meaning, such as fostering supportive connections. These elements are crucial as individuals navigate the challenges of debilitating symptoms that can confound even experienced medical practitioners.

We can use the biopsychosocial model to consider many factors affecting the health of people infected with COVID-19 (Haslam et al. 2021). Clinicians may learn more about a person's supports and beliefs by asking the following questions:

- Can the person gather support from their family or participate in their community?
- Does the person have supports checking in on them regularly?
- Do they have any deeply held beliefs that can help guide them or provide meaning in times of concern or crisis?
- Are there supportive people, institutions, or other resources in their environment that contribute to stabilizing their world? This can help address any fears they may hold or transitions they need to prepare for.
- Can their suffering be isolated to the experience of their illness? Or are they at risk of it spilling out and affecting other areas of their life, like their relationships or financial stability?

Looking at the biopsychosocial impacts from another perspective involves examining whether their home life is filled with acrimony, or challenging beliefs around illness or the body that might make their recovery more challenging. A team of researchers (Balboni et al. 2022) from Harvard's Dana-Farber Cancer Institute found that unaddressed spiritual needs in patient care are often associated with poorer patient quality of life, and addressing patients' spiritual needs is associated with improved end of life outcomes. Further, they found that attending religious services as part of a religious community lowered overall mortality, alcohol use, cannabis use, and illicit drugs use. In short, fostering a spiritual dimension in patients' healthcare not only avoids harm but also appears to improve both health outcomes and quality of life.

Psychotherapy: Acceptance and Commitment Therapy (ACT)

Among different treatments for anxiety and depression related to COVID-19 infection, psychotherapy stands out. Many types of therapy can treat depression and anxiety associated with COVID-19 including cognitive behavioral therapy (CBT), problem solving therapy (PST), and supportive therapy. Acceptance and commitment therapy (ACT) also has advantages related to coming to terms with the pandemic. This model consists of six interdependent and overlapping processes (Gibson Watt et al. 2023) that can happen simultaneously or at different times, depending on the patient's capacity to regulate their own emotions. You may already be familiar with CBT, as it is often considered a first-line therapy. However, there are a few notable differences. Whereas CBT focuses on regulating emotions, ACT focuses on identifying values. CBT encourages patients to observe their emotions from a distance, and ACT takes this one step further, by asking patients to notice when they are resisting emotions. Instead of observation, patients are encouraged to move closer to painful emotions, paradoxically helping patients manage their resistance to negative feelings.

The core processes of ACT are listed in Table 3.1 (Gibson Watt et al. 2023).

The combination of unpredictable symptoms, and sometimes a life-limiting prognosis, makes ACT an intriguing treatment option for people affected by COVID-19. For patients managing chronic illness and or pain, making small changes can appear challenging, especially for those with a history of accomplishment or high achievement. Noticing incremental improvements is a necessary part of their journey.

Furthermore, ACT can help patients in becoming more attuned to their daily experience through mindfulness practices. Defusing from their identification with pain, limitations, or distress helps patients get some necessary distance from suffering. Asking patients to reexamine their values is a critical way ACT supports them in regulating their emotions when frustrated, anxious, or depressed (and

Table 3.1 Core processes of Acceptance and Commitment Therapy (ACT).

Acceptance	Allowing challenging thoughts and emotions rather than engaging in avoidance and suppression of difficult feelings
Defusion	Identifying and disconnecting the patient's identity from their symptoms of suffering, thereby reducing the negative power and influence of challenging or unpleasant emotions
Engagement with the present	The patient is encouraged to remain curious, allowing a flexible awareness of the present rather than a rigid sureness about the past or the future
Self as context	Engaging in a contextual and flexible perspective on the self-narratives rather than a rigidly held set of beliefs about who we are
Values	Identification of the qualities and behaviors that are important to the individual, identifying for the individual, how meaningful life is made rather than rigid expectations
Committed action	Requiring the patient to take a clear-eyed examination of where they are and what they are capable of, and then in connection with the other five processes, decide what they can do to participate and move forward

ties back to R/S above). Defusing, mindfulness practices, and reinvesting in one's personal values in ACT encourages individuals to focus on the present rather than dwelling on the past or worrying about the future. Many ACT interventions take the form of metaphors, guiding patients in simple meditations or asking them to focus on observing their mind as though watching something, for example, a flowing stream with leaves floating on top, each representing a thought, worry, or idea.

Helping COVID-19 patients regulate their emotions regarding symptoms and the challenges of treatment requires a compassionate and flexible approach from their team of physicians, psychologists, family, and friends. Patients confronting these symptoms often struggle with doubts about the authority of medicine. The medical profession has yet to provide satisfactory answers to their questions of "What is happening?" or "Why me?" ACT teaches that one of the most effective ways to promote healing is for the patient to learn to be present, tolerate pain, and apply acceptance rather than resistance to stress or discomfort. In other words, the patient learns to be comfortable with being uncomfortable.

Telehealth and COVID-19

Patients experiencing COVID-19 symptoms and complications often have complex fears of both being alone and potential reexposure to the virus in social settings. This dual concern, whether stemming from isolation or debilitating symptoms like fatigue, dizziness, difficulty breathing, tachycardia, or tinnitus, contributes to a profound sense of loneliness. We can use telehealth to keep patients in communication with their care team.

Telehealth, commonly associated with internet-mediated video visits using a computer, phone, or tablet, extends beyond visual encounters. Telephone calls and distance monitoring via network-integrated data collection are also integral components (Weightman 2020). Despite barriers to telehealth, such as internet access challenges and unpredictable insurance coverage, video visits have emerged as a cost-efficient option post-pandemic.

Efforts to refine telehealth best practices emphasize a patient-centered approach, underscoring the significance of both verbal and nonverbal cues in patient interactions. This can be challenging if the clinician is not familiar with the patient's history, prompting some to begin with a standardized, short set of questions answered on a numeric scale. Understandably, video visits may be frustrating for those confined at home, yet they remain an essential starting point in certain cases.

In complementing psychotherapy, a few mental health mobile applications offer support for people with COVID-19-related mental health issues. An excellent example is the COVID Coach mobile app developed by the US Department of Veterans Affairs, which can be found at https://mobile.va.gov/app/covid-coach. The surge in downloads during the pandemic indicates an increased interest in seeking mental health support through technology. While these apps enhance convenience and accessibility, we must acknowledge the lack of conclusive evidence regarding their impact on mental health outcomes. Additionally, privacy and security concerns accompany many apps. They should be considered supportive tools rather than substitutes for the therapeutic relationship between patients and therapists. Therefore, if you find yourself struggling, it is still advisable to establish care with a clinician when possible. This allows for a thorough evaluation to find the right diagnosis and treatment, while benefiting from the human connection inherent in the therapeutic process.

Conclusion

Beyond medications, there are many avenues to explore for addressing mental health challenges related to COVID-19 infection. These include MBTs, psychotherapy, pacing, supplements, aromatherapy, and online technology. Recognizing and tending to your mental health involves confronting challenging topics like mortality and disability, and for many people, also incorporating spiritual dimensions into their care.

Learning Points

- There are no approved treatments for the neuropsychiatric symptoms associated with COVID-19.
- MBTs can be used alone or in conjunction with pharmacotherapy to treat neuropsychiatric symptoms of COVID-19.
- Spirituality appears to improve both health outcomes and quality of life.
- Treatments may take your biology, social situation, and psychological factors into consideration.
- ACT is a therapeutic approach that can help people suffering from mental disorders become more attuned to their daily experience through mindfulness practices.
- Telehealth can improve treatment access.

References

Balboni, T.A., VanderWeele, T.J., Doan-Soares, S.D. et al. (2022). Spirituality in serious illness and health. *JAMA* 328 (2): 184–197. https://doi.org/10.1001/jama.2022.11086.

Del Castillo, F.A. (2021). Health, spirituality and Covid-19: themes and insights. *Journal of Public Health (Oxford, England)* 43 (2): e254–e255. https://doi.org/10.1093/pubmed/fdaa185.

Douaud, G., Lee, S., Alfaro-Almagro, F. et al. (2022). SARS-CoV-2 is associated with changes in brain structure in UK biobank. *Nature* 604 (7907): 697–707. https://doi.org/10.1038/s41586-022-04569-5.

Engel, G.L. (1977). The need for a new medical model: A challenge for biomedicine. *Science* 196 (4286): 129–136.

Fesharaki-Zadeh, A., Lowe, N., and Arnsten, A. (2022). Clinical experience with the a2A-adrenoceptor agonist, guanfacine, and N-acetylcysteine for the treatment of cognitive deficits in "Long-COVID19". *Neuroimmunology Reports* 3: 100154.

Gibson Watt, T., Gillanders, D., Spiller, J.A., and Finucane, A.M. (2023). Acceptance and commitment therapy (ACT) for people with advanced progressive illness, their caregivers and staff involved in their care: a scoping review. *Palliative Medicine* 37 (8): 1100–1128. https://doi.org/10.1177/02692163231183101.

Haslam, S.A., Haslam, C., Jetten, J. et al. (2021). Rethinking the nature of the person at the heart of the biopsychosocial model: exploring social changeways not just personal pathways. *Social Science & Medicine* 272: 113566. https://doi.org/10.1016/j.socscimed.2020.113566.

Hawkins, J., Hires, C., Keenan, L., and Dunne, E. (2022). Aromatherapy blend of thyme, orange, clove bud, and frankincense boosts energy levels in post-COVID-19 female patients: a randomized, double-blinded, placebo controlled clinical trial. *Complementary Therapies in Medicine* 67: 102823. https://doi.org/10.1016/j.ctim.2022.102823.

Karosanidze, I., Kiladze, U., Kirtadze, N. et al. (2022). Efficacy of adaptogens in patients with long COVID-19: a randomized, quadruple-blind, placebo-controlled trial. *Pharmaceuticals (Basel)* 15 (3): https://doi.org/10.3390/ph15030345.

Kas, A., Soret, M., Pyatigoskaya, N. et al. (2021). The cerebral network of COVID-19-related encephalopathy: a longitudinal voxel-based 18F-FDG-PET study. *European Journal of Nuclear Medicine and Molecular Imaging* 48 (8): 2543–2557. https://doi.org/10.1007/s00259-020-05178-y.

Koenig, H.G. (2009). Research on religion, spirituality, and mental health: a review. *Canadian Journal of Psychiatry* 54 (5): 283–291. https://doi.org/10.1177/070674370905400502.

Laird, K.T., Krause, B., Funes, C., and Lavretsky, H. (2019). Psychobiological factors of resilience and depression in late life. *Translational Psychiatry* 9 (1): 88. https://doi.org/10.1038/s41398-019-0424-7.

Lavretsky, H., Laird, K.T., Krause-Sorio, B. et al. (2020). A randomized double-blind placebo-controlled trial of combined Escitalopram and Memantine for older adults with major depression and subjective memory complaints. *The American Journal of Geriatric Psychiatry* 28 (2): 178–190. https://doi.org/10.1016/j.jagp.2019.08.011.

Michos, E.D. and Cainzos-Achirica, M. (2021). Supplements for the treatment of mild COVID-19-challenging Health beliefs with science from A to Z. *JAMA Network Open* 4 (2): e210431. https://doi.org/10.1001/jamanetworkopen.2021.0431.

Nguyen, S.A. and Lavretsky, H. (2020). Emerging complementary and integrative therapies for geriatric mental health. *Current Treatment Options in Psychiatry* 7 (4): 447–470. https://doi.org/10.1007/s40501-020-00229-5.

Nguyen, S.A., Oughli, H.A., and Lavretsky, H. (2022). Complementary and integrative medicine for neurocognitive disorders and caregiver Health. *Current Psychiatry Reports* 24 (9): 469–480. https://doi.org/10.1007/s11920-022-01355-y.

Olczak-Pruc, M., Swieczkowski, D., Ladny, J.R. et al. (2022). Vitamin C supplementation for the treatment of COVID-19: a systematic review and meta-analysis. *Nutrients* 14 (19): https://doi.org/10.3390/nu14194217.

Pandya, S.P. (2021). Older women and wellbeing through the pandemic: examining the effect of daily online yoga lessons. *Health Care for Women International* 42 (11): 1255–1278. https://doi.org/10.1080/07399332.2021.1932897.

Parker, M., Sawant, H.B., Flannery, T. et al. (2023). Effect of using a structured pacing protocol on post-exertional symptom exacerbation and health status in a longitudinal cohort with the post-COVID-19 syndrome. *Journal of Medical Virology* 95 (1): e28373. https://doi.org/10.1002/jmv.28373.

Thomas, S., Patel, D., Bittel, B. et al. (2021). Effect of high-dose zinc and ascorbic acid supplementation vs usual care on symptom length and reduction among ambulatory patients with SARS-CoV-2 infection: the COVID A to Z randomized clinical trial. *JAMA Network Open* 4 (2): e210369. https://doi.org/10.1001/jamanetworkopen.2021.0369.

Tosato, M., Ciciarello, F., Zazzara, M.B. et al. (2022). Nutraceuticals and dietary supplements for older adults with Long COVID-19. *Clinics in Geriatric Medicine* 38 (3): 565–591. https://doi.org/10.1016/j.cger.2022.04.004.

U.S. Department of Veterans Affairs (2022). Psychological distress among religious nonbelievers: a systematic review Whole Health System Approach to Long COVID practice. https://www.publichealth.va.gov/n-coronavirus/docs/Whole-Health-System-Approach-to-Long-COVID_080122_FINAL.pdf (accessed 16 July 2024).

Weber, S.R., Pargament, K.I., Kunik, M.E. et al. (2012). Psychological distress among religious nonbelievers: a systematic review. *Journal of Religion and Health* 51 (1): 72–86. https://doi.org/10.1007/s10943-011-9541-1.

Weightman, M. (2020). Digital psychotherapy as an effective and timely treatment option for depression and anxiety disorders: implications for rural and remote practice. *The Journal of International Medical Research* 48 (6): 300060520928686. https://doi.org/10.1177/0300060520928686.

Yang, H.J., Setou, N., and Koh, E. (2022). Utilization of mind-body intervention for integrative health care of COVID-19 patients and survivors. *International Journal of Environmental Research and Public Health* 19 (11): https://doi.org/10.3390/ijerph19116618.

Zope, S.A., Zope, R.A., Biri, G.A., and Zope, C.S. (2021). Sudarshan Kriya Yoga: a breath of hope during COVID-19 pandemic. *International Journal of Yoga* 14 (1): 18–25. https://doi.org/10.4103/ijoy.IJOY_102_20.

4

Delirium Related to COVID-19 Infection

Ryan L. Ta[1], Mallory Bryant[2], and Maria C. Duggan[1,3]

[1] Division of Geriatric Medicine, Vanderbilt University Medical Center, Nashville, TN 37232, USA
[2] Department of Medicine, Vanderbilt University Medical Center, Nashville, TN 37232, USA
[3] Critical Illness, Brain Dysfunction and Survivorship Center, Vanderbilt University Medical Center, Nashville, TN 37232, USA

Introduction

What Is Delirium?

You might have come across the term delirium, perhaps recalling it as that sleep-deprived and foggy state of mind during a college all-nighter for finals. Delirium is tossed around in various contexts, but it is not just a casual term. Delirium is a serious medical condition with potentially harmful consequences. Let us explore delirium, focusing on its definition, symptoms, and why it is often confused with dementia.

At its core, delirium is akin to sudden "brain failure." The medical definition describes delirium as an acute or fluctuating change in cognition, marked by inattention, altered levels of consciousness, and disorganized thinking (American Psychiatric Association 2013, pp. 596–601). In simpler terms, it is a disorder of impaired attention that happens quite suddenly, oftentimes in a waxing and waning pattern, rather than developing gradually over time. Additionally, if your friend or loved one has delirium, you might notice increased fatigue, restlessness, and difficulty following their thoughts.

The symptoms of delirium are often mistaken for dementia by healthcare workers. Dementia is a syndrome that progressively impairs thinking and memory, affecting a person's ability to function independently over time. In contrast to delirium, dementia usually develops gradually over time. Mistaking a confused patient for having dementia, or dismissing it as a consequence of aging, is a critical error for healthcare workers. This misjudgment can lead to serious consequences, as a delayed recognition of delirium can lead to serious medical complications and an increased risk of death.

Delirium does not present the same way in every person. It is commonly classified based on arousal levels into three types: hypoactive, hyperactive, and mixed. Hypoactive delirium, also known as quiet delirium, may make individuals appear drowsy or sedated, with reduced movement and limited communication (Neufeld and Thomas 2013). They may decline food, medications, and physical therapy. Unfortunately, its subtle presentation often leads to misinterpretation as fatigue or depression, resulting in more than half of cases being overlooked (Oldham et al. 2018). On the other hand, hyperactive delirium, characterized by restlessness, pulling at catheters and lines, and aggressive behaviors, is rarer than one might think. Most people with delirium have mixed delirium, with both hypoactivity and hyperactivity happening within minutes to hours of each other (Neufeld and Thomas 2013).

What Causes Delirium?

Understanding the causes of delirium is important because it is the first step in treating delirium. It is akin to addressing an overflowing kitchen sink – you do not grab your mop first. Instead, you ask: why is the sink overflowing? You identify the faucet as the source and promptly turn it off. But finding the cause of delirium is trickier than locating a running faucet. Typically, delirium is caused by multiple factors rather than a single culprit.

These factors fall into two main categories: predisposing and precipitating factors (Inouye et al. 2014). Predisposing factors are existing conditions in your usual state of health that increase your risk of delirium. Examples of predisposing and precipitating factors are listed in Table 4.1. Predisposing factors include older age ($\geq$75 years), dementia, functional impairment (requiring assistance with self-care), sensory impairment (e.g. vision difficulties and hearing loss), depression, history of alcohol misuse, and excessive medications (polypharmacy).

On the other hand, precipitating factors are new triggers that may set off delirium. Examples include medications that affect the brain (psychoactive medications) or induce drowsiness (sedative-hypnotic medications), sleep deprivation, physical restraints, bladder catheters, organ failure, electrolyte problems, infections, surgeries, and acute hospitalizations.

Predisposing and precipitating factors interact with each other in a way that a highly vulnerable patient with many predisposing factors can develop delirium with only minimal precipitating factors. In contrast, a robust individual without

Table 4.1 Common predisposing and precipitating risk factors for delirium.

Predisposing risk factors	Precipitating risk factors
Advanced age ($\geq$75 years)	Medications (psychoactive, sedative-hypnotic)
Cognitive impairment/dementia	Physical restraints
Functional impairment	Bladder catheters
Sensory impairment (e.g. vision, hearing)	Organ failure/electrolyte problems
Depression	Infections
History of alcohol misuse	Surgeries
Polypharmacy	Hospitalizations

predisposing factors typically requires exposure to many more precipitating factors to develop delirium (Inouye et al. 2014).

Let us consider the car you have just inherited from your great-uncle Albert. Albert drove that rear-wheel drive car 100 000 mi on one set of tires that never saw a rotation or replacement. Imagine the worn-down tread on those tires. Now, when this car cruises at 25 mph on roads with just an eighth of an inch of rain, it loses traction and spins out of control. Contrast this with your all-wheel-drive truck, equipped with brand new tires. This truck resists spinning out of control until it drives 100 mph over 2-inch puddles of water. The predisposing factors in this scenario are the rear-wheel drive (as opposed to all-wheel drive) and Albert's worn-down tire tread (compared to your new tires). The precipitating factors are the speed of the car and the depth of water. It takes fewer precipitating factors to cause a disaster in a system that has more predisposing factors.

Here are a few examples. Consider an older adult with severe dementia, bed-bound at baseline and living at a long-term care facility. This individual can become delirious with a seemingly simple trigger like constipation. On the other hand, a young and healthy patient may require much more to become delirious: a prolonged stay in the intensive care unit (ICU), a severe infection, reliance on a breathing machine, multi-organ failure, and sedation. The accumulation of predisposing risk factors comes with aging, which puts older adults at increased risk for delirium. In older adults, it is important to recognize that nearly anything can act as a precipitating factor for delirium.

What do we know about what is happening in the brain at the microscopic level to cause delirium? Due to the multiple complex factors that can lead to delirium, each episode of delirium is likely to have its own unique combination of pathophysiologic causes. These causes can vary from one episode to another and from person to person. It is unlikely that a single, definitive mechanism explains all cases of delirium (Inouye et al. 2014). Instead, growing evidence suggests that various combinations of biological factors interact in the brain, disrupting its large-scale communication networks and causing sudden problems with thinking and memory (Watt et al. 2012). These biological factors include imbalances of neurotransmitters (brain chemicals), inflammation (immune system storms), physical stressors, metabolic problems, electrolyte disorders, and genetic factors (Inouye et al. 2014).

How Common Is Delirium?

While delirium can occur in any setting, it is very common in the hospital. It affected a significant portion of patients even before the onset of the COVID-19 pandemic. In intensive care and palliative units, it has been shown to affect 70–80% of patients, while up to 35% of older adults in medical and surgical units experience delirium (Oldham et al. 2018). In the emergency department, delirium affects up to 20% of older adults (Barron and Holmes 2013).

During the pandemic, delirium commonly affected hospitalized patients with COVID-19. Among older adults with COVID-19 in the emergency department, delirium affected 28% of patients and was regularly seen without the typical signs and symptoms of a respiratory infection, such as fever and shortness of breath (Kennedy et al. 2020). Up to two-thirds of patients with COVID-19-induced acute respiratory distress syndrome (ARDS), a life-threatening lung condition characterized by inflammation and fluid in the lungs, reportedly had delirium (Helms et al. 2020). Studies done primarily during the early pandemic yielded mixed results for rates of delirium. However, a recent study extending beyond the early pandemic phase demonstrated significantly increased delirium rates (Reppas-Rindlisbacher et al. 2023). This study also pointed to an increased use of newly prescribed antipsychotics and benzodiazepines after hospital discharge, two classes of medications commonly used to temporarily treat delirium symptoms that are only meant for short-term use.

The COVID-19 pandemic has been aptly described as a "delirium factory." Several factors contributed to the increased risk for delirium during the pandemic. First, the COVID-19 virus itself is not confined to the respiratory system; it can invade the central nervous system (CNS), which houses the brain. This invasion can cause inflammation, akin to an "immune system storm," in the brain, potentially leading to delirium. Beyond the direct impact of the virus on the brain, COVID-19 can cause other medical consequences known to be delirium triggers. These include extended periods on a breathing machine, prolonged immobilization in bed, multi-organ failure, and use of medications that pose potential harm to the brain, such as antipsychotics and sedatives (Inouye 2021).

In addition to the physiological impact of the virus, infection control measures introduced environmental factors that further elevated the risk of delirium in patients. Visitor restrictions isolated patients from their support networks, separating them from family members and caregivers. Healthcare providers, in an effort to minimize exposure and preserve personal protective equipment, limited their time with patients, resulting in isolation of patients from the very individuals providing care. The use of personal protective equipment like gowns, masks, and eye protection, further compounded the communication challenge by obscuring faces and muffling voices. This made communication especially cumbersome and confusing, especially for patients with hearing or vision impairments (Inouye 2021).

Public Health Impacts of Delirium

Delirium poses a substantial health risk, extending beyond its immediate impact on thinking and memory. It increases the risk for death, with patients experiencing delirium in the hospital facing mortality rates ranging from 25% to 33% (Witlox et al. 2010). The threat of death persists even after the hospital, remaining elevated for up to two years after discharge. The severity of this risk has been quantified best in the ICU, where for every day affected by delirium, the risk of death increases by 10% (Vasilevskis et al. 2010). Survivors of delirium also experience a myriad of complications. They are more likely to fall, acquire an infection, remain on a breathing machine longer, stay in the hospital and ICU longer, and experience readmissions after discharge from the hospital (Ely et al. 2004).

The repercussions of delirium extend beyond the hospital stay. Delirium affects a person's thinking and memory, mood, and overall function well after hospitalization discharge. In ICU survivors, this is known as post-intensive care syndrome (PICS), which is a collection of new or worsening changes in cognitive (i.e. memory and thinking), psychological, and physical function that persist after a period of critical illness, continuing after hospitalization. Patients can experience memory and thinking problems beyond the initial episode of delirium, and these symptoms may last for years. Disturbingly, the odds of developing dementia skyrocket by 12.5 times after an episode of delirium (Witlox et al. 2010). Mental health problems like post-traumatic stress disorder (PTSD) and depression are also common after delirium. Physical function is often affected, leading to a loss of independence that often necessitates residence in a nursing home or rehabilitation facility, which may worsen depression (Witlox et al. 2010).

The toll of delirium is not only measured in human suffering but also in economic terms. The additional healthcare spending attributed to delirium in the United States is estimated to reach up to a staggering $152 billion per year (Leslie et al. 2008). Fortunately, delirium is preventable in up to 40% of cases (Inouye et al. 1999). Prevention requires using non-pharmacological approaches to minimize risk factors for delirium and conducting regular screenings to identify early signs of delirium. By prioritizing prevention and early recognition of delirium, there is a potential to mitigate both the human and the financial costs associated with delirium.

Recognizing Delirium

Mrs. Tran is an 87-year-old woman who presents to the ED with a few days of productive cough and shortness of breath with associated fevers, chills, and generalized malaise. She lives at home with her husband, and both are functionally independent at baseline. She has a medical history of hypertension and type 2 diabetes mellitus. She is found to have viral pneumonia due to COVID-19 with low oxygen levels and is admitted to the in-patient medicine unit for antiviral therapy, steroids, and supplemental oxygen.

Eventually, Mrs. Tran's respiratory status improves, and she is gradually taken off oxygen. Her husband is not able to visit due to visitor restrictions. On the fourth day of her hospitalization, her nurse, who has been caring for her since admission, notices that she has remained lethargic since the morning and has not been eating her meals. She awakens to voice but intermittently cannot pay attention when conversing. The nurse decides to let her rest, and she drifts off to sleep shortly after.

The Importance of Early Recognition of Delirium

Mrs. Tran's case illustrates the common mistake of failing to detect delirium early. Recognizing delirium as soon as it develops is imperative to lessen the negative consequences associated with it, especially considering that the patients who are affected the most (i.e. very sick patients and older adults) are already quite vulnerable (Oldham et al. 2018). Even in the hospital, recognizing delirium is a challenge, as up to 75% of delirium cases are missed when a validated screening tool is not used (Spronk et al. 2009). Twice daily monitoring for delirium has been recommended by a number of expert guidelines and professional societies and organizations, including the ICU Pain, Agitation, and Delirium Clinical Practice Guidelines by the Society of Critical Care Medicine, the updated Pain, Agitation, Delirium, Immobility, and Sleep (PADIS) guidelines (Devlin et al. 2018), hospital standards to promote optimal surgical care of the older adult by the Coalition for Quality in Geriatric Surgery (Berian et al. 2018), and the Age-Friendly Health Systems (AFHS) Initiative of the Institute for Healthcare Improvement (IHI) (Age-Friendly Health Systems: Guide to Using the 4Ms in the Care of Older Adults 2020).

How to Recognize Delirium

The Confusion Assessment Method (CAM) is one of the most validated screening tools for identifying delirium (Figure 4.1). It consists of determining the presence of four features: (i) acute onset and fluctuating course, (ii) inattention, (iii) altered level of consciousness, and (iv) disorganized thinking. The CAM is considered a positive test for delirium if both the first and second criteria are present along with the presence of either the third or fourth feature (Inouye et al. 2008).

For feature 1, "acute onset" refers to the way that delirium develops quickly, usually over a couple of hours to days. This contrasts with dementia, a chronic progressive loss of memory with impaired thinking that develops more gradually over time, usually over many months to years. Feature 1 can also be abnormal with "fluctuating course," meaning that symptoms can worsen and improve throughout the day, often worsening at night. Feature 2, inattention, is the hallmark feature of delirium. A patient with inattention may appear easily distracted, "space off" or stare during conversations, may be unable to complete a thought, or may ask the same questions repeatedly. Feature 3, "altered level of consciousness," can appear as either drowsiness or lethargy (i.e. hypoactive) or restlessness or agitation (i.e. hyperactive) (American Psychiatric Association 2013, pp. 596–601). Delirious patients can have difficulty staying awake during the day and asleep at night. In extreme cases, patients' night-day sleep-wake cycles can become completely reversed, a vicious cycle that further worsens delirium.

If you notice yourself having difficulty following a delirious patient's thoughts, there is a good chance they are experiencing feature 4, "disorganized thinking." They may have difficulties with communication and understanding what you are saying. Distortions in their perception of reality can also occur, manifesting as delusions and hallucinations (American Psychiatric Association 2013,

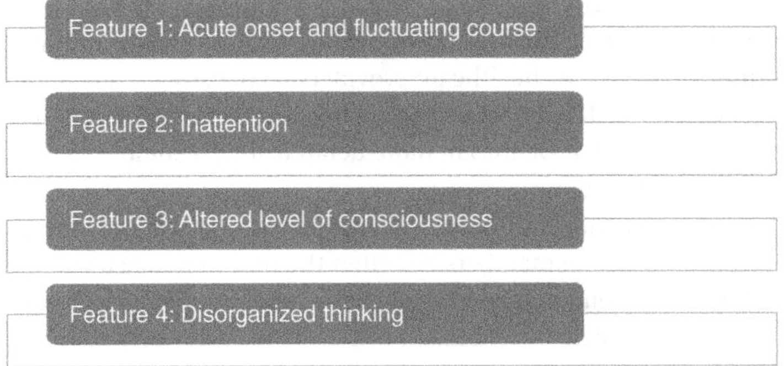

Figure 4.1 Features of the confusion assessment method (CAM).

pp. 596–601). Delusions are persistent, false beliefs despite evidence for the contrary, such as a patient believing their nurse is stealing money from their purse, when in fact, they are not. Hallucinations are perceptions in the absence of external stimuli. Examples include seeing people or hearing voices that aren't there.

People with delirium often experience emotional disturbances, such as depression, anxiety, fear, irritability, anger, euphoria, and even apathy (a complete lack of emotion). These emotional disturbances are especially common at night and can happen suddenly, with unpredictable shifts between emotions (American Psychiatric Association 2013, pp. 596–601).

Challenges to Recognizing Delirium During the COVID-19 Pandemic

Although recognizing delirium was already a challenge prior to the COVID-19 pandemic, the circumstances surrounding the pandemic made delirium recognition much more problematic. To reduce the risk of transmission and preserve personal protective equipment, healthcare workers often limited contact with patients, resulting in fewer opportunities to observe patients' thinking and behavior. Surges in patient volume resulted in shortages in personnel. Family visitation restrictions meant the absence of those often quick to notice changes in a patient's thinking and behavior. In addition, removing families from the bedside meant they could not help to facilitate communication in patients with difficulties understanding and expressing speech, such as those with dementia or a history of stroke. Face masks worn by healthcare workers interfered with patients' understanding of delirium screening questions, especially for those with hearing impairment. Personal protective equipment (i.e. masks, face shield, gowns, and gloves) intimidated some patients with dementia who already had paranoia, making them less likely to participate in delirium screening. Lastly, many patients affected by COVID-19 had such bad lung failure that they required deep sedation and paralysis while on a breathing machine, making proper assessment for delirium unfeasible (Duggan et al. 2021).

If you were hospitalized during the COVID-19 pandemic, it is possible that you experienced delirium without your healthcare providers recognizing it, given the challenges mentioned above. If you are experiencing lingering symptoms like memory problems, which we'll delve into in more detail below, it could be a consequence of undiagnosed delirium.

Although we have gained better control over the pandemic, challenges in recognizing delirium persist. As family members are often the first to notice a change in a patient's thinking, we strongly recommend having a family member present with the patient throughout their hospitalization to help identify early changes. For families unable to be physically present, regular phone calls and frequent communication can also be helpful in spotting early signs of delirium.

Prevention of Delirium

"An ounce of prevention is worth a pound of cure," wrote Benjamin Franklin of fire prevention in eighteenth century Philadelphia. In today's terms, with a brain weighing 3 lb, we might say, "An ounce of prevention is worth three pounds of neurons (brain cells)." While early recognition of delirium is crucial for further workup and management, prioritizing the prevention of delirium should take precedence. Up to 40% of delirium can be prevented without medications (Inouye et al. 1999). This is particularly important in high-risk patients with numerous predisposing and precipitating risk factors for delirium.

The Hospital Elder Life Program (HELP) is an evidence-based approach to prevent delirium through non-pharmacological means (Inouye et al. 1999). Having been widely disseminated throughout many healthcare systems, it effectively reduces the incidence of delirium (Hshieh et al. 2018). The major components of HELP are implemented in the recommendations by the AFHS, an initiative by the IHI (Age-Friendly Health Systems: Guide to Using the 4Ms in the Care of Older Adults 2020). These recommendations are as follows:

- Provide appropriate oral hydration and nutrition.
- Reorient frequently to time, place, and situation, inviting family members for assistance and personal approaches.
- Encourage early, frequent, and safe mobility, with a goal of walking three times per day.
- Assess for pain and ensure pain is well-controlled, scheduling non-opioid pain medications if needed.
- Ensure personal adaptive equipment, such as eyeglasses, hearing aids, and dentures.
- Optimize the environment by keeping the blinds open during the day and minimizing the use of tethering devices such as Foley catheters.
- Minimize sleep disruptions during the night and use non-pharmacological interventions to promote sleep, such as earplugs and sleeping masks.

The mnemonic HOMMMEESS, which includes the recommendations from HELP and AFHS, is one useful way to remember these measures to prevent delirium (Table 4.2). Most of the interventions are high-yield and can be done by families and caregivers.

Acute Management of Delirium

Mrs. Tran is eventually diagnosed with delirium and has persistently positive CAM assessments five days into her hospital stay. Growing more restless and unable to report specific symptoms, she starts moaning and attempting to get out of bed. After

Table 4.2 Non-pharmacological measures for delirium prevention and treatment.

Hydration/nutrition
Orientation
Mobilize
Manage pain
Minimize medications
Eliminate devices
Engage family
Sensory restoration
Sleep optimization

The HOMMMEESS mnemonic is a useful way to remember the non-pharmacological measures to prevent and treat delirium.

talking to her nurse and reviewing her medical chart, the doctor discovers that Mrs. Tran has not had a bowel movement since admission. She starts a laxative and has a bowel movement the next morning. Nurses continue delirium precautions such as frequent reorientation, assistance with meals, and quiet hours at night. Over the next few days, Mrs. Tran demonstrates improvement in attention and orientation. Her medical team lifts her COVID-19 isolation precautions on the seventh day, allowing her family to spend more time at her bedside. On the day of hospital discharge, Mrs. Tran, although not yet back to her baseline cognitive function, is taken home by her family with home health services.

Mrs. Tran's case demonstrates how treating underlying contributors to delirium coupled with meeting basic needs (e.g. hydration, sleep, pain control, and movement) is the best approach to managing delirium. When a patient is delirious, clinicians use the prevention strategies discussed in the previous section: reorienting the patient, removing potential contributors such as monitoring devices or medications, and encouraging the use of glasses or hearing aids (Age-Friendly Health Systems: Guide to Using the 4Ms in the Care of Older Adults 2020). Family and friends, whether at the bedside or over the phone, can play an important role in identifying the need for and assisting with many of these interventions.

When looking for the causes of delirium, you may see multiple members of the healthcare team collaborate to conduct a careful history, physical examination, and chart review. Pharmacists are particularly helpful in reviewing medications that could be contributing and developing plans, if appropriate, to discontinue or taper off such medications. Your role, as a family member or caregiver, is particularly important, providing additional valuable history. The healthcare team may look for changes in vital signs or laboratory values, which can help identify organic causes like infections, pain, dehydration, constipation, and urinary retention. The nursing team also plays a critical role in early identification of delirium and provides information to brainstorm potential causes. As non-pharmacological treatments are initiated, healthcare providers will regularly follow up with the bedside nurse and any family present, including yourself, to assess changes in mental status.

In general, medications used to treat delirium are aimed at the underlying cause, such as acetaminophen for suspected pain. However, for certain symptoms, behavioral medications may be warranted. For example, if a person becomes so agitated or aggressive that they are a danger to themselves or staff, then calming medications can be used to maintain safety. For the United States Food and Drug Administration (FDA) to approve medications for certain conditions, a comprehensive multistep process is followed to make sure these medications are safe and effective for certain conditions; however, the medications often used for delirium are not FDA-approved. They can cause side effects and even worsen delirium. Antipsychotic medications are a class of drugs that are commonly used for hyperactive delirium. Sedating medications such as benzodiazepines have been shown to worsen delirium and are avoided in most cases. When clinicians use antipsychotics or other medications targeted at behavioral disturbances from delirium, they generally aim for the lowest dose of the medicine and for the shortest duration, as medications only help with managing symptoms and do not reverse delirium (Girard et al. 2018).

Long-term Management After Delirium

Mrs. Tran is accompanied by her husband to a follow-up appointment with her primary care physician six months after her hospitalization. At the visit, Mrs. Tran shares that she has felt more depressed since getting out of the hospital. She is discouraged about having to use a walker to walk long distances and is easily fatigued despite working with physical therapists three times per week. Her husband notes that she is more forgetful than she was before her hospital admission. The primary care doctor administers both a Patient Health Questionnaire-9 (PHQ-9) to screen for depression and a Montreal Cognitive Assessment (MoCA) to screen for cognitive impairment. The PHQ-9 is consistent with moderate depression. Her MoCA score decreased from 28 one year prior to 22, now consistent with mild cognitive impairment.

Delirium can lead to long-term problems well after its initial presentation. Many survivors of delirium experience PICS. PICS encompasses a range of new or worsening changes in cognitive, psychological, and physical function that persist after severe illness and hospitalization. Patients affected by delirium are particularly prone to PICS. In a study looking at over 16 000 critically ill patients, delirium was related to higher rates of cognitive and functional impairment up to 12 months after discharge from the hospital (Salluh et al. 2015). If you have had an episode of delirium, the journey ahead may involve enduring challenges such as cognitive impairment, mental health disorders, and physical and functional limitations.

The likelihood of long-term cognitive impairment following an intensive care stay is estimated to range from 30% to 80% with delirium being the most significant and consistent risk factor (Pandharipande et al. 2013). Other risk factors, aside from delirium, include older age, male sex, previous strokes, and poor self-reported health (Teeters et al. 2016). A longer duration of delirium is associated with more severe cognitive deficits, affecting areas like memory and executive function – the ability to plan, organize, and complete tasks (Pandharipande et al. 2013). While some experience cognitive improvement, particularly in the first six months after hospitalization, others may face a progressive decline. Despite initial improvement, many people experience long-term cognitive impairment lasting beyond a year after hospitalization. Those with preexisting cognitive impairment might see a further decline (Wilcox et al. 2021). These changes to thinking and memory present challenges to maintaining employment, functional independence, and optimal quality of life. In the outpatient setting, your healthcare clinician may use tools like the MoCA and the Eight-item Interview to Differentiate Aging and Dementia (AD8) to screen for cognitive impairment at various points after hospitalization(s) complicated by delirium. If screening indicates cognitive impairment, your healthcare clinician may consider referring you for further neuropsychological testing and possibly cognitive rehabilitation, akin to physical rehabilitation but tailored for the brain.

Anxiety, depression, and PTSD stand out as the most common mental health disorders following a period of critical illness, with reported rates exceeding 50% in some cases (Colbenson et al. 2019). Factors contributing to these disorders, beyond delirium, include reliance on a breathing machine, sedation, and an extended hospital stay (Patel et al. 2016). The prevalence of depressive symptoms after delirium has been reported at 22%, nearly three times higher than in patients without delirium (Langan et al. 2017). Anxiety symptoms after delirium has been reported at 8% (Langan et al. 2017). Given the potential negative impact of critical illness on mental health, your healthcare clinician may use validated screening tools like the PHQ-9 for depression, General Anxiety Disorder-7 (GAD-7) for anxiety, and Primary Care PTSD Screen for DSM-5 (PC-PTSD-5) for PTSD during follow-up appointments. If you screen positive, your healthcare clinician may recommend psychotherapy or support groups, and, if needed, start medication.

Delirium is often complicated by the presence of new physical and functional impairment, reported in 25–80% of patients after an ICU stay (Colbenson et al. 2019). Whether the impairment is a worsening chronic symptom or a new symptom, such as weakness or fatigue, your healthcare clinician may screen for deficits that could be preventing you from taking care of yourself and living independently in the months following hospitalization. This can be accomplished through validated tools such as the Katz Index of Independence in Activities of Daily Living. Many people engage in physical therapy and occupational therapy following hospitalization to address limitations in identified areas.

As researchers are starting to understand the many complications that COVID-19 survivors are experiencing, especially those who experienced delirium, more resources are becoming available. For example, the Critical Illness, Brain Dysfunction, and Survivorship (CIBS) Center hosts weekly virtual support groups for survivors of delirium and those with long-term complications of COVID-19 (www.icudelirium.org). There are also support groups for families and caregivers, as the effects of acute illness have a ripple effect beyond the patient (www.icudelirium.org). These support groups can help patients, their families, and caregivers cope with the lingering effects of COVID-19 and delirium.

Conclusion

Delirium is a common complication for patients with COVID-19. Oftentimes mistaken for dementia or simply written off as old age, delirium can cause serious consequences both during and after hospitalization that extends beyond the patient, negatively impacting families, caregivers, and healthcare systems. By identifying those at risk to implement early preventative non-pharmacological measures, delirium can often be prevented. When delirium occurs, strategies for delirium prevention are also the recommended treatment for delirium: finding and treating the underlying causes and making sure patients' basic needs are met. Families and caregivers play a crucial role in the management of delirium. After resolution of delirium, patients may experience long-term cognitive impairment, mental health disorders, and physical and functional impairment.

Learning Points

- Delirium is characterized by a sudden or fluctuating change in thinking, marked by inattention, with altered levels of consciousness and disorganized thinking.
- Delirium typically develops over hours to days, commonly affecting patients with COVID-19.

- Delirium should not be confused with dementia. Dementia is a syndrome of gradually worsening thinking and memory that negatively affects a person's ability to function independently, but it typically develops over months to years.
- Delirium can cause serious complications and can even increase the risk of death.
- Consequences of delirium can negatively impact families, caregivers, and healthcare systems.
- Delirium is often preventable by identifying high risk individuals and implementing early non-pharmacological interventions.
- Delirium screening tools can identify delirium early. One tool is the CAM.
- Non-pharmacological interventions for delirium prevention are also the recommended treatment for delirium.
- Families and caregivers have a crucial role in delirium prevention and management.
- Families can also help implement non-pharmacologic treatment interventions at the bedside, like orienting, assisting with feeding, assessing for pain, and helping with mobility.
- Long-term effects of delirium include problems in memory and thinking, mental health disorders, and physical and functional impairment.

References

American Psychiatric Association (ed.) (2013). *Diagnostic and Statistical Manual of Mental Disorders: DSM-5*, 5e. American Psychiatric Association.

Barron, E.A. and Holmes, J. (2013). Delirium within the emergency care setting, occurrence and detection: a systematic review. *Emergency Medicine Journal* 30 (4): 263–268. https://doi.org/10.1136/emermed-2011-200586.

Berian, J.R., Rosenthal, R.A., Baker, T.L. et al. (2018). Hospital standards to promote optimal surgical care of the older adult: a report from the coalition for quality in geriatric surgery. *Annals of Surgery* 267 (2): 280–290. https://doi.org/10.1097/SLA.0000000000002185.

Colbenson, G.A., Johnson, A., and Wilson, M.E. (2019). Post-intensive care syndrome: impact, prevention, and management. *Breathe* 15 (2): 98–101. https://doi.org/10.1183/20734735.0013-2019.

Devlin, J.W., Skrobik, Y., Gélinas, C. et al. (2018). Clinical practice guidelines for the prevention and management of pain, agitation/sedation, delirium, immobility, and sleep disruption in adult patients in the ICU. *Critical Care Medicine* 46 (9): e825. https://doi.org/10.1097/CCM.0000000000003299.

Duggan, M.C., Van, J., and Ely, E.W. (2021). Delirium assessment in critically ill older adults: considerations during the COVID-19 pandemic. *Critical Care Clinics* 37 (1): 175–190. https://doi.org/10.1016/j.ccc.2020.08.009.

Ely, E.W., Shintani, A., Truman, B. et al. (2004). Delirium as a predictor of mortality in mechanically ventilated patients in the intensive care unit. *JAMA* 291 (14): 1753–1762. https://doi.org/10.1001/jama.291.14.1753.

Girard, T.D., Exline, M.C., Carson, S.S. et al. (2018). Haloperidol and ziprasidone for treatment of delirium in critical illness. *New England Journal of Medicine* 379 (26): 2506–2516. https://doi.org/10.1056/NEJMoa1808217.

Helms, J., Kremer, S., Merdji, H. et al. (2020). Neurologic features in severe SARS-CoV-2 infection. *New England Journal of Medicine* 382 (23): 2268–2270. https://doi.org/10.1056/NEJMc2008597.

Hshieh, T.T., Yang, T., Gartaganis, S.L. et al. (2018). Hospital elder life program: systematic review and meta-analysis of effectiveness. *The American Journal of Geriatric Psychiatry: Official Journal of the American Association for Geriatric Psychiatry* 26 (10): 1015–1033. https://doi.org/10.1016/j.jagp. 2018.06.007.

Inouye, S.K. (2021). The importance of delirium and delirium prevention in older adults during lockdowns. *JAMA* 325 (17): 1779–1780. https://doi.org/10.1001/ jama.2021.2211.

Inouye, S.K., Bogardus, S.T., Charpentier, P.A. et al. (1999). A multicomponent intervention to prevent delirium in hospitalized older patients. *The New England Journal of Medicine* 340 (9): 669–676. https://doi.org/10.1056/ NEJM199903043400901.

Inouye, S.K., van Dyck, C.H., Alessi, C.A. et al. (2008). Clarifying confusion: the confusion assessment method. *Annals of Internal Medicine.* https://www. acpjournals.org/doi/10.7326/0003-4819-113-12-941.

Inouye, S.K., Westendorp, R.G., and Saczynski, J.S. (2014). Delirium in elderly people. *The Lancet* 383 (9920): 911–922. https://doi.org/10.1016/S0140-6736(13)60688-1.

Institute for Healthcare Improvement (2020). *Age-Friendly Health Systems: Guide to Using the 4Ms in the Care of Older Adults.* Institute for Healthcare Improvement. https://forms.ihi.org/hubfs/IHIAgeFriendlyHealthSystems_ GuidetoUsing4MsCare.pdf.

Kennedy, M., Helfand, B.K.I., Gou, R.Y. et al. (2020). Delirium in older patients with COVID-19 presenting to the emergency department. *JAMA Network Open* 3 (11): e2029540. https://doi.org/10.1001/jamanetworkopen. 2020.29540.

Langan, C., Sarode, D.P., Russ, T.C. et al. (2017). Psychiatric symptomatology after delirium: a systematic review. *Psychogeriatrics: The Official Journal of the Japanese Psychogeriatric Society* 17 (5): 327–335. https://doi.org/10.1111/psyg.12240.

Leslie, D.L., Marcantonio, E.R., Zhang, Y. et al. (2008). One-year health care costs associated with delirium in the elderly. *Archives of Internal Medicine* 168 (1): 27–32. https://doi.org/10.1001/archinternmed.2007.4.

Neufeld, K.J. and Thomas, C. (2013). Delirium: definition, epidemiology, and diagnosis. *Journal of Clinical Neurophysiology* 30 (5): 438. https://doi.org/10.1097/WNP.0b013e3182a73e31.

Oldham, M.A., Flanagan, N.M., Khan, A. et al. (2018). Responding to ten common delirium misconceptions with best evidence: an educational review for clinicians. *The Journal of Neuropsychiatry and Clinical Neurosciences* 30 (1): 51–57. https://doi.org/10.1176/appi.neuropsych.17030065.

Pandharipande, P.P., Girard, T.D., Jackson, J.C. et al. (2013). Long-term cognitive impairment after critical illness. *The New England Journal of Medicine* 369 (14): 1306–1316. https://doi.org/10.1056/NEJMoa1301372.

Patel, M.B., Jackson, J.C., Morandi, A. et al. (2016). Incidence and risk factors for intensive care unit-related post-traumatic stress disorder in veterans and civilians. *American Journal of Respiratory and Critical Care Medicine* 193 (12): 1373–1381. https://doi.org/10.1164/rccm.201506-1158OC.

Reppas-Rindlisbacher, C., Boblitz, A., Fowler, R.A. et al. (2023). Trends in delirium and new antipsychotic and benzodiazepine use among hospitalized older adults before and after the onset of the COVID-19 pandemic. *JAMA Network Open* 6 (8): e2327750. https://doi.org/10.1001/jamanetworkopen.2023.27750.

Salluh, J.I.F., Wang, H., Schneider, E.B. et al. (2015). Outcome of delirium in critically ill patients: systematic review and meta-analysis. *BMJ (Clinical Research Ed.)* 350: h2538. https://doi.org/10.1136/bmj.h2538.

Spronk, P.E., Riekerk, B., Hofhuis, J., and Rommes, J.H. (2009). Occurrence of delirium is severely underestimated in the ICU during daily care. *Intensive Care Medicine* 35 (7): 1276–1280. https://doi.org/10.1007/s00134-009-1466-8.

Teeters, D.A., Moua, T., Li, G. et al. (2016). Mild cognitive impairment and risk of critical illness. *Critical Care Medicine* 44 (11): 2045. https://doi.org/10.1097/CCM.0000000000001842.

Vasilevskis, E.E., Pandharipande, P.P., Girard, T.D., and Ely, E.W. (2010). A screening, prevention, and restoration model for saving the injured brain in intensive care unit survivors. *Critical Care Medicine* 38 (10): S683. https://doi.org/10.1097/CCM.0b013e3181f245d3.

Watt, D.F., Koziol, K., and Budding, D. (2012). Delirium and confusional states. In: *Disorders in Neuropsychiatry* (ed. C.A. Noggeland and R.S. Dean). New York: Springer.

Wilcox, M.E., Girard, T.D., and Hough, C.L. (2021). Delirium and long term cognition in critically ill patients. *BMJ* 373: n1007. https://doi.org/10.1136/bmj.n1007.

Witlox, J., Eurelings, L.S.M., de Jonghe, J.F.M. et al. (2010). Delirium in elderly patients and the risk of postdischarge mortality, institutionalization, and dementia: a meta-analysis. *JAMA* 304 (4): 443–451. https://doi.org/10.1001/jama.2010.1013.

www.icudelirium.org (2024). www.icudelirium.org (accessed 16 July 2024).

5

Mood Disorders as a Result of COVID-19 Infection: Depression and Bipolar Disorder

Drew Cumming and Gregory Fricchione

Department of Psychiatry, Massachusetts General Hospital, Boston, MA, 02114, USA

Introduction

There's been a recent surge in discussions about the mental health crisis, not just in the United States but globally. But let's start by clarifying what we mean by "mental health." Depending on whom you ask, it can refer to anything from personal well-being to chronic, severe mental illness. Here, we will narrow our focus to mood disorders – understanding the term, the diagnostic process, and exploring how they may be affected by COVID-19.

The term "mood disorders" encompasses both depressive disorders and bipolar spectrum disorders. In this chapter, we'll clarify what doctors mean when they refer to "depression" and "bipolar." We'll delve into how symptoms from these illnesses may overlap with symptoms of COVID-19 infection and explore how COVID-19 could potentially trigger or worsen depressive and bipolar spectrum disorders.

Now, turning our attention to COVID-19, it emerged in 2019 catapulting the world into a global pandemic. Regarded as one of the most serious public health challenges in modern history, the virus has adopted a seasonal pattern of infection over the past few years, giving rise to various forms or variants at different times. While several variants have been associated with certain symptoms and severities, for simplicity, we will use the umbrella term "COVID-19" to refer to all SARS-CoV-2 variants (or severe acute respiratory syndrome coronavirus 2 variants).

We think of COVID-19 as an infection primarily infecting the lungs, evaluating the severity of the illness based on the challenge it poses to breathing. However, the impact of the infection extends far beyond the respiratory system. Infection can affect a diverse array of organs by increasing inflammation – a response our body initiates against microbes and perceived threats. To respond to the threat of infection, our bodies engage the immune system, which includes specialized organs, cells, and proteins. The immune system acts both locally, addressing threats where they emerge, and systemically, acting throughout the entire body. Our body's defense comprises a rapid, nonspecific "innate" immune response and a subsequent "acquired" immune response that holds a memory of past exposures, allowing for specific actions. Systemic effects of inflammation include experiences commonly associated with feeling unwell, such as fever, fatigue, loss of appetite, and difficulty concentrating (Dantzer et al. 2008, pp. 46–56).

We've all experienced what it's like to be sick – think about having the flu. Our energy and motivation plummet, socializing becomes unappealing, and all we want to do is curl up under a blanket until we recover. This "sickness behavior" is believed to serve a purpose. It helps our bodies save energy for fighting off the infection and protects us from potentially dangerous situations when we're sick and weak (Khandaker et al. 2021, pp. 109–138). These changes in our feelings and behaviors are thought to be driven by the immune system, with inflammation in our brain playing a pivotal role. Specialized immune cells called microglia make up 15–20% of all brain cells and are gaining recognition for their important role in changing how the brain works (Bourgognon et al. 2021, pp. 51–72). Interestingly, these sickness behaviors are very similar to the changes in mood and behavior seen in depression.

Major Depressive Disorder (MDD)

Mrs. Andrews is a 47-year-old woman with high blood pressure and hypothyroidism, for which she takes daily medications. Her doctor has also told her that she has "pre-diabetes." She had major depressive episodes after both of her children were born but responded well to an antidepressant medication; she stopped taking this several years ago, as she felt she no longer needed it.

Mrs. Andrews lives with her husband and two children. She works part-time at her church and volunteers at her children's school. One week after flying home from vacation with her family, she began to feel aches in her body and low energy, which didn't improve after a nap. She took an at-home COVID-19 test after developing a fever and tested positive. On her doctor's advice, she isolated from her family and initiated Nirmatrelvir/Ritonavir treatment.

Mrs. Andrews encountered various symptoms, including fever, chills, and body aches. Despite improvements in her fever, chills, and aches, she continued to experience low energy and decreased appetite. Upon returning to work, she faced challenges in staying organized and completing her usual tasks, evoking embarrassment about her performance. At night she woke up frequently and experienced difficulties falling back asleep. Her boss recommended taking time off work, which triggered feelings of shame, as Mrs. Andrews had previously taken great pride in her work. Gradually, daily activities such as getting out of bed, getting dressed, and showering became more challenging, which worried her family.

Concerned about Mrs. Andrews's well-being, her family brought her to the doctor, who considered the possibility of depression or Long COVID. The doctor then referred Mrs. Andrews to a psychiatrist. In a thorough evaluation, the psychiatrist delved into Mrs. Andrews's medical history, recent experiences, performed a physical exam, and reviewed blood work. The psychiatrist diagnosed Mrs. Andrews with a major depressive episode and started her on an antidepressant. Fortunately, Mrs. Andrews's symptoms improved, allowing her to regain a sense of well-being and return to work.

When doctors, particularly psychiatrists, discuss depression, they often refer to something much more specific than the casual use of the term in society. You might hear a friend say, "I can't believe my hockey team lost again, it's depressing," or read a post on social media expressing, "Ugh, I'm going to be so depressed if it rains and the concert is cancelled!"

When we talk about depression in a medical context, we are usually referring to major depressive disorder (MDD), also known as clinical depression. The term "clinical" is used because it goes beyond feeling sad or upset; it becomes "clinical" when it persists for an extended period, makes it difficult to meet requirements at home, work, or school, and leads to changes in how your body's nervous, endocrine (hormonal), and other systems function.

MDD stands out with the highest lifetime prevalence among psychiatric illnesses, affecting 15–20% of individuals during their lifetime (Sadock et al. 2017, pp. 60–82). While people with MDD initially experience feelings of sadness or low mood, the condition evolves over time, significantly affecting various aspects of their lives. A study by the American Medical Association showed that clinical depression results in an annual loss of over 30 billion dollars in productivity (Stewart et al. 2003, pp. 3135–3144).

Beyond the emotional impact, MDD introduces challenges such as difficulty concentrating and a lack of motivation, creating a detrimental cycle that worsens over time. Changes in the brain during depression disrupt normal sleep patterns, leading to daytime fatigue. Loss of appetite is common, exacerbating the decrease in energy levels. As depression progresses, the brain's ability to produce hopeful or optimistic thoughts diminishes, leading to a limited loop of negative thoughts. This loop can make it difficult for someone to imagine experiencing joy or having fun, causing a loss of interest in once-enjoyable hobbies. Trapped in this depressive loop of low energy, difficulty concentrating, and a pervasive sense of hopelessness, people may start contemplating suicide.

For a diagnosis of MDD, the depressed mood and associated symptoms must be present for a minimum of two weeks. With appropriate treatment, episodes of major depression typically last around three months; however, if left untreated, they can last for more than a year (Sadock et al. 2017, pp. 60–82). People who experience a major depressive episode are more likely to experience similar episodes later in life compared to those who haven't experienced depression before. Stressors, such as physical illness or an emotional crisis, can trigger another episode of depression in individuals with a history of depressive episodes.

Depression and COVID-19

In reading the case of Mrs. Andrews, you were hopefully struck by the similarities between her depressive symptoms and some of the sickness behaviors discussed earlier in this chapter. There is growing recognition of, and interest in, the role of inflammation in depression. People with MDD have more active inflammatory processes. Increasing brain inflammation negatively alters the communication between the frontal lobes (involved in higher-order functions) and the limbic system (involved in emotional and behavioral responses) (Khandaker et al. 2021, pp. 109–138). Markers of inflammation also correlate with depression severity, according to a study evaluating patients hospitalized with COVID-19 (Mazza et al. 2021, pp. 138–147).

Women and people with previous episodes of major depression are at higher risk for developing depression after COVID-19 infection. People with mood disorders also have significantly higher odds of hospitalization or death from COVID-19 (Ceban et al. 2021, pp. 1079–1091). It's currently unclear whether the severity of infection increases the risk for depression. However, rates of depression are higher in people who require hospitalization. A meta-review of published articles suggests an astonishingly high rate of depression (21–45%) after COVID-19 infection (Mazza et al. 2022, pp. 681–702). These statistics are complicated by the fact that many of the original studies were performed during the tumultuous period of lockdowns and strict quarantines. A more recent longitudinal study showed that the incidence of major depression was higher following a COVID-19 infection for over a year compared to the general population, but returned to baseline, on average, after 13–14 months (Taquet et al. 2022, pp. 815–827).

People with persistent symptoms following a COVID-19 infection, as discussed in Chapter 8, often experience neuropsychiatric difficulties. As previously mentioned, inflammation negatively impacts the communication system between the frontal lobes and limbic system in the brain, and unfortunately, COVID-19 has a strong preference for these areas. People with persistent symptoms may experience difficulties with concentration, organization, or memory. They may have trouble feeling motivated, with some feeling that they just can't "get going." Additionally, emotional regulation may become more challenging for them (Newhouse et al. 2022, pp. 619–627).

Diagnosing Depression

Due to historical, societal, and cultural factors, there are misconceptions that depression shouldn't be treated like other medical illnesses, and individuals with depression are often told to simply "toughen up." However, this perception couldn't be further from the truth. Regardless of its cause, depression leads to long-standing changes in how the brain functions. It also causes changes in the rest of the body, affecting hormones and parts of the nervous system. The longer someone experiences depression, the more entrenched these changes become, making them more challenging to treat and increasing the likelihood of future episodes of depression.

You should seek treatment for yourself or loved ones when depressive symptoms persist for at least two weeks and/or interfere with your regular activities. A helpful mnemonic to remember common depressive symptoms is SIG E CAPS:

Sleep: Changes in sleep patterns, often finding it harder to fall asleep or stay asleep.
Interest: Loss of interest in usual hobbies or activities that were once enjoyable.
Guilt: Feelings of guilt, particularly about your impact on others.
Energy: Decreased energy levels throughout the day, leading to fatigue.
Concentration: Difficulty concentrating and maintaining focus on tasks.
Appetite: Changes in appetite, often with decreased interest in food.
Psychomotor: Slowed movements and responses.
Suicidality: Thoughts related to self-harm or suicide; a psychiatric emergency.

The Patient Health Questionnaire-2 (PHQ-2), a brief screening tool for depression, is readily available. It asks about symptoms over the past two weeks, including whether you have experienced little interest or pleasure in doing things, or whether you feel down, depressed, or hopeless. A positive screen is more suggestive of depression.

MDD is diagnosed when a patient has a depressed mood and four or more of the symptoms above for at least two weeks. Depression can look very different in different people. Some people may experience "atypical depression," which is characterized by increased sleep and appetite. In some people, severe depression can lead to psychotic symptoms, such as hallucinations or fixed beliefs that are not based in reality (delusions).

It can be challenging to diagnose depression in someone who is currently sick or experiencing lingering symptoms. Using the SIG E CAPS mnemonic, you can see that many of these symptoms are common parts of being ill. To diagnose depression in someone who is also sick, we often focus on the nature of a person's thoughts. When people are depressed, they often think about themselves in a very harsh and negative way. They may also feel guilty or lose hope that they could feel well again.

Suicidality is a psychiatric emergency (refer to Chapter 9 for more details on psychiatric emergencies). Suicidal thoughts exist along a spectrum, ranging from passive thoughts that life may not be worth living to active thoughts of wanting to harm oneself. If you or your loved one are experiencing suicidal thoughts, take action. You can visit the nearest Emergency Room, or you can call the emergency or crisis number (e.g. 911 for emergencies; 988 for the National Suicide and Crisis Lifeline in the US).

Treating Depression

Fortunately, there are several effective treatments for depression. Your doctor may discuss the option of starting an antidepressant medication with you. When prescribed antidepressants, it's typical to continue treatment for at least three months, especially during a first episode of depression. People with recurrent episodes of depression often require medication for much longer.

The most commonly prescribed antidepressants belong to a group called selective serotonin reuptake inhibitors (SSRIs). Despite slight differences in their properties, these medications share a common mechanism related to serotonin, a crucial neurotransmitter in the brain. These medications are typically taken daily, either in the morning or at night. However, altering communication pathways in the brain is a gradual process, and it may take a month or longer to observe the full effects of these medications.

As our stomach and intestines also use serotonin, some people may experience nausea when initiating these medications. This side effect tends to improve over the first few days, with the first day often being the most challenging. To mitigate this, try taking the medication with a full stomach, right after breakfast or dinner. Initial anxiety is another common experience during the first few days on the medication, but this typically diminishes over time. We often use these medications to treat anxiety! Some people may also notice changes in their sex drive or in their body's sexual responses. If these side effects persist, your doctor can provide solutions. It's important not to abruptly stop these medications, as withdrawal effects may occur. These can manifest as flu-like symptoms or rebound anxiety and depression. A rare but critical side effect associated with any antidepressant is the emergence of suicidal thoughts. If you experience such thoughts, contact your doctor immediately or go to the nearest emergency department. Additionally, antidepressants can potentially trigger mania in people at risk for bipolar disorder, a topic that will be further discussed below.

While SSRIs are the most commonly prescribed class of antidepressants, there are other types of antidepressant classes, including serotonin-norepinephrine reuptake inhibitors (SNRIs), which clinicians might recommend to address specific symptoms like pain. Other antidepressants can help with sleep and appetite, such as mirtazapine (Remeron). For those struggling with activation and energy, bupropion (Wellbutrin) is often a good consideration. Determining the most suitable medication can be challenging, so it's often helpful to inform your doctor if a close family member responded well to a particular medication. Your doctor might also consider medications from other medication groups to target particularly severe depression, including antipsychotics, mood stabilizers, or stimulants, or discuss neuromodulatory procedures, such as electroconvulsive therapy (ECT) or transcranial magnetic stimulation (TMS).

Therapy is an equally effective treatment for depression, and many individuals prefer it. There are various types of therapy, such as cognitive behavioral therapy (CBT), mindfulness-based cognitive therapy (MBCT), and acceptance and commitment therapy (ACT) that can help relieve depressive symptoms. CBT is sometimes recommended as a first-line treatment. These therapies also play a role in preventing future depressive episodes.

Bipolar Disorder

Leonardo is a 22-year-old male who has had several episodes of depression, beginning at age 16. He took an antidepressant for a few months but stopped because he didn't feel it was necessary. He is in his last year of college and lives several states away from the rest of his family.

While studying for exams, he began to feel more tired than usual. He developed a persistent cough and body aches. He tested positive for COVID-19 at the student health center and was quarantined in his room in accordance with his college's guidelines. He quickly felt better, but missed his exams. As a result, he had to stay up late "cramming" for several days to be ready for the make-up exam date.

Leonardo borrowed some of his roommate's "concentration pills" in order to stay up late. After several days with only three or four hours of sleep, he felt full of energy. He told his friends that he had discovered multiple mistakes by his professors. He wrote long, confusing emails highlighting his plans to expose his professors as secret government agents, installed on campus to monitor student activists. He did not attend his examinations, as he felt they were no longer relevant. Instead, he walked 20 miles to the state capitol, demanding to speak with the Governor.

Leonardo was sent to the hospital, where he was diagnosed with bipolar disorder with concern for an active manic episode. He was admitted to the psychiatry unit and started on medication. As his symptoms improved, he worked with his family and college to reschedule his exams, planning to return the following semester.

We all have days when our mood is a little better or a little worse, especially if something extraordinary happens in our lives. In most cases, a depressed or elevated mood for a couple of days is no cause for worry. However, in people with bipolar disorder, their abnormally low (or high) mood can persist and become disabling.

You may have heard the term "bipolar" used to describe someone who becomes easily upset or angry. Bipolar disorder, however, is a psychiatric illness. People with bipolar disorder experience recurrent, prolonged periods of both very low mood (depression) and very high mood (mania), which alternate over time. People diagnosed with bipolar disorder often have several family members with the same illness, which can be an important clue.

Periods of depression and mania in bipolar disorder are called "mood episodes." For the vast majority of people with bipolar disorder, their first mood episode, or even their first couple of episodes, are depressive episodes. These often first occur when people are in their late teen years or in their early twenties. The majority of people with bipolar disorder will have more depressive episodes than manic episodes. However, bipolar disorder cannot be diagnosed until a person experiences an episode of mania.

Bipolar disorder is a chronic condition, meaning that affected individuals will likely encounter numerous mood episodes throughout their lives. With appropriate medications, we can reduce the frequency and severity of these episodes, significantly enhancing the quality of life for patients. Like depression, if left untreated, manic episodes can persist for several months. The severity of manic episodes often requires hospital admission for stabilization and rapid medication adjustment.

Like depression, mania has a constellation of related symptoms. While some people experiencing mania may experience an abnormally elevated mood, others may feel extraordinarily irritable. Beyond mood changes and irritability, a critical aspect of recognizing mania is the presence of an exceptional level of energy. This can be seen in various ways – not sleeping for several days, constant movement, rapid speech, or increased distractibility. Typically, these features develop over several days or a few weeks. During a manic episode, an individual may also behave differently, seemingly indifferent to potential consequences. They may start new projects or spend a lot of money on unnecessary purchases. They may engage in new, risky behavior, such as excessive drinking, using drugs, gambling, fighting, reckless driving, or engaging in unsafe sexual behaviors. Importantly, during a manic episode, people lose the ability to make decisions as they normally would. When the episode ends, individuals often report feelings of grief and shame as they learn about their behavior during the episode.

Both manic and depressive episodes can include additional changes in thinking, particularly psychosis. Psychotic symptoms can include hallucinations or disorganized, unclear thought patterns that others find hard to follow and understand. Mood episodes with psychotic features can also include delusional thinking. This occurs when a person comes to firmly believe ideas detached from reality. These delusions can be grandiose ("I discovered the secret to both physics and the economy, and now God is sending me on a secret mission to implement it"), persecutory or paranoid ("My neighbor hates me because I have blonde hair, so he has put cameras in my apartment and poisoned my food"), or erotic ("I can't tell you who, but a famous singer is in love with me, and we're actually married, and all their songs are about me"). You will not be able to convince them that these delusions are false. Instead, their belief in these thoughts will weaken over the course of the treatment and usually fade away with time.

Bipolar Disorder and COVID-19

Similar to MDD, inflammation is increased in bipolar disorder and plays a role in changing how the brain operates. Since inflammation in these mood disorders is already increased, and since the impact of severe COVID-19 infection on the body comes about through effects of increased inflammation, it is unfortunate but not surprising that people with mood disorders face an increased risk of poor outcomes from COVID-19. Indeed, a meta-review involving 91 million participants revealed that people with mood disorders had an increased risk of hospitalization and death from COVID-19 compared to their healthy counterparts (Ceban et al. 2021, pp. 1079–1091).

Psychiatrically, studies indicate an increased incidence of depressed mood, fatigue, and cognitive changes following a COVID-19 infection in bipolar disorder (Campos et al. 2022, pp. 2435–2455). There are also reported cases of initial manic episodes during or after a COVID-19 infection in people with no history of psychiatric disorders (Park et al. 2021, pp. 847–849).

As discussed earlier, people with mood disorders experience increased inflammation, which can trigger depressive symptoms. Markers of inflammation have been shown to be higher during manic episodes than in depression (Modabbernia et al. 2013, pp. 15–25). Several anti-inflammatory medications have shown a positive impact on depressive symptoms, and antidepressants have been shown to decrease inflammation, though the relationship between these findings remains unclear (Kappelmann et al. 2021, pp. 139–163).

Diagnosing Bipolar Disorder

As mentioned earlier, individuals with bipolar disorder typically have multiple depressive episodes before experiencing mania. Depression in bipolar disorder tends to be more severe and prolonged than in MDD. It may also pose greater challenges in treatment with antidepressant medications. Certain manic episodes can be triggered by starting an antidepressant, as the mood boost from the medication causes the patient's mood to rise too high. Occasionally, this serves as the first indication of bipolar disorder, as such a reaction does not occur in people with MDD.

To diagnose a manic episode, doctors look for evidence of abnormally elevated or irritable mood and three of the following (four if mood is only irritable): grandiosity or inflated self-esteem, decreased need for sleep (without lowered energy levels), very talkative and hard to interrupt, ideas that jump around and are hard to follow, distractibility, greatly increased movement, excessive involvement in dangerous or risky behaviors. To qualify as mania, these symptoms should persist for at least one week. They do not qualify if they occur in the setting of drug use. If these symptoms are severe enough to necessitate hospital admission, it qualifies as mania, regardless of duration.

Features of Mania
- Abnormally elevated, expansive, or irritable mood
- Persistently increased activity or energy
- Significantly inflated self-esteem or grandiosity
- Decreased need for sleep
- Much more talkative, pressure to keep talking
- Racing thoughts
- Distractibility
- Increased projects or other goal-directed activity; increased movements
- Excessive involvement in potentially risky behaviors

People with manic episodes are diagnosed with Bipolar I disorder. There is another diagnosis, Bipolar II disorder, which involves "hypomanic" episodes – these are less severe episodes of the same symptoms that last for at least four days. Hypomanic episodes are distressing but not severe enough to require hospitalization.

Mood episodes may also be "mixed episodes," which include both depressive and manic features. For example, someone may have an abnormal level of energy, racing thoughts, and impulsivity, but they may also feel incredibly sad and hopeless. Mixed episodes are considered dangerous, as there is an increased risk of suicide associated with the mixture of depressed thoughts and impulsivity.

Mania can also result from neurological or medical conditions. In these cases, it's called secondary mania. Secondary mania can be due to neurological lesions, like strokes and tumors, or medical conditions like systemic lupus erythematosus, "lupus." It can also be due to toxic and metabolic conditions.

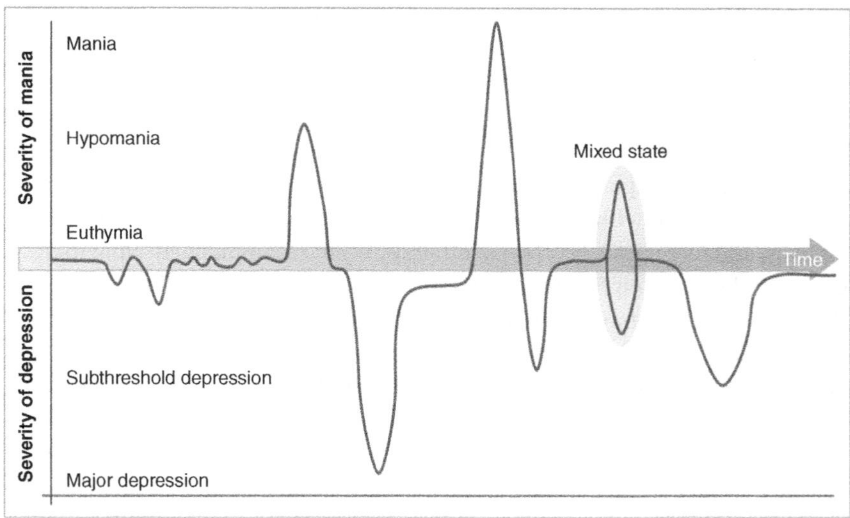

Figure 5.1 Life chart showing progression of bipolar disorder. *Source:* Reproduced with permission from Grande et al. (2016)/Elsevier.

Figure 5.1 shows the ups and downs of people's mood in bipolar disorder, including major depressive episodes, mania, hypomania and mixed states. The term "euthymia" refers to someone's baseline, or "normal" mood.

Treating Bipolar Disorder

While MDD is often treated by a PCP, bipolar disorder is considered a severe mental illness and requires the expertise of a psychiatrist. Like with depression, your psychiatrist will take a careful history of your lifelong symptoms, perform a physical exam, and collect blood work. They may assess other areas of your health to consider if a medical condition is contributing to your symptoms. In areas without access to psychiatrists, some PCPs consult with psychiatrists to help guide their care, even if the patient cannot be seen by the specialist.

The goal of treatment in bipolar disorder is to stabilize the patient's mood between the extremes of depression and mania. This is frequently accomplished through a group of medications called "mood stabilizers," including lithium, valproic acid, and lamotrigine. Managing these medications is more complicated than antidepressants, as they need to be maintained at a certain level within the body without reaching excessively high levels, which can lead to potentially life-threatening side effects. Hence, it is important for patients to adhere to medication instructions, undergo careful monitoring by their psychiatrist, and attend regular appointments.

The initial treatment of manic episodes may include medications to help the patient sleep, such as benzodiazepines or antipsychotics, typically not prescribed for extended periods. However, some antipsychotics also demonstrate efficacy in treating bipolar depression and can be used on their own. As medications are usually started during mood episodes, involving family members in the treatment planning process is highly beneficial for them to understand the associated risks and benefits. People with bipolar disorder often require medication throughout their lives, and relying solely on psychotherapy is not recommended. Nonetheless, therapy can be very helpful for patients in coping with a chronic illness.

We cover the use of mood stabilizers during pregnancy and postpartum in more detail in Chapter 10. For women with bipolar disorder, it's crucial to acknowledge that all medications pose potential risks to the baby. However, an often-overlooked risk arises from untreated depressive and manic episodes. The extreme levels of inflammation and stress during these episodes have been correlated with worse pregnancy outcomes. There is also an increased risk of recurrent mood episodes during and after pregnancy if medication is stopped. Our understanding of ideal medication choices and doses continues to evolve, so collaboration with a psychiatrist who is knowledgeable about women's mental health is essential.

Special Considerations: Treating Mood Disorders During COVID-19

A couple of points about treating mood disorders during COVID-19 merit special attention. We discussed how to differentiate illness behaviors and symptoms of depression earlier in the chapter. It helps to pay particular attention to certain symptoms in people with bipolar disorder. For example, pay special attention to a person's daily routine and sleep patterns during infection, as disrupted sleep can trigger mania. Pay attention to a person's water intake when sick – it is easy to become dehydrated during illness (from sweating, diarrhea, fever, etc.), which can alter the concentration of mood stabilizers. Dehydration can lead to dangerous levels of medications in a person's blood and may even lead to hospitalization. Similarly, drinking too many fluids can lower medication concentrations, making them less effective.

The medication Nirmatrelvir/Ritonavir (Paxlovid) deserves special mention. It's prescribed to people at high risk for developing serious symptoms as a result of COVID-19 infection. Importantly, it decreases the activity of certain liver enzymes, which are responsible for processing many psychiatric medications. Taking Nirmatrelvir/Ritonavir with certain psychiatric medications can lead to an increased concentration of psychiatric medications in the body. If a person is taking medications that increase serotonin, they are at increased risk for a dangerous condition called "serotonin syndrome." Initial symptoms of serotonin syndrome may overlap with symptoms of COVID-19 infection: restlessness, nausea, diarrhea, and sweating. However, as serotonin levels rise, symptoms become more severe and can include shaking, confusion, increased heart rate, and increased blood pressure. If untreated, serotonin syndrome can become life-threatening and result in seizures and coma. Although serotonin syndrome is very rare, it can happen to people starting Paxlovid who are already taking certain psychiatric medications.

Conclusion

We are increasingly recognizing the toll of mood disorders, such as major depressive disorder and bipolar disorder, exacerbated by the COVID-19 pandemic. This chapter explores how COVID-19 infection may affect these mood disorders. While sickness behaviors are a normal and appropriate response to illness, they become problematic in the context of mood disorders. Most individuals with mood disorders are seen by their primary care physician (PCP), who can assess their symptoms and discuss treatment options, including antidepressant medications or a referral to therapy.

Learning Points
• Infection with COVID-19, like other viral infections, can affect brain functioning through directly or indirectly triggering neuroinflammation, resulting in secondary mood disorders. • The physical and emotional stress of contracting COVID-19 can trigger recurrences or exacerbations of MDD and bipolar disorder. • People with bipolar disorder experience recurrent, prolonged periods of both very low mood (depression) and very high mood (mania), which alternate over time. • People with mood disorders have significantly higher odds of hospitalization or death from COVID-19. • Antidepressants and mood stabilizers can treat mood disorders, but watch out for interactions with Paxlovid.

References

Bourgognon, J.-M., McColl, A., Suessmilch, M. et al. (2021). Stress, immune system and the brain. In: *Textbook of Immunopsychiatry* (ed. G. Khandaker, N. Harrison, E. Bullmore, and R. Dantzer), 51–72. UK: Cambridge University Press.

Campos, J.A.D.B., Campos, L.A., Martins, B.G. et al. (2022). The psychological impact of Covid-19 on individuals with and without mental health disorders. *Psychological Reports* 125 (5): 2435–2455.

Ceban, F., Nogo, D., Carvalho, I.P. et al. (2021). Association between mood disorders and risk of Covid-19 infection, hospitalization, and death: a systematic review and meta-analysis. *JAMA Psychiatry* 78 (10): 1079–1091.

Dantzer, R., O'Connor, J.C., Freund, G.G. et al. (2008). From inflammation to sickness and depression: when the immune system subjugates the brain. *Nature Reviews. Neuroscience* 9 (1): 46–56.

Grande, I., Berk, M., Birmaher, B., and Vieta, E. (2016). Bipolar disorder. *Lancet* 387 (10027): 1561–1572. https://doi.org/10.1016/S0140-6736(15)00241-X. Epub 2015 Sep 18. PMID: 26388529.

Kappelmann, N., Bullmore, E., and Khandaker, G. (2021). Immunotherapies for depression. In: *Textbook of Immunopsychiatry* (ed. G. Khandaker, N. Harrison, E. Bullmore, and R. Dantzer), 139–163. UK: Cambridge University Press.

Khandaker, G., Colasanti, A., and Harrison, N. (2021). Inflammation, sickness behaviour and depression. In: *Textbook of Immunopsychiatry* (ed. G. Khandaker, N. Harrison, E. Bullmore, and R. Dantzer), 109–138. UK: Cambridge University Press.

Mazza, M.G., Palladini, M., De Lorenzo, R. et al. (2021). Persistent psychopathology and neurocognitive impairment in Covid-19 survivors: effect of inflammatory biomarkers at three-month follow-up. *Brain, Behavior, and Immunity* 94: 138–147.

Mazza, M.G., Palladini, M., Poletti, S., and Benedetti, F. (2022). Post-Covid-19 depressive symptoms: epidemiology, pathophysiology, and pharmacological treatment. *CNS Drugs* 36 (7): 681–702.

Modabbernia, A., Taslimi, S., Brietzke, E., and Ashrafi, M. (2013). Cytokine alterations in bipolar disorder: a meta-analysis of 30 studies. *Biological Psychiatry* 74 (1): 15–25.

Newhouse, A., Kritzer, M.D., Eryilmaz, H. et al. (2022). Neurocircuitry hypothesis and clinical experience in treating neuropsychiatric symptoms of postacute sequelae of severe acute respiratory syndrome coronavirus 2. *Journal of the Academy of Consultation-Liaison Psychiatry* 63 (6): 619–627.

Park, J.H., Kummerlowe, M., Gardea Resendez, M. et al. (2021). First manic episode following Covid-19 infection. *Bipolar Disorders* 23 (8): 847–849.

Sadock, B., Sadock, V.A., and Ruiz, P. (2017). *Kaplan & Sadock's Concise Textbook of Clinical Psychiatry*, 4e. Philadelphia: LWW.

Stewart, W.F., Ricci, J.A., Chee, E. et al. (2003). Cost of lost productive work time among US workers with depression. *Journal of the American Medical Association* 289 (23): 3135–3144.

Taquet, M., Sillett, R., Zhu, L. et al. (2022). Neurological and psychiatric risk trajectories after SARS-CoV-2 infection: an analysis of 2-year retrospective cohort studies including 1 284 437 patients. *The Lancet. Psychiatry* 9 (10): 815–827.

6

Anxiety and Trauma-related Disorders due to the COVID-19 Pandemic

Mara Kailin[1], Virmarie Diaz Fernandez[2], Cynthia Peng[3], and Carmen Black[4]

[1] *The University of Denver, Counseling Psychology Program, Morgridge College of Education, Denver, CO, 80208, USA*
[2] *Concert Health, Orange Park, FL, 32073, USA*
[3] *Department of Psychiatry, Brigham and Women's Hospital, Boston, MA, 02115, USA*
[4] *Department of Psychiatry, Yale School of Medicine, New Haven, CT, 06510, USA*

Introduction

COVID-19 and anxiety go hand in hand. Anxiety is a natural response to real or perceived threats or dangers, and COVID-19 falls squarely within that category. Anxiety and fear allow us to access a state of heightened alertness and preparedness to ward off potential harm. This protective mechanism can become a source of distress. For some, however, it can develop into anxiety disorders, which can significantly disrupt life and get in the way of a person's ability to function effectively in the world.

Neurobiology of Anxiety

The brain is a complicated and fascinating organ, and the way it responds to anxiety is no exception. Let's think about how the brain reacts to anxiety through its structure and also its function.

There are several brain structures that play key roles in anxiety. Looking at Figure 6.1, you can see where these structures are located. The part of the brain

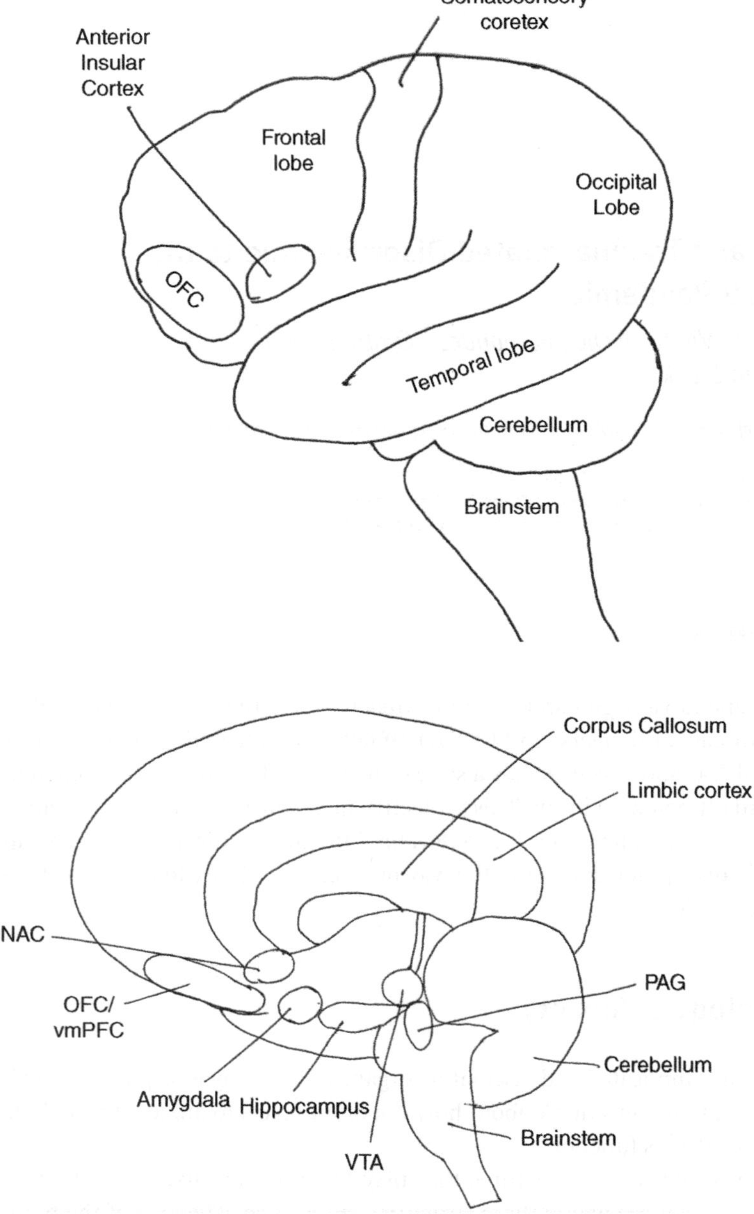

Figure 6.1 Important structures of the brain related to anxiety.

called the cortex is a great place to get started. Scientists and doctors refer to the cortex as the "higher cognitive centers" of the brain, meaning that the cortex is a group of brain structures that do the thinking and the feeling. These include structures such as the prefrontal cortex (PFC) near the front, which helps us with planning, making decisions, deciding the steps we need to take (or not take) to achieve our goals, and trying to predict what will happen if we choose to act (or not act) in a certain way. The lower part of the PFC is called the orbitofrontal cortex (OFC). It is involved in learning and reward, meaning that it is responsible for remembering which choices and actions have (or have not) led to success in the past. Accordingly, a part of the cortex called the limbic system is responsible for our emotions and feelings. The limbic system is located deep inside the middle portion of our brains. Individual parts of the limbic system include the amygdala, hippocampus, thalamus, and hypothalamus. The limbic system is considered to be more evolutionarily primitive than other parts of the brain because many of us often feel emotions without having the words or awareness to describe what we feel with words.

A small, almond-shaped structure called the amygdala plays a central role in the limbic system (Martin et al. 2009) – it takes in emotions of fear and anxiety from one's perception of daily experiences and communicates that fear and anxiety to the brain's cortex to plan and predict our behavior. The brain can then use the perceptual information and the "alert!" signal from the amygdala to decide what to do in that moment. The amygdala is connected to various brain structures, such as the hippocampus (responsible for memory), the thalamus (which processes sensory information from our five senses and directs it to the relevant brain regions for processing and action), and the hypothalamus (the main link between the endocrine system that manages hormones and the nervous system that governs our senses and movement). These brain regions must work together to keep our bodies relaxed and stable. In people with anxiety, the connections between these structures are more intense and robust. Consequently, their response to anxiety-provoking situations can be more pronounced and heightened compared to those without anxiety.

Let's contextualize this with a few examples. Think about how our ancient ancestors navigated their world while hunting and gathering food for survival. When they stumbled upon berries or other food sources, that was cause for celebration. However, if they happened to encounter a predator like a lion during their foraging, it posed a significant and immediate threat to their existence. Their visual (and possibly auditory) system would perceive this danger, and the amygdala would swiftly register it, sounding the alarm of "danger!" to the cortex. The PFC would then kick into action, strategizing to ensure the safety and survival of all. In response to the environment, the hunter-gatherer might decide to flee as fast as possible, hide in the grasses or trees, fight back against the lion, or take another action. Once the lion had departed, the hypothalamus would signal to the brain and the rest of the body, conveying that the threat had subsided, allowing everyone to return to a baseline state of relaxation. The hippocampus would encode and store this memory for future reference, a reminder of what actions worked in the past and serving as a guide for future encounters with predators.

Though this may seem far-fetched to us in modern times, many situations in our lives also mimic this pattern. The onset of the pandemic is a clear example. Recall back to the beginning of the pandemic when a mysterious set of symptoms started to appear that no scientist or doctor had seen before – that was certainly anxiety-provoking! The TV and internet were filled with worrisome information about climbing hospital rates and deaths. The information processing centers of our brain were rapidly communicating with the amygdala and other areas to figure out what was going on and what to do about it. The amygdala detected a modern threat – the threat of an invisible and possibly lethal virus that was perhaps even more scary than the threat of a lion.

Do you remember when we learned that COVID-19 was spreading around the world at a rapid pace? Constantly seeing worrisome things in the media can make the fear of the unknown even more frightening. At that time, we may have used our frontal lobes, as previously discussed, to make decisions. Should we wear a mask? Should we go to the grocery store or have groceries delivered? Should we cancel upcoming travel? Is it safe to go to work? Is it safe to visit sick or elderly loved ones? As scientists and public health officials gathered more information, our higher-order cognitive centers used the information to direct our actions. Sure, our limbic system may have signaled "threat!" and felt acutely anxious when another person came too close to us in public. Hopefully, however, parts of the cortex said "Oh, I can see that they are wearing a mask; let me assess other factors rationally before making a hasty decision."

We can also apply this to social situations. COVID-19 has changed our social interactions and the way we relate to each other and the world. Think back to the peak of COVID-19 when we quarantined ourselves and only interacted with the people we lived with for many months. As vaccines started to roll out and the world gradually reopened, we began to gather again and attend events. Though we may have felt good that life seemed to be returning to normal, we may have also felt anxiety about reengaging in social interactions after such a long time. Seeing a large crowd of people may have been anxiety-provoking, triggering a response in the amygdala, which then transmitted this information to their cortex. We may have thought "Gosh, that's a bigger crowd of people than I've seen in a while. I am anxious about the possibility of catching COVID-19." Alternatively, we may have thought "After so many months in quarantine, my social and conversational skills have declined; I hope my friends don't think I'm socially awkward." Situations such as these in our modern lives can be as anxiety-provoking as predatory lions were for our ancestors!

Disproportionate Impact of COVID-19 on Anxiety

The COVID-19 pandemic disproportionately affected minoritized racial and ethnic populations. Minoritized populations endured the additional stress and anxiety resulting from discrimination in society and within healthcare institutions. In the United States, African American and Latinx communities faced higher rates of COVID-19-related illnesses and deaths as a result of racism. Limited social and employment opportunities concentrated racially minoritized communities into less glamorous and more dangerous jobs that could not be performed remotely, often in more crowded settings with fewer resources. They were also more likely to live in crowded housing, which often included multiple generations and elderly loved ones. Furthermore, people living in minoritized communities experienced the media broadcasting the effects of the pandemic on people and communities that looked like them – including having to bury more loved ones due to COVID-19.

Stress Responses to Trauma and Loss

We hope that you are comforted by learning about how anxiety is rooted in our anatomy and evolutionary history. Stress is our inevitable companion throughout life, yet our responses to stress can vary significantly depending on the nature of the stressor and our individual coping mechanisms. Stress reactions are normal physiological and psychological responses to events perceived as threatening or harmful. Understanding these reactions is crucial for maintaining our mental well-being and navigating life's adversities.

Acute Stress Reactions

Acute stress reactions (also known as acute stress responses) are immediate, short-term reactions to sudden, unexpected, or traumatic events. These events could range from witnessing an accident, experiencing a natural disaster, or being in a life-threatening situation. The symptoms of acute stress reactions can be both physical and psychological. Physical symptoms may include rapid heartbeats (called heart palpitations), shortness of breath, trembling, sweating, or discomfort or pain in your stomach. Psychological symptoms can include confusion, anxiety, or difficulty sleeping. These reactions are your body's way of responding to a perceived threat or danger. It is the body's "fight or flight" response kicking into gear. That is, when considering the lion analogy from the previous section, the "fight or flight" response is the body's physical and mental preparation to either fight the lion or sprint away to safety.

Acute stress reactions are quite common in both children and adults. The good news is that while these reactions can be distressing, they typically only last a short period of time. Many people have experienced acute stress reactions due to COVID-19. You may have experienced financial hardship from job loss, burnout as a healthcare or other essential professional working on the frontlines to keep the country safe and running, parental hardship due to virtual schooling and closed daycares, sudden isolation from loved ones, hospitalizations of loved ones battling the virus, a loss of access to healthy coping mechanisms like religious services or community activities, and so much more.

Post-traumatic Stress Disorder (PTSD)

When an acute stress reaction lasts for more than one month, it may be a sign of Post-Traumatic Stress Disorder (PTSD), a more severe and long-term condition that often requires professional intervention. PTSD involves the same physical and psychological reactions of the acute stress response mixed with unwanted, frequent, scary memories or thoughts of the traumatic event. Over time, people with PTSD avoid situations, places, or actions that remind them of the traumatic event, which interferes with their ability to function.

Grief

Grief, on the other hand, is a reaction to a significant loss, most commonly the death of a loved one. It is a complex emotional process that involves a range of feelings such as sadness, anger, guilt, and despair. Grief is not a process that follows any expected pattern, and it does not stick to a specific timeline. Some people may start to feel better within weeks or months, while the grieving process may take years for others. Everyone grieves in their own way, and there is no "right" or "wrong" way to grieve. Grief may also come with physical symptoms, such as changes in appetite or sleep, fatigue, or physical discomfort. Many people are grieving the loss of loved ones infected with the virus, with particularly high levels of grief among older adults and in people from minority communities.

Prolonged Grief Disorder

Grief is a normal and natural response to loss. By contrast, people experiencing "complicated grief" or prolonged grief disorder experience symptoms for an extended period of time (at least one year for adults and at least six months for children and adolescents). People with prolonged grief disorder avoid reminders of the deceased loved one and may struggle to function well (for example, they may not be able to work due to their sadness). In such cases, grief counseling or therapy can help.

Both acute stress reactions and grief are normal processes that reflect our body's natural response to traumatic events and loss. PTSD and prolonged grief disorder are only diagnosed when a person's symptoms last for longer than expected and significantly affect their ability to function. If you're not sure whether you (or your loved one's) symptoms are more severe than expected, it may be a good idea to reach out for support and seek professional help.

Anxiety Disorders

Anxiety disorders can develop at different stages of life and follow distinct courses. Many of us experienced anxiety during and after the pandemic, and for good reason. Common reasons for heightened anxiety during pandemics include a fear of germs, a fear of crowded spaces, work, and social hardships, a fear of financial hardships, a fear of falling behind academically, and isolation. For some of us, our minds and bodies responded to the stress and anxiety of the COVID-19 pandemic in ways that caused long-lasting and significant suffering, as well as impairment in our daily activities. The sections below describe the anxiety disorders and cover effective interventions that can effectively treat anxiety disorder symptoms.

Anxiety disorders are a group of mental health conditions characterized by excessive fear, anxiety, or behavioral disturbances. Many people feel anxious from time to time, and this is completely normal. Mental health professionals define the difference between normal anxiety and an anxiety disorder by whether or not the anxiety is causing negative life consequences or functional impairments – like feeling so anxious throughout the day that your boss gets mad that you cannot complete your work. Anxiety disorders have different triggers, but they all have one common symptom: excessive fear or worry in situations that are not threatening. The most common anxiety disorders are specific phobias, generalized anxiety disorder (GAD), social anxiety disorder, obsessive-compulsive disorder (OCD), and panic disorder.

Specific Phobias

Specific phobias are intense, irrational fears of specific objects or situations that pose little or no real danger – like extreme fear of blood or fear of being trapped in an elevator. To be diagnosed with a specific phobia, you must spend a great deal of energy trying to avoid the fear or endure it only with great discomfort over a prolonged period of time. Specific phobias can happen at any age, even in early childhood. They are most often first seen between the ages of 15 and 20. Phobias can persist for several years or, in 10–30% of cases (Eaton et al. 2018), even decades. They often accompany other anxiety, mood, and substance use disorders. The course and severity of specific phobias can vary greatly. Some individuals may experience a gradual decrease in symptoms over time, while others may continue to experience symptoms over many years.

Generalized Anxiety Disorder (GAD)

Katie is a 40-year-old single parent who lost her job during the pandemic. She has constant worries and loses sleep due to her concerns about finances, the education of her children, and her job security.

Generalized anxiety disorder (GAD) is characterized by chronic and excessive worry about a number of different things like health, finances, or job security. Typically, It has a later onset than other anxiety disorders (Lijster et al. 2017) and often starts around age 30, although it can also occur in childhood. The disorder is more common in women than in men. As seen in Figure 6.2, symptoms include losing sleep, feeling irritable, experiencing muscle aches, fatigue from being nervous, and having difficulty concentrating – all for at least six months. The severity and duration of symptoms can vary widely among individuals, but many people experience periods of intense anxiety mixed in between periods of relative calm. These worries can be about everything and nothing specific at the same time, but must be beyond the limits of realistic consequences. In Katie's case above, once her life has fully restabilized, she would only meet criteria for a diagnosis of GAD

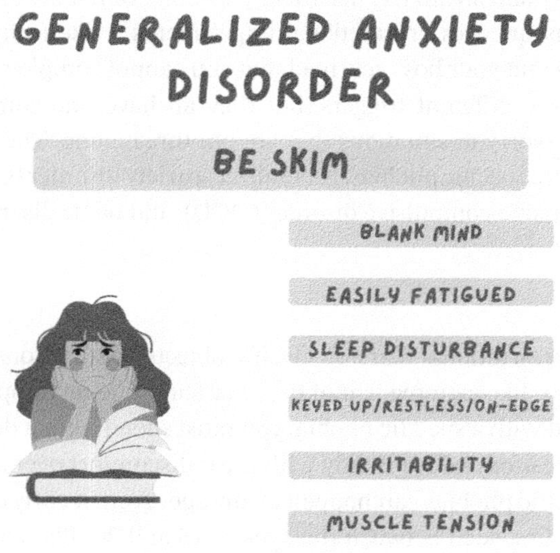

Figure 6.2 GAD symptoms.

if the intensity of her worries and sleeplessness do not improve after six months. If Katie's symptoms remain severe and she meets the criteria for GAD, the severity of her symptoms may still fluctuate and worsen during times of stress. Without treatment, GAD can become a chronic condition with distressing symptoms.

Social Anxiety Disorder

Social anxiety disorder, also known as Social Phobia, is characterized by an intense fear and avoidance of social situations that lasts for at least six months. The main concern for people experiencing social anxiety is a fear that other people are judging them or criticizing them. Social anxiety disorder typically presents during the teenage years, although it can also emerge in early childhood (Rosellini et al. 2013). It can be debilitating, with individuals often avoiding social interactions to the point where their normal daily life is significantly disrupted. We might think about social anxiety in a person who avoids social situations due to an intense fear of being embarrassed about wearing (or not wearing) a mask. Without treatment, social anxiety disorder can persist for many years or a lifetime.

Obsessive-compulsive Disorder (OCD)

Obsessive-Compulsive Disorder (OCD) is characterized by repetitive, unwanted, intrusive thoughts of something bad happening (obsessions) followed by irrational, excessive urges to do certain actions that are thought to reduce the risk of that something bad happening (compulsions).

For example, Ruth may have an overwhelming fear of germs (her obsession), leading her to wash her hands so frequently (her compulsion) that her hands start to bleed, and she misses hours of work as a result.

OCD usually begins in adolescence or early adulthood, but in rare cases it can start in childhood. OCD is generally believed to follow a chronic waxing and waning course.

We would also consider OCD in Jonas, who experiences such an intense fear of viral contagion (his obsession) that he checks and rechecks his masks so frequently (his compulsion) that he is fired from his job for being late too often (his life consequence). The course of OCD can vary among individuals. Unfortunately, some experience a gradual worsening of symptoms if their OCD is not treated.

Panic Disorder

Kendra is a 23-year-old mathematics student who lives alone. She studied remotely during the COVID-19 pandemic. Once her university opened back up, she made the decision to attend a close friend's party. There she experienced her first panic attack, which caused her to leave the party. She had two more panic attacks over the next week, which she attributed to school stress. Concerned that her panic attacks were due to a medical condition, Kendra makes a doctor's appointment. She tells her doctor that she has started to avoid crowded social gatherings entirely due to her fear of having another panic attack. Her doctor diagnoses Kendra with panic disorder.

Panic disorder involves a fear of having panic attacks that is so intense that it changes behavior. People with panic disorder avoid situations in which they believe they may have another panic attack. Panic attacks are sudden periods of intense fear that may include rapid heartbeats, sweating, shaking, shortness of breath, numbness, or a feeling that something terrible is about to happen. Panic disorder is twice as common in women as it is in men (McLean et al. 2011). Symptoms often begin before age 25. Children can also have panic disorder, but it is often not diagnosed until they are older. Without treatment, panic disorder can become a chronic condition and may interfere significantly with a person's functioning.

Different Experiences of Anxiety

While some symptoms are common across all anxiety disorders, the way they are expressed and interpreted can vary significantly depending on one's personality, cultural identity, and lived experiences. Together, these factors influence how individuals perceive, express, and manage their stress, anxiety, and grief. We are all unique. For some people, it can be difficult for them to share that they are struggling, or they may feel like they cannot talk about work or financial stress. For others, their particular environment may encourage the open expression of emotions like fear and stress, like coping with a pandemic-related job loss (Morales-Rodríguez 2021). Anxiety may be expressed in terms of bodily complaints such as headaches or stomachaches, or it may be expressed in terms of emotional symptoms such as worry and nervousness. These different expressions are all valid. This is the reason why mental health clinicians consider so many different symptoms and struggles when diagnosing anxiety.

Social, historical, and cultural factors influence how a person experiences anxiety (Hoffman and Hinton 2014). For example, "Ataque de Nervios" is a culturally-bound syndrome found in Latinx communities. This syndrome is characterized by uncontrollable shouting, crying, trembling, sensations of heat rising in the chest and head, and verbal or physical aggression. Sometimes, fainting or seizure-like episodes may occur. In Japan, a condition known as "Taijin Kyofusho" is characterized by intense fear that a person's body, bodily functions, or physical appearance are offensive to others (Essau et al. 2012). This condition could be viewed as a variant of social anxiety disorder, but it is culturally unique in its focus on offending others rather than fear of personal embarrassment. In the Inuit culture, "Kataoyak" or "Arctic Hysteria" refers to episodes of intense fear, disorientation, and perceptual disturbances during long periods of darkness in winter.

Human beings are diverse, and so are our experiences of anxiety. Overall, these cultural variations highlight the importance of cultural sensitivity and understanding in the diagnosis and treatment of anxiety disorders. We should never make assumptions that someone from a certain background will automatically feel any particular way. Rather, it helps to maintain a healthy curiosity that allows us to approach each person as an individual and humbly ask how they feel. If you have concerns about whether your symptoms could be due to anxiety, it can be helpful to meet with a clinician, who can guide you toward appropriate resources and treatments.

Anxiety With COVID-19 and Other Chronic Health Conditions

The COVID-19 pandemic has placed health-related anxiety in the spotlight. The virus's novelty, the severity of symptoms and potential for severe illness, social isolation, the constant stream of often-conflicting information about the virus, and its rapid rate of spread have generated significant anxiety globally. Individuals may fear contracting the virus and worry about their own health or the health of their loved ones. Those of us who have been infected may experience anxiety related to the course of the illness, the long-term health effects, and the social stigma associated with the disease. Some COVID-19 infections result in persistent symptoms called Long COVID. Its symptoms, including changes in blood pressure, heart rate, and digestion, can potentially be confused with an anxiety disorder.

The unique social context of the COVID-19 pandemic also contributes to anxiety. This is largely due to isolation, fear of infection, and significant changes in daily routines. These external stressors can exacerbate anxiety and other mental health issues. However, these situational triggers for anxiety are separate from the physiological changes that might occur due to the virus itself. Some research suggests that in severe cases, the virus may cause changes in brain function, potentially affecting serotonin levels, a neurotransmitter that contributes to feelings of well-being and happiness (Eteraf-Oskouei and Najafi 2022). When serotonin levels drop, this can lead to symptoms of depression and anxiety. It is important to note, however, that the relationship between COVID-19 and serotonin levels is still not fully understood and is an ongoing area of research. Also, it is likely that the majority of anxiety related to the pandemic is due to the socio-emotional impact, rather than direct physiological changes caused by the virus (Eteraf-Oskouei and Najafi 2022). Thus, while the pandemic's social context and isolation can lead to anxiety, this is distinct from the potential brain changes and serotonin level fluctuations that might be caused by the virus. Both aspects, however, can coexist and interact, making it critical to address both the psychological and physiological dimensions when treating COVID-19-related anxiety. Anxiety is not exclusive to COVID-19. Other infections, such as Influenza, HIV, or Hepatitis, can also trigger anxiety by mimicking the physical components of anxiety disorders, such as a rapid heartbeat, shortness of breath, and fatigue. Furthermore, the stress of knowing you have an infection, the uncertainty about complications and outcomes, the burden of managing the infection, and the potential impact on lifestyle and lifespan can all increase anxiety.

Chronic medical conditions are medical conditions that often do not fully resolve, like high blood pressure, diabetes, cancer, and asthma. These illnesses can also be a source of anxiety, a common response to various health conditions. For instance, heart disease can provoke anxiety due to symptoms that resemble those of panic attacks, like chest pain and palpitations. Hormonal imbalances, as seen in thyroid disease, can lead to anxiety symptoms such as restlessness and irritability. People with chronic medical conditions are more likely to have severe complications from COVID-19, including a higher likelihood of death. They have valid reasons to be more anxious about catching COVID-19 than healthier or younger adults.

Treatment of Anxiety Disorders

Susan is a 34-year-old woman working as a biologist conducting experiments in a lab. At the start of the COVID-19 pandemic, the lab had to shut down all operations. Susan tells you that she is now constantly worried about her experiments to the point that she feels "crazy." She believes that her career is doomed because of her unfortunate situation, and she finds it increasingly difficult to concentrate. She also feels inadequate and unmotivated, which keeps her from doing other research at home. Physically, she mentions feeling cold sweats, heart racing, and muscle aches. She also shares that she struggles to sleep due to an inability to "shut off" her brain at night.

Recognizing and addressing anxiety can improve a person's quality of life. There are a variety of treatment options for anxiety. Health professionals can provide valuable support by educating patients about their condition, addressing fears and misconceptions, and offering strategies to manage anxiety. Treatments may include medications, therapy, lifestyle modifications, and relaxation techniques.

Medications

Susan is experiencing severe anxiety every day, affecting her ability to work. She sees her primary care clinician and is diagnosed with GAD.

When thinking about medication options to treat anxiety, antidepressants are often the first choice. On the one hand, among antidepressant classes, many clinicians start with a trial of a daily medication, such as a Selective Serotonin Reuptake Inhibitors (SSRI). On the other hand, if someone finds themselves anxious as a result of specific situations – let's say, a big test coming up, meeting someone new for the first time, or speaking in front of a crowd – an "as needed" medication may be appropriate to take right before or during the anxiety-provoking situation. Categories of "as needed" anxiety medication include antihistamines (the same medications commonly used to treat allergies), blood pressure medications called beta blockers that prevent the body's "fight or flight" responses from fully kicking in, or benzodiazepines, which are very effective but can produce tolerance when used regularly.

Psychotherapy

Whereas medications target anxiety symptoms through neurotransmitters, psychotherapy treats anxiety through changes in a person's thoughts and behavior (Sanderson et al. 2020). Some of the most common forms of therapy for anxiety disorders are Cognitive Behavioral Therapy (CBT) and Acceptance and Commitment Therapy (ACT), supportive talk therapy, mindfulness therapies, and body-based therapies. CBT focuses on what therapists call the "cognitive triangle", which are the links between cognitions (thoughts), emotions, and behaviors. In our case above, Susan is understandably anxious because her experiments could not progress. Her concerns about her career (thoughts) lead her to feel anxious, as she now perceives herself as a failure of a scientist (emotions). Her anxiety and sense of inadequacy lead Susan to stop her work during quarantine (behaviors). During CBT sessions, a therapist may help Susan identify her thoughts as "catastrophizing" thoughts. These are thoughts where the perceived consequences of a problem are thought to be more severe than they really are. Her therapist may help her identify that the pandemic is outside of her control and not a reflection of her abilities as a scientist. Developing this understanding can influence Susan's self-esteem. Rather than stopping her work, she may find motivation and ways to use her time away from the lab to read papers in her field, for example.

CBT in action:

After infection with COVID-19, Susan recovers after a few weeks. However, she develops a fear of crowds, initially due to her concern about becoming reinfected with COVID-19. She sees her therapist for CBT who helps her (i) acknowledge her thoughts: she had been educated to refrain from crowds during the peak of the pandemic, and seeing a crowd of people can still be anxiety-provoking, (ii) relate that thought to the emotion of anxiety or fear, but ultimately recognize that the threat of COVID-19 reinfection is less now than it was at the peak of the pandemic, and (iii) direct her behavior to proceed in crowded areas with reasonable caution (not to flee).

Lifestyle Modifications

Susan can actively counteract anxiety by changing her routine. Either through therapy or personal goal-setting, she can develop a routine of getting out of bed at the same time each morning, exercising, preparing meals, and participating in leisure activities.

These are a set of actions we call "behavioral activation" and form part of lifestyle modification.

Spiritual Connections

Many people turn to spiritual traditions when facing life stressors. This is also a very important form of coping. Research demonstrates how a healthy spiritual life can improve mental health and anxiety (Lucchetti et al. 2021). In the United States, certain groups may be less trusting of formal medical institutions, such as refugees who have experienced mistreatment by official institutions in their country of origin. Social factors lead to the COVID-19 pandemic impacting many of these same communities worse than others. So, for people who have experienced discrimination in the past, witnessing and experiencing discrimination during the pandemic may have reinforced their reasons for not trusting formal mental health systems in the future. Not only is spiritual coping an evidence-based form of dealing with anxiety, faith institutions are seen by many communities who have experienced discrimination to be a more trustworthy alternative than working with a clinician. Oftentimes, collaborating with spiritual advisors like a hospital chaplain or church pastor forms useful allyship in reducing stress and anxiety.

Relaxation Techniques and Mindfulness Practices

Figure 6.3 outlines methods that Susan can use to manage anxiety at home. There are other methods and exercises to help Susan relax when anxiety feels out of control, or when she feels nervous about an anxiety-provoking situation. Breathing exercises, especially when one breathes from the deep belly (diaphragmatic breathing), counteract the sympathetic nervous system (the "fight or flight" system) and stimulate the parasympathetic nervous system (the "rest and digest" system). You can try them when you feel your heart beating faster, when you start to breathe faster, if you feel dizzy or jittery – these are signs that a situation is triggering your sympathetic nervous system, and it is time to

Figure 6.3 Tips to relieve anxiety.

activate the parasympathetic nervous system. You can learn relaxation techniques in many ways (including YouTube videos, mobile apps, therapy, or workbooks). One effective and easy-to-learn breathing technique is called "boxed breathing." You can try this right now: Inhale through your nose for four seconds, hold your breath for four seconds, exhale through your mouth for four seconds, then hold your breath again for four seconds. Boxed breathing stimulates the vagus nerve, which is a major player in the parasympathetic nervous system (see Figure 6.4).

Imagery exercises are relaxation techniques where a person is guided to create a soothing scene in their mind's eye. There are numerous guided imagery exercises that can be accessed online or *via* apps, and many are free. Similarly, progressive muscle relaxation is another tool you can use to decrease anxiety. You can find guided progressive muscle relaxation exercises, or you can do them on your own by getting in a comfortable position in a quiet space and focusing on relaxing one muscle group at a time, starting with the bottom of the feet and moving slowly all the way up to the top of the head. These are excellent tools for relaxation or to help you fall asleep at night, whether you are feeling anxious or not.

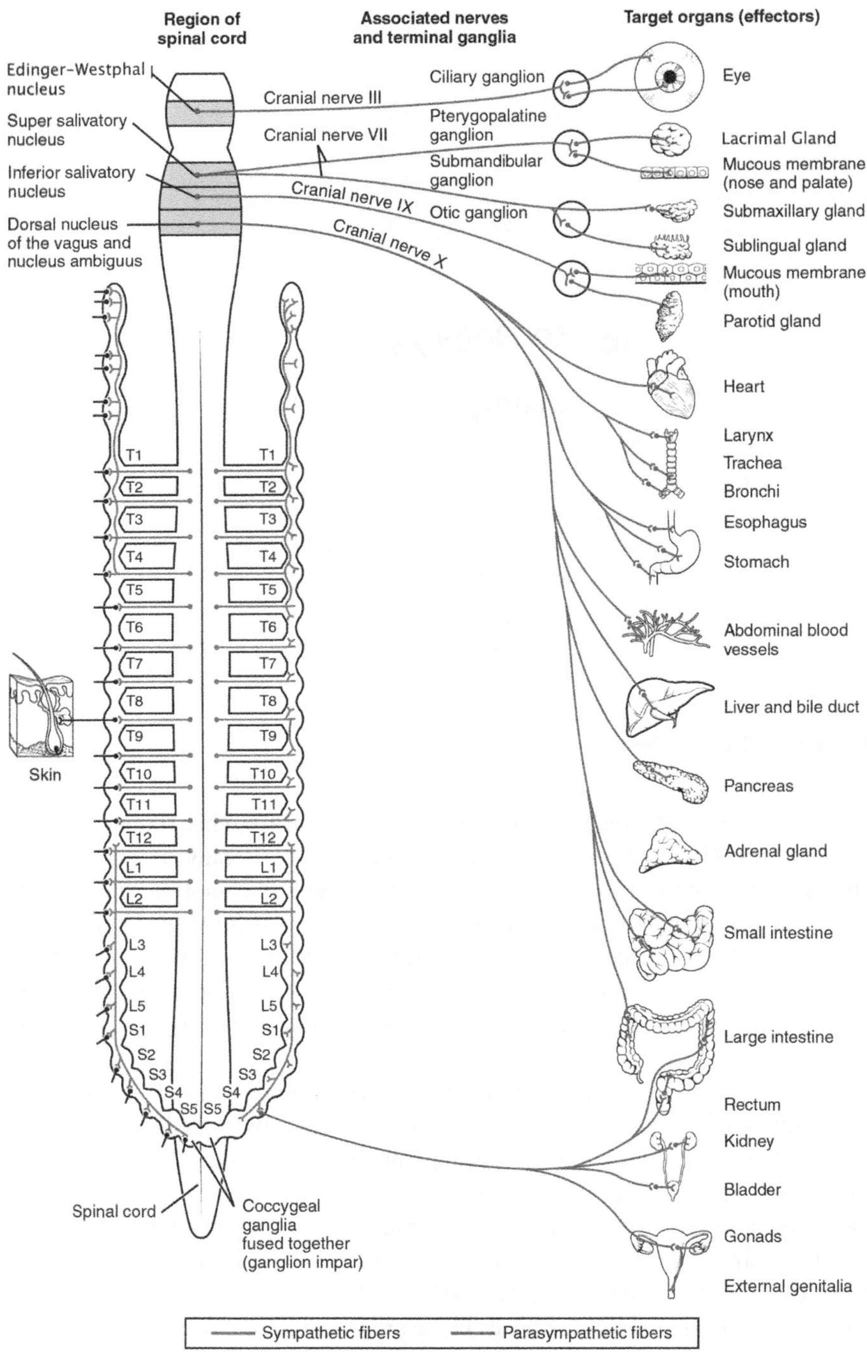

Figure 6.4 The sympathetic and parasympathetic nervous system. *Source:* Illustration from Anatomy & Physiology, Connexions Web site. http://cnx.org/content/col11496/1.6/, Jun 19, 2013. Date 23 May 2013, 21:12:14. *Source:* Anatomy & Physiology, Connexions Web site. http://cnx.org/content/col11496/1.6/, Jun 19, 2013. AuthorOpenStax College.

Mindfulness techniques are another way to calm anxiety and engage the parasympathetic nervous system. A mindfulness practice involves focusing on only one thing in the moment, such as focusing on your breathing. As your mind wanders away from that one thing during the mindfulness practice, you gently and nonjudgmentally bring your mind back to that one thing as often as needed. You can turn almost any activity into a mindfulness exercise. Some people like to try mindful walking, mindful eating, or mindful swimming. Yoga or Tai Chi can also serve as a mindfulness or relaxation practice where one focuses exclusively on the movements of the body and the breathing associated with those movements.

Environmental Modifications: Greenspace

What if a healthcare professional told you they could prescribe something known to help your anxiety, is low-cost or no-cost, and has no side effects? Your clinician might suggest something called "greenspace" for you. We can broadly think about greenspace as any urban park, tree-lined street, or natural open space. We know that being outdoors decreases the risk of transmitting the virus. Recall the last time you were outside, and it made you feel good. Greenspace doesn't necessarily have to be literally "green." Wintry landscapes, bursting fall colors, blue waves crashing against sand, and everything in between count as well – the main idea is that one is immersed in nature. Though it may seem like common sense, being in greenspace has many benefits for mental and physical health (Twohig-Bennett and Jones 2018). These include better heart health, lower cholesterol, lower blood pressure, improved pregnancy outcomes, increased attention, and decreased stress (Twohig-Bennett and Jones 2018). Think about the last time something happened that caused you anxiety. Now, think – in that moment – if you could be transported to a forest where the wind is whistling through the trees, the running water of a brook is nearby, the scent of pine needles is around you, and the sun is warming your skin. Hopefully, even in that quick, multisensory example, you felt some twinge of relief. Nature is a powerful medicine!

One of the very few silver linings from the pandemic is that our society has rethought the way we see and use greenspace. Remember the days when gathering indoors and in large numbers was not safe? Relatively speaking, being outdoors was safer, and many people chose to gather outside in smaller groups to socialize. Precisely because we could not gather in restaurants or each other's houses, and perhaps because we were tired of "socializing" virtually, we became creative. It was quite the sight to see people gathering on picnic blankets or bed sheets and enjoying public parks and other greenspaces. It opened our eyes as to how simple and fun this could be, and some people started to include visits to local parks into their busy lives. People can continue to use greenspace as an effective and simple way of connecting with others, connecting with themselves, and connecting with nature.

How to Assist a Loved One with Anxiety

Experiencing anxiety is challenging, but it can be even more difficult to watch a loved one go through a difficult time. Here are ways you can provide support to someone dealing with prolonged or significant anxiety:

- Encourage them to seek professional help from a mental health clinician who can assess, diagnose, and provide treatment options.
- Provide a safe and nonjudgmental environment for them to express their feelings and thoughts.
- Educate yourself about anxiety disorders to better understand their experiences.
- Help them maintain a healthy lifestyle by promoting balanced eating, regular exercise, and adequate sleep.

Remember to prioritize your own mental health too, as supporting someone with a mental health condition can be taxing.

We have shared extensive information about anxiety and its manifestations in the aftermath of the COVID-19 pandemic. Now, we will consolidate all this theoretical information and explore how anxiety plays out in real-world scenarios through two case studies.

Joseph is a 40-year-old man who sought therapy because his anxiety had increased since the onset of the COVID-19 pandemic. He first remembered experiencing anxiety in elementary school, mostly in social situations or when he needed to speak in front of a group, but he was able to manage his symptoms by keeping a small, close-knit group of friends and focusing his studies on computer programming, which did not require group work or presentations.

After college, Joseph moved to a new, small city where he did not have many social contacts. He got a job working remotely with a technology company. Joseph found that he preferred staying at home and isolating during the pandemic. When the initial months of the pandemic turned into more than a year and it became safe to go out, he continued to stay at home, only leaving when he needed to get groceries or go on an essential errand. He did not seek out or develop a new social network in his new hometown.

Joseph rarely interacted with others in his job, and he found that he was no longer reaching out to family or friends, even virtually, as the pandemic wore on. Joseph's fear of social situations that he first noticed in elementary school returned and became more pronounced. He felt extreme anxiety even at the thought of reaching out to friends. When others would try to connect with him, he would not answer the phone and would ignore messages. He started to develop anxiety around checking his texts or messages, knowing that he would be too anxious to know how to respond in a way that felt good to him. Eventually, he stopped communicating even with family members. He began to experience panic attacks that seemed to come on randomly and very suddenly. He started to isolate even more at the fear of having more panic attacks in public. After more than two years of the pandemic, Joseph ended up being taken by ambulance to the emergency room with shortness of breath, lightheadedness, chest pain, and difficulty breathing. The clinicians in the emergency room examined Joseph and determined that nothing was wrong with him medically, and he was diagnosed with panic disorder.

It was after his ER visit that Joseph sought therapy. The therapist identified that he was experiencing anxiety in multiple domains of his life, including Social Anxiety Disorder due to his fear of being embarrassed in public, Agoraphobia due to his extreme fear of leaving his home to enter crowded spaces or places where it would be hard for him to escape, as well as Panic Disorder, where his choices to isolate were also driven by an intense fear of having more panic attacks (described previously in this chapter).

Joseph participated in individual therapy weekly for approximately nine months. The therapist used CBT techniques to help Joseph examine his irrational beliefs and cognitive distortions and replace them with more adaptive thinking patterns. Joseph learned to examine the evidence for his thoughts and beliefs in order to determine whether they were accurate or might be distorted. Joseph learned about the Cognitive Triangle, which illustrates how our thoughts, emotions, and behaviors affect one another and are interconnected.

The therapist taught Joseph anxiety reduction and grounding techniques, which he practiced weekly. The grounding techniques that Joseph found most helpful were mindfulness practices. Joseph engaged in a variety of mindfulness practices where he focused on only one thing in the moment. Joseph found he could do mindfulness in all sorts of creative ways, including mindful teeth brushing, where he focused only on brushing his teeth. This was especially effective when he used his nondominant hand! He also tried mindful dishwashing, mindful eating, and mindful walking.

The therapist also worked with Joseph to identify the triggers for his panic attacks by working backwards to identify the thoughts and feelings that lead to the sudden spike in anxiety that causes panic. During therapy, Joseph's panic attacks became less frequent, and he began to leave the house more and more. By the end of therapy, his panic attacks were completely gone. Joseph also began to enjoy some of the social situations and friendships that he used to cherish. He reestablished close relationships with family members and old friends and began new relationships in his new hometown. He still occasionally experienced anxiety, but he was able to manage anxious thoughts and feelings when they arose using grounding techniques he learned in therapy.

Alma is a 56-year-old woman who immigrated to the US from Guatemala as a young child with her mother and younger brother. The journey was very difficult, and Alma was worried about whether she and her family would survive. Along the way, she saw the bodies of migrants that had passed away on their journey. They had little food and had to sleep outside in unsafe conditions most nights. Her younger brother, who was a toddler at the time of their arrival to the US, developed a life-threatening illness during the difficult journey. He was hospitalized for several months, but he thankfully ended up recovering fully. After her son's illness, Alma's mother was always fearful of her children getting sick. Any cough or sneeze would get her worried; she took Alma to the doctor quite often, concerned she might have some sort of illness, but Alma never developed anything more serious than a common cold.

Alma was in her early 50s when the COVID-19 pandemic started. Her mother had passed away of natural causes 10 years prior, and her brother was a happy, healthy adult living in a different city. In her adult life, Alma had struggled with anxiety around illness like her mother. She cleaned her apartment daily and washed her hands frequently to try to prevent the spread of germs. Sometimes, she would shower multiple times per day and had a particular ritual that she needed to follow when cleaning herself in order for her to believe that she would not fall ill. As the months of COVID-19 quarantine wore on, Alma's anxiety, and the behaviors she used to try to control the anxiety, became more and more pronounced. She continued to stay at home, even after quarantine orders were lifted. She stopped accepting any mail or packages, worrying that they were contaminated. She constantly cleaned the surfaces in her home. She found she was washing her hands dozens of times per day despite never leaving her home. She developed rituals where she needed to put items in her closet in a certain order and check that her doors were locked over and over again in order to try to keep her fears at bay.

Alma, along with her work colleagues, had been working remotely for the first two years of the pandemic. When the organization asked all of the employees to return to the office, Alma was so worried about getting ill that she refused to return. For a number of months her boss let her continue to work from home, but eventually she was unable to complete her duties as a project manager without returning to the office, so she lost her job. A colleague suggested she seek therapy to help with her anxiety and job loss.

Alma was wary of seeking therapy, as it was not something that was common in her culture. She participated in a consultation with a therapist, who helped her understand that her increased anxiety with the pandemic was common and treatable. The therapist was an immigrant herself, also from Central America, and was able to work with Alma in her native Spanish. The therapist explained to Alma that behavioral health treatment, especially around traumatic experiences, is more effective when it can be conducted in a client's native language.

Because Alma felt that the therapist could relate to her, she quickly developed trust with the therapist and they started treatment together. The therapist helped Alma understand and process her early traumatic experience of migration to the US. Alma had not previously realized that she had experienced trauma on the journey. With the help of the therapist, she came to understand that trauma is a lasting emotional response that often results from living through a distressing event. She came to understand that experiencing a traumatic event can harm a person's sense of safety, sense of self, and ability to regulate emotions and navigate relationships. Alma's mother also had a difficult time with the residual effects of the migration and her son's illness, which manifested in medical anxiety for her children that lasted throughout their childhoods. Alma internalized similar worries around illness. This became very hard to manage and sort out from the rational fears around COVID-19 and its dangers.

Alma's anxiety spiked during the pandemic and developed into OCD. As described in greater detail above, OCD is a type of anxiety disorder characterized by a pattern of unwanted thoughts and fears known as obsessions leading to repetitive behaviors designed to alleviate the distress of the obsessions, called compulsions. Alma felt driven to do compulsive acts in an attempt to ease anxiety, but even when she would try to ignore or get rid of bothersome thoughts or urges, they kept coming back. Her obsessions and compulsions got in the way of her daily activities and caused a lot of distress. OCD often centers around certain themes, such as being overly fearful of getting contaminated by germs. To ease contamination fears, Alma washed her hands over and over again, cleaned her house, and engaged in other compulsions motivated by her obsessive fear of COVID-19.

Alma participated in individual therapy twice per week for two months and then once per week for six more months. Therapy focused first on processing Alma's trauma history and then targeted her OCD symptoms. First, the therapist helped Alma learn and practice anxiety management techniques. Alma learned diaphragmatic breathing, progressive muscle relaxation techniques, and imagery exercises designed to reduce anxiety. Alma also learned how to engage relaxation via the parasympathetic nervous system. Once Alma was better able to regulate her emotions, she and the therapist constructed a "trauma narrative" over a series of appointments. The narrative allowed Alma to process her worries and fears and share them with another supportive, trained individual. Ultimately, Alma was able to share her completed trauma narrative with her brother. This process was very healing for her and helped her brother continue to support her in her journey.

The second part of therapy focused on Alma's OCD symptoms. The therapist used an evidence-based therapy called Exposure and Response Prevention (ERP) to help her overcome her fears of catching COVID-19 and becoming ill. Alma and the therapist created a "fear hierarchy" of her fears and rated the intensity of the fear for each item on the list. Alma then participated in imaginal exposure where *the therapist guided her through imagery exercises featuring some of her fears. As Alma was able to successfully complete imaginal exposure, she then transitioned to live or "in vivo" exposure exercises. She gradually tackled her fears one by one until she and the therapist completed the list. Examples of some of the in vivo exposure exercises that Alma and the therapist did included not washing her hands after walking around the block, and not washing down the counter before eating a meal. With the exposure exercises, Alma's OCD symptoms were dramatically reduced, as was her overall level of anxiety. She was able to return to her job and enjoy her life, despite the fact that COVID-19 has not disappeared.*

Conclusion

The COVID-19 pandemic unleashed a surge of emotional challenges, with anxiety and trauma-related disorders taking center stage. The fear and uncertainty surrounding the virus, coupled with experiences like losing loved ones or adapting to new ways of living, have significantly impacted our mental well-being. It is important for all of us to recognize that these reactions are a typical response to an abnormal situation, and seeking help demonstrates strength, not weakness.

Remember, you don't have to navigate this alone. Numerous resources are available to help you. Therapy, medications, and other supports have all proven effective in managing anxiety and trauma-related disorders. Do not hesitate to connect with healthcare professionals who can guide you toward what is right for you.

This chapter aims to enhance your understanding of the emotional repercussions of the pandemic. Moving forward, prioritize your mental health just as you would your physical well-being. By supporting one another and extending a hand when needed, we can collectively navigate these challenging times.

Learning Points

- Anxiety is a normal, biologically adaptive physiological and psychological response to events perceived as threatening or harmful.
- The COVID-19 pandemic heightened anxiety universally. Its impact was particularly pronounced among marginalized populations.
- For some individuals, the increased anxiety induced by COVID-19 caused or intensified anxiety disorders.
- Seeking assistance from a mental health professional can be an effective approach to address these challenges.
- There are numerous treatments for anxiety disorders including medications, therapy, lifestyle modifications, and relaxation techniques.

References

Eaton, W.W., Bienvenu, O.J., and Miloyan, B. (2018). Specific phobias. *Lancet Psychiatry* 5 (8): 678–686. https://doi.org/10.1016/S2215-0366(18)30169-X. PMID: 30060873; PMCID: PMC7233312.

Essau, C.A., Sasagawa, S., Ishikawa, S. et al. (2012). A Japanese form of social anxiety (taijin kyofusho): frequency and correlates in two generations of the same family. *The International Journal of Social Psychiatry* 58 (6): 635–642. https://doi.org/10.1177/0020764011421099. Epub 2011 Sep 12. PMID: 21911434.

Eteraf-Oskouei, T. and Najafi, M. (2022). The relationship between the serotonergic system and COVID-19 disease: a review. *Heliyon* 8 (5): e09544. https://doi.org/10.1016/j.heliyon.2022.e09544. Epub 2022 May 26. PMID: 35652122; PMCID: PMC9132783.

Hofmann, S.G. and Hinton, D.E. (2014). Cross-cultural aspects of anxiety disorders. *Current Psychiatry Reports* 16 (6): 450. https://doi.org/10.1007/s11920-014-0450-3. PMID: 24744049; PMCID: PMC4037698.

Lijster, J.M., Dierckx, B., Utens, E.M. et al. (2017). The age of onset of anxiety disorders. *Canadian Journal of Psychiatry* 62 (4): 237–246. https://doi.org/10.1177/0706743716640757. Epub 2016 Jul 9. PMID: 27310233; PMCID: PMC5407545.

Lucchetti, G., Koenig, H.G., and Granero Lucchetti, A.L. (2021). Spirituality, religiousness and mental health: a review of the scientific evidence. *World Journal of Clinical Cases* 9 (26): 7620–7631. https://doi.org/10.12998/wjcc.v9.i26.7620. PMCID: PMC8462234; PMID: 34621814.

Martin, E.I., Ressler, K.J., Binder, E., and Nemeroff, C.B. (2009). The neurobiology of anxiety disorders: brain imaging, genetics, and psychoneuroendocrinology. *The Psychiatric Clinics of North America* 32 (3): 549–575. https://doi.org/10.1016/j.psc.2009.05.004. PMID: 19716990; PMCID: PMC3684250.

McLean, C.P., Asnaani, A., Litz, B.T., and Hofmann, S.G. (2011). Gender differences in anxiety disorders: prevalence, course of illness, comorbidity and burden of illness. *Journal of Psychiatric Research* 45 (8): 1027–1035. https://doi.org/10.1016/j.jpsychires.2011.03.006. Epub 2011 Mar 25. PMID: 21439576; PMCID: PMC3135672.

Morales-Rodríguez, F.M. (2021). Fear, stress, resilience and coping strategies during COVID-19 in Spanish university students. *Sustainability* 13 (11): 5824. https://doi.org/10.3390/su13115824.

Rosellini, A.J., Rutter, L.A., Bourgeois, M.L. et al. (2013). The relevance of age of onset to the psychopathology of social phobia. *Journal of Psychopathology and Behavioral Assessment* 35 (3): 356–365. https://doi.org/10.1007/s10862-013-9338-5. PMID: 23935239; PMCID: PMC3736863.

Sanderson, W.C., Arunagiri, V., Funk, A.P. et al. (2020). The nature and treatment of pandemic-related psychological distress. *Journal of Contemporary Psychotherapy* 50 (4): 251–263. https://doi.org/10.1007/s10879-020-09463-7.

Twohig-Bennett, C. and Jones, A. (2018). The health benefits of the great outdoors: a systematic review and meta-analysis of greenspace exposure and health outcomes. *Environmental Research* 166: 628–637.

7

Psychotic Disorders Related to COVID-19 Infection

Chris Kenedi

Duke University Medical Center, Durham, NC 27720, USA

Pedro was 18 and a freshman at Carleton College in Minnesota when he came down with COVID-19 for the first time. Pedro had left his small town in New Zealand to study in the United States with feelings of trepidation about leaving his family, but also excitement about forging his own path away from his loving, but sometimes overprotective, family. He had immigrated from Chile to New Zealand when he was 4 years old, but he had wanted to study and live in the United States since he was 14 years old, inspired by the movie "Good Will Hunting."

In his first two weeks before the school year started, Pedro immersed himself in meeting other new students, setting up his dorm room, and adapting to American culture and language. His friends teased him about cultural differences, like not going barefoot while going out to eat – which would not be an issue in his small New Zealand town!

Starting his fourth week at college, Pedro began feeling sluggish and unable to keep up with friends during the day or when they partied in the evening. He had no appetite and found himself sniffling constantly, which he attributed to seasonal allergies. He dragged himself to class on Monday, but skipped dinner. On Tuesday morning he woke up exhausted, with a runny nose, a cough, and a sore throat. He had not been out the night before and his roommate wasn't ill. As he dragged himself to his computer science class, and then volleyball practice later that day, he began shivering and shaking in the warm fall air; even before he went on to the volleyball court he was sweating profusely, and he felt dizzy and unwell. His friend Eva touched his forehead and told him "You are burning up." A rapid antigen test showed that he had COVID-19, leading the college to relocate him to a designated house for positive cases.

Pedro's first two nights were difficult with fevers, shaking chills, an aching body, and no appetite. On the third day, his fever subsided and he began to recover. By the fifth day, his body had stopped aching, leaving only a lingering cough. He returned to his dorm by the seventh day.

Pedro's family worried about him, and they were relieved by his recovery. They knew Pedro would be tired as he recovered, but they did not expect the confusing texts that started to appear at all hours of the day. Convinced of a conspiracy against him, Pedro believed his roommate planted hidden cameras as part of a social experiment, and professors used secret language to conspire due to his New Zealand origin. He believed cafeteria staff was mocking him by serving fish and chips. Family and friends intervened when Pedro's isolation escalated, and he refused communication. They persuaded Pedro to go to the hospital for a medical evaluation.

The emergency department staff found him to have a fast heart rate, but otherwise normal vital signs. No abnormalities were noticed on physical examination, blood-work, or imaging. A CT scan of his brain revealed no issues. Dr. Ilya Lewis from the Consultation Liaison Psychiatry Services evaluated Pedro, noting his suspicion, withdrawal, malodorous state, and thin appearance, indicating days without eating. She observed that he responded to voices only Pedro seemed able to hear. Pedro's awareness that something was wrong was striking; he frequently experienced distress, grappling with the unsettling realization that he could not trust his own senses or his own mind.

Doctors at the community hospital agreed that Pedro was experiencing psychosis – but the cause and nature of his disorder – and how it should be treated, became a topic for discussion, requiring collaboration between the in-patient medical teams, liaison psychiatrists, neurologists, and laboratory specialists.

Introduction

Psychosis, at its most basic, is a word used to describe the experiences of people who have lost touch with reality. This chapter will explore different types of psychotic experiences and symptoms, and how and why patients who are suffering from, or recovering from, COVID-19 may be more susceptible to experiencing psychosis.

The medical community has explored the connection between COVID-19 and psychosis since early on in the pandemic. A systematic review in 2021 found descriptions of 48 patients across 17 countries with documented psychotic disorders (Smith et al. 2021). Fast forward to 2024, where a search on PubMed – the National Library of Medicine's freely accessible online repository for scientific journals and books – reveals a substantial increase, with thousands of articles discussing the correlation between COVID-19 and psychotic symptoms in patients.

In this chapter, we delve into questions that confronted Pedro's clinicians, family, and friends: Did the virus cause his symptoms, or was it inflammation related to the viral infection? Could a preexisting mental health disorder, triggered by the illness, have eventually declared itself even without COVID-19? Was recreational drug use a contributing factor? Each of these questions bears substantial weight for Pedro's treatment plan, providing insights into the potential course of his recovery.

What Is Psychosis?

One of best-known scientists who studied psychosis was Emil Kraepelin. In 1896 (for what is now called schizophrenia) he described "dementia praecox" as "a peculiar destruction of the inner cohesiveness of the … personality with predominant damage to the emotional life and the will" (Sass 1994). Psychosis is devastating because it affects, and has the power to devastate, the very essence of our humanity. It can disrupt the brain's ability to generate and maintain our sense of who we are as unique individuals in the world – we can lose part or all of our identity when psychotic. It can also destroy our ability to understand and relate to other people, leading to a terrible form of loneliness. This is reinforced when psychotic symptoms scare or disgust other people, which then contributes to isolation and hopelessness and can reinforce psychotic delusions, paranoia, and self-disgust, and in some instances lead to suicide.

While psychotic experiences can be subdivided many ways, one of the first and most important questions in assessing someone experiencing psychosis is whether or not the person has insight into their loss; some people with psychosis will question their paranoia, delusions, and hallucinations – this is called reality testing. However, others will experience their psychotic phenomena as very real, and instead discount or ignore the people who do not agree with, or acknowledge, their psychotic beliefs.

Insight

For individuals experiencing psychosis, there is a spectrum of awareness. Some may be aware or terrified by their psychotic symptoms – seeing things they cannot explain or that they know are not real. These individuals are "reality testing." They can compare the actual circumstances with their expectations, navigating the dissonance between what their senses convey and what their mind is telling them.

Other patients accept that the voices they are hearing are real without questioning them. They may even follow the instructions of the voices to do bizarre or dangerous things. This is less common but referred to as "command auditory hallucinations." These auditory hallucinations can be dangerous to the individual or to others – for instance, if the hallucinating voice tells them to fly off a rooftop or step into traffic.

Insight is important, as people without an understanding of the risks, benefits, and alternatives to choices are deemed to "lack capacity." This means they cannot consent to contracts or enter into agreements. Take, for instance, a person who is psychotic, guided by voices telling them to leave all their money for the care of rabbits. Most likely they cannot legally make a new will to set up a trust fund for rabbits based on the voice's directive.

Moreover, insight is important in navigating the challenges faced by people with psychotic symptoms and COVID-19. The absence of insight can evoke fear, making them appear intimidating or, conversely, causing them to experience heightened fear themselves. This can be a very difficult experience for their friends, family, and clinicians. People lacking insight might resist medication that could help them, fearing they may be poisoned. Impaired insight can also lead to delayed help-seeking, erode trust in others, and foster self-isolation, which can make their symptoms even worse.

Types of Psychotic Symptoms

Psychosis can affect the mind in many ways, but usually, we talk about various forms of primary psychosis such as schizophrenia. There is also secondary psychosis, seen in people with severe major depression or bipolar disorder who become manic. If left untreated, their mood disorder can escalate, leading to psychosis.

As seen in Table 7.1, people with psychosis can experience positive symptoms, negative symptoms, or dissociative symptoms. While this is an incomplete list of what we see in psychosis, it serves to identify some of the issues that confront patients with COVID-19- related psychosis and those caring for them.

The positive symptoms get the most attention, but it is the negative symptoms that destroy people's lives and contribute to the increased rate of suicide in people with psychosis. Positive symptoms typically scare people and result in police being called and mental health service involvement. Positive symptoms are also more often seen in delirium – when the brain becomes confused in the setting of a medical condition. Dissociative, positive, and negative symptoms are all seen together in primary psychotic disorders (like schizophrenia or post-traumatic stress disorder (PTSD)).

Dissociative symptoms are associated with the brain's response to adverse experiences in development (such as physical, sexual, or emotional abuse or neglect),

Table 7.1 Symptoms of psychosis.

Type of symptoms	Examples
Positive symptoms (adding things that are not reality based)	*Delusions* • FBI is out to get me • The bus driver works for the FBI • The newscaster is speaking directly to me • People can read my thoughts *Hallucinations* • Voices, people, smells, tastes that are not real *Paranoia* • The doctor was late, therefore she must hate me
Negative symptoms (take away from a person's ability to thrive)	*Apathy*: not caring about life *Alogia*: trouble with expressing feelings or speaking *Avolition*: lack of follow through, such as not bathing or going to work *Anhedonia*: lack of pleasure
Dissociative symptoms (disconnections between you and world, or even you and your body)	*Derealization*: you believe things around you are distorted and not real *Depersonalization*: seeing yourself from outside your body, or seeing your body as a thing rather than part of you as a whole *Identity disturbance* an unstable and ever-changing sense of who you are that shifts with each relationship or situation.

or severe psychological trauma as an adult (for example, violations such as rape, or near-death experiences involving a loss of control). Dissociative symptoms revolve around a loss of awareness of time, or feeling one's own body is not real or having out of body experiences. They can be re-triggered by severe illness, assault, or injuries. Some dissociative medications (like ketamine) and drugs of abuse (MDMA, LSD) can sometimes cause dissociative psychosis.

One model for understanding dissociative symptoms is the elephant and rider – where the elephant represents the autonomic nervous system and the unconsciousness/emotional mind. It is responsible for much of the function of the brain, such as controlling circulation, breathing, and hormones, and the stomach and liver. It is also connected with the emotional mind and feelings like anger, shame, fear, hunger, and sexual attraction to name a few. This part of the brain has been evolving for approximately 600 million years.

The rider represents consciousness. It has only been around for 150–200 thousand years and is likely an evolutionary add-on module designed to improve communication and to allow social interaction and cooperation.

Most of the time they work together. The rider says go, they go; work, they work; eat, they eat. However, if the elephant is hungry, sexually excited, scared, or angry, sometimes the elephant will charge ahead and run away. This may occur even if the rider is pleading/begging/explaining to the elephant (themselves) that it is okay and not be so scared or angry, or to think of the consequences (such as kissing someone who is not their partner, or eating something that is unhealthy).

The disconnect between the rider (the conscious mind) and the elephant (the emotional/autonomic part of the brain) can lead to a person feeling "out of body" (derealization) or "disconnected from myself" (depersonalization), which are dissociative psychotic symptoms. This is important because these kinds of dissociative psychotic experiences can become more severe when a person with autonomic hypervigilance is very ill or in recovery from COVID-19. This occurs when the hypervigilant person is triggered into a further threat state by the body's immune response to COVID-19 or by disruptions caused by the body repairing itself in recovery from COVID-19 (which is also governed by the immune and nervous systems).

One of the most important things to keep in mind is that experiencing psychotic symptoms does not necessarily mean that a person has a psychotic disorder. Everyone in their life will likely have dissociative experiences. For instance, during a heated argument with a loved one, you may hear yourself saying things that, in hindsight, feel hurtful or unnecessary. This response often stems from the emotional pain of the moment. Similarly, consider instances when you are eating a bag of candy, intending to save some for later. However, you suddenly realize your hand is fumbling around the empty bag – and you realize you ate all the candy "on autopilot."

These are both examples of dissociative symptoms, which can be a normal part of the human experience. Isolated dissociative symptoms are not a medical or psychiatric disorder as long as people can "reality test" – realize when they have dissociated – and as long as it does not affect their functioning, affecting their capacity to have relationships, participate in society, and work. Even hallucinations, delusions, or paranoia can exist within a person's mind, as long as they can challenge them (indicating insight) and as long as these symptoms do not hinder their daily functioning. However, if the presence of psychotic symptoms leads to job loss, relationship breakdowns, and isolation within their community, it indicates a psychotic disorder that would likely benefit from treatment.

How Can COVID-19 Infection Lead to Psychosis?

A number of factors or conditions can lead to psychosis in COVID-19 as listed in Table 7.2.

Delirium

Clinical experience has shown that the most common cause of psychotic symptoms, such as delusions or hallucinations in patients infected with COVID-19 (or any serious illness), is delirium. As detailed in Chapter 4, delirium is a state of confusion and loss of brain function/coordination that is typically associated with older adults and those with acute illnesses (such as COVID-19). Symptoms fluctuate hour to hour and through the day – both in the nature and type of the symptoms, as well as their intensity. Confusion and difficulty maintaining attention – an inability to focus or remember new material – are the hallmarks of delirium. Other classic signs of delirium include poor attention, disorientation, compromised memory formation or memory loss, as well as symptoms like agitation, hallucinations, and restlessness. Delirium also frequently includes paranoia and delusions, as people misinterpret the actions of people around them and misinterpret their fears or fantasies as being real (for example, believing that the CIA is following them with drones). It's noteworthy that many of these symptoms are also hallmarks of the positive symptoms of psychosis (hallucinations, delusions, disorganization, and confusion).

Around one third of delirious patients present in the opposite manner, characterized by quietness and withdrawal – referred to as "hypoactive delirium." These patients have symptoms which include disorientation, loss of attention, and confusion, but their psychotic symptoms mimic the negative symptoms of psychosis. Clinicians and care workers of vulnerable people should be careful to look for hypoactive delirium. These patients can be easily missed because of their immobility, stupor, and refusal, which can be seen as obstinacy or laziness, or they can be ignored if there are other patients asking for assistance.

In people with COVID-19, delirium can be triggered by the immune response, causing neuroinflammation (Marshall 2023). This inflammation, in turn, creates a further raft of problems, disrupting the regulation of brain physiology – the chemical processes that allow the brain to function as an organ. This regulation includes coordinating thinking, managing feelings, and overseeing the functioning of our other organs like the heart, lungs, stomach, as well as executing tasks such as moving our fingers and toes, using our eyes and ears, and keeping our balance, among other critical tasks.

Delirium is not considered a stand-alone neurocognitive disorder; rather, it is influenced by inflammatory and hypoxic-ischemic mechanisms induced by acute stressors (Tyson et al. 2022), such as surgery or COVID-19 infection. Even in mild

Table 7.2 Mechanisms leading to psychosis.

Trigger	Mechanism leading to psychosis
Delirium	• Immune response due to viral infection leads to neuroinflammation • Neuroinflammation is also likely responsible for the loss of taste and smell in COVID-19
Drugs	• Steroids such as prednisone disrupt the nervous system and degrade or eliminate sleep – which protects the brain • Recreational drugs like cannabis, methamphetamine, cocaine, hallucinogens and others can make a brain vulnerable to psychosis – especially when there is also a systemic infection.
Mental illness	• Patients with known psychotic disorders whose symptoms were previously under control. • Patients with previously undiagnosed mental illness • Patients who develop mental illness while infected with, or recovering from, COVID-19.
Viral damage to brain cells	• The virus itself (uncommonly) can directly impact the brain (COVID-19 Encephalitis) • When virus causes enough irritation or damage to the frontal, prefrontal, temporal lobes or other areas • Clearly demonstrated in similar infections such as SARS and MERS; more commonly seen in H1N1 influenza
Secondary effects of COVID-19	• Pro-coagulant effect of the virus and immune response can cause clotting, cerebrovascular damage or strokes • Severe COVID-19 can cause respiratory collapse and hypoxia (low oxygen), which starves and damages the brain
Other medical or neurological conditions in COVID-19 patients	• Alzheimer's disease • Autoimmune disorders like Lupus • Epilepsy • Huntington's disease • Multiple sclerosis • Parkinson's disease
Isolation	• Stress due to isolation can trigger psychotic symptoms – particularly dissociative psychosis • Secondary effects of COVID-19, such as sleep deprivation and cognitive fatigue, may strip away the compensatory capacity of some patients to reality test – which may allow (previously unexpressed) psychotic thought structures or processes to "run amok" in their minds
Long COVID	• Dissociative psychosis symptoms mimic fatigue, apathy, and derealization • Also associated with functional neurological disorders, which can occur in the context of the body's response to COVID-19 and pre-COVID-19 vulnerabilities

cases of COVID-19 with limited inflammation, significant delirium can manifest in individuals with vulnerable brains. These individuals lack the capacity to compensate for the disruption in the brain caused by the inflammatory response, making the elderly (especially those with dementia), people with brain injuries, or those with severe intellectual disabilities particularly susceptible.

The inflammation associated with COVID-19, compounded by the environment of a hospital or care setting, can also impact an individual's gastrointestinal tract biome – the healthy bacteria lining the gut – leading to symptoms like diarrhea, and in extreme cases, life-threatening loss of bowel control. Changes in the gut biome can worsen inflammation, causing the gut to fail and potentially leading to sepsis as the underlying cause of delirium and psychotic symptoms. Even in cases where gut dysfunction is mild, with symptoms like diarrhea or constipation, it can cause dehydration or poor oral intake, exacerbating brain dysfunction and psychosis. While such disturbances may not disrupt brain regulation in most people, in frail and older patients, it can be the proverbial "straw that breaks the camel's back."

In elderly patients, even seemingly isolated conditions like a urinary tract infection can produce enough inflammation to trigger delirium, with resolution typically observed in the days following treatment of the infection.

Medication-induced Psychosis

The primary issue related to COVID-19-induced psychosis and prescribed medication is undeniably steroids. The mechanism of neuropsychiatric side effects is complex, but it involves suppression of the hypothalamic-pituitary-adrenal axis, which contributes to hormone regulation and sleep disturbances. While there are direct impacts of long-term steroid use on the brain, the primary indicator of adverse side effects of steroids on the central nervous system is the patient's sleep patterns (Warrington and Bostwick 2006).

As COVID-19 infection causes respiratory difficulty, and the immune response causes fevers, rigors (shaking), chills, aches, and mucus production, sleep is already impacted. When a person is hospitalized, sleep is even more compromised by checking vital signs, administering medication, and medical rounds and meals happening on the hospital system's schedule rather than the affected person's body/brain schedule. Adding steroids to this mix – even when necessary or life-preserving for respiratory function – may fragment and discombobulate what remains of neuroendocrine stability, leading to fragmented sleep, agitation, and exhaustion. This impacts executive function (decision making), cognition, and the circuity and chemistry of the brain that regulates mood, and increases a person's risk of delirium. Furthermore, the disruption of the protective structure of the brain and kindling of mood disorders can cause depression and mania – both of which generate psychotic symptoms if unrecognized and untreated.

Finally, steroids can trigger dissociative psychosis by removing the coping mechanisms in place, especially when sleep is fragmented or compromised. Sleep is protective against all forms of mental illness, but it is particularly crucial for people with developmental trauma, PTSD, or at genetic risk for dissociative symptoms. This is why some patients can experience a return of PTSD symptoms when hospitalized – for instance, military veterans who experienced battlefield trauma may struggle with COVID-19 in the ICU or medical wards.

Many other prescribed medications can trigger delirium or "drug-induced thought disorders" (psychosis), but these are medications that are not used for COVID-19; they are medications prescribed for other purposes that when combined with COVID-19, the inflammatory responses can trigger psychosis. These reactions are rare, but some individuals may be more susceptible than others due to genetics and how they metabolize the medication.

While there are a few reports in the medical literature of COVID-19 antiviral treatments such as favipiravir causing psychosis, these are only a few patients among the millions who have taken the medication. Some of these patients may have had other risk factors for psychosis. Reassuringly, pharmacovigilance monitoring by public health teams does not suggest an increased risk for psychosis in people taking antiviral medication used to treat COVID-19.

Recreational Drugs

All patients with preexisting risk factors for psychosis – brain injury, severe mental illness such as schizophrenia or bipolar disorder, intellectual impairment, or people at higher genetic risk – can suffer psychotic reactions from recreational drugs. The highest risks are from drugs such as methamphetamine, cocaine, LSD and other hallucinogens, MDMA, ketamine, and PCP (phencyclidine), as well as cannabinoids/synthetic cannabinoids (marijuana), but almost any neuroactive recreational drug can put someone vulnerable at risk for psychosis (Fiorentini et al. 2021). In most cases the risks are low. However, when a person has COVID-19 and uses recreational drugs, they may develop psychosis in one of two ways:

i) They have an underlying psychotic disorder (for example, schizophrenia) that overwhelms their coping mechanisms in the setting of substance use and the neuroinflammation from COVID-19. This leads to a drug-induced psychosis, which triggers a presentation of the underlying disorder, which can last for weeks to years.

ii) The drug induces delirium, which typically lasts for hours to days.

Medication/Substance Withdrawal

A bigger issue for patients with COVID-19 is not the prescribed medications they are taking, but rather when they stop taking their medications. This is particularly true for patients on routine benzodiazepines such as diazepam (Valium), lorazepam (Ativan), or alprazolam (Xanax). People who have been on these medications continuously for a month or longer are at risk of physiologic dependence – when the brain adjusts to the drug's active chemical as being part of its physiology. This means that withdrawal of the drug leads to the brain chemistry experiencing loss of the chemical. This can trigger withdrawal delirium with seizures and psychotic symptoms in some cases. Benzodiazepine-related withdrawal symptoms can occur for up to 14 days after the medication is stopped.

This withdrawal can happen if the patient is too ill to take the medication, or when admitted to a medical unit where the clinical staff are not aware of the medication's regular use. This may happen, for instance, if the patient is embarrassed about taking an "as needed" antianxiety medication every day, or if they have been taking a spouse or partner's medication or pills obtained illegally, perhaps from a clinician their primary doctor was not aware of. Withdrawal symptoms typically begin within 24–48 hours after the medication is stopped but may worsen, and psychotic symptoms can progress over the course of 14 days. If unrecognized, up to 35% of patients with this type of withdrawal may die. However, in the modern age, when promptly identified, the mortality rate is closer to 2% (Khan et al. 2008).

Another commonly encountered problem in patients admitted to the hospital for COVID-19-related illness is withdrawal from alcohol. From the brain's point of view, alcohol and benzodiazepines are very similar as neuroactive substances. The early signs of severe alcohol withdrawal may be missed due to the COVID-19 inflammatory response, especially if a person minimized or hid their drinking from others. In these patients, early recognition can prevent life-threatening withdrawal symptoms (seizures, delirium, psychosis, and death). Clinicians treat alcohol withdrawal with benzodiazepines until withdrawal symptoms are controlled; they then gradually reduce the dose, weaning the brain off the dependence rather than stopping "cold turkey." The analogy is a person standing at the top of a mountain (built up by chronic alcohol or benzodiazepine use/dependence). They can either jump off the cliff and get injured, or they can go down the bumpy path – they might stumble and be uncomfortable, but it will not kill or harm them.

Other substance withdrawals can increase the risk of psychosis – particularly dissociative psychosis – such as nicotine withdrawal from patients smoking or vaping large amounts of tobacco/nicotine prior to COVID-19. As COVID-19 patients may struggle to breathe, they will often cease smoking or vaping. While this typically leads to symptoms such as nervousness, increased appetite, anxiety, depressed mood, and agitation, it can also contribute to helplessness and trigger dissociative psychosis in patients at risk. It can also contribute to the risk of delirium in patients with fragile brains, such as the elderly with COVID-19 who have preexisting cognitive impairment.

Mental Illnesses and COVID-19-related Psychosis

Patients with preexisting severe mental illnesses, such as schizophrenia, bipolar disorder, or PTSD, or those with severe personality disorders, may be at higher risk of experiencing psychotic symptoms when ill with COVID-19, or in recovery from it. In general, medical illness can act as a trigger for their psychotic symptoms.

Some people experiencing mild mental illness might not have received a diagnosis or treatment, managing to keep their symptoms under control through various coping mechanisms. These strategies could involve distraction, adhering to rigid schedules, or intentionally avoiding social interactions to conceal their symptoms. However, in the event of a severe illness such as COVID-19, these previously effective coping mechanisms may no longer be accessible. This could lead to destabilization of their mental state, causing a worsening or unmanageable manifestation of psychotic symptoms that the individual can no longer hide.

Another example of this is major depression, which is discussed in Chapter 5. When depression becomes severe, it can lead to psychosis in addition to depressive symptoms.

COVID-19 Virus Attacking Brain Tissue Directly

Can respiratory infections damage brain pathways and cause mental illness and psychosis?

Karl Menninger, one of the most prominent American psychiatrists of the twentieth century and a cofounder of the Menninger Clinic mental health hospital system, wrote a seminal paper on influenza and psychosis in 1919 (Menninger 1919). He reviewed 100 cases of patients with severe mental illness symptoms – around half of them with psychotic disorders and two thirds with hallucinations. While previous clinician-scientists had noted that pandemic outbreaks can lead to increased rates of psychosis (reports from St Petersburg, Russia in 1889 and United Kingdom medical journals in the 1890s referred to "psychosis of influenza"), Menninger's paper is one of the most-cited in this field. He described patients with psychotic symptoms that developed during or after serious bouts of influenza.

However, a follow-up paper by Menninger in 1926 looked at 50 patients diagnosed with "dementia praecox" (schizophrenia) where the symptoms developed in the context of the 1918 influenza epidemic. He found that in more than half of the patients, the psychotic symptoms resolved – as opposed to our modern understanding of schizophrenia, which is a psychotic disorder that is lifelong (Menninger 1926).

Another study estimated that around 0.9–4% of individuals exposed to H1N1 influenza, Ebola, SARS, MERS, or COVID-19 developed psychosis or psychotic symptoms, a significantly higher percentage than the median incidence of 0.015% observed among the general population (Brown et al. 2020). A similar investigation specifically looking at COVID-19 patients and psychosis found that for 236 379 patients followed over six months, patients with COVID-19 were 2.2 times more likely to develop psychosis than patients with influenza (Taquet et al. 2021).

A critique often raised against studies like these is that patients with identified blood samples and tests demonstrating specific viral infections are, by definition, generally quite unwell and under medical care. Consequently, they receive closer monitoring. This implies that psychotic symptoms expressed by these patients are more likely to be identified compared to individuals in the general population or those managing their illness at home. This observation is supported by the fact that the symptoms noted in medical studies of COVID-19 and psychosis are predominantly delusions and hallucinations. These psychotic symptoms are the most dramatic and tend to elicit greater concern among clinicians and family members.

COVID-19 Exposure During Pregnancy and Later Psychotic Disorders

Alan Brown, a psychiatrist at Colombia University, published a study in 2004 looking at the records of more than 12 000 women who were pregnant between 1959 and 1966 and had blood samples. He followed up on women who had antibodies positive for the influenza virus and found that pregnant women exposed to influenza during the first half of pregnancy (when the central nervous system/brain is developing at the fastest rate) were three times more likely to have children who go on to develop schizophrenia compared to pregnant women who were not exposed to influenza. It is not clear from this work if it is the virus, or the immune response, that impacted the fetus's developing brain (Brown et al. 2004).

A psychologist named Mednick noted that people born during the 1957 influenza pandemic, as opposed to shortly after it had ended, found the pandemic group had a higher rate of developing schizophrenia later in life (Mednick et al. 1988).

Many studies have suggested that exposure to infection can lead to higher rates of psychotic disorders – for instance, 200+ papers have demonstrated that children born in winter/early spring months (when viral infections are more common) have a greater risk of schizophrenia. However, it is not only exposure to viral infections that is associated with the later development of psychotic disorders.

Toxoplasmosis, a parasite, is also implicated as a microbial exposure during pregnancy that may contribute to the development of psychotic disorders. This implies that it is not the agent, but the body's immune response which may play the primary role in an increased risk of a mental health disorder, including psychotic disorders.

How Does COVID-19 Damage the Brain and Cause Psychosis?

COVID-19 can directly damage the brain *via* direct invasion of brain cells and their support structure. However, the brain cells are not the main target of the virus, so this type of injury is not typically a major concern for patients or clinicians. The COVID-19 virus primarily attacks the cellular lining of the lung and to a lesser extent, gut cells. It does this by linking to an enzyme called ACE2, which it uses as a key to enter the cell. The problem is that the brain likes to reuse some keys in different locks, and some of those locks allow the virus to enter cells of the central nervous system. When the virus gets into a cell, it takes over the cell until it is depleted and dead. The only way the body has to eradicate it is to kill the cell; so, the more brain cells the virus gets into, the more brain cells that die.

An important point is that the ACE2 key (enzyme) tends to fit brain cells which have a particular focus on brain chemistry that influences the mind including serotonin, glutamine, and dopamine. These are particularly important for the pathways that stabilize our ability to take in sensory information and connect it to memories and emotions. Disruptions of these pathways are what lead to the symptoms of psychosis such as delusions and hallucinations.

There are 80–120 billion brain cells in the human brain, so the loss of some cells (a few hundred thousand or even a few million), will not be noticed or cause problems for most people. However, for people with prior brain damage from injury or atrophy, mental illness, persistent recreational drug use, poor nutrition, or genetic susceptibility, the loss can be devastating. To complicate things, sometimes the repair process can itself be a contributor to brain dysfunction. COVID-19 is like a house fire (if the brain and body are the house) – for some people the fire is small and contained to an appliance or one room (like the throat or lungs). For others who have severe illnesses with hospitalization or who end up on a ventilator, it is a fire that spreads through many rooms of the house or gets into the walls or smoke drifts up to the attic and causes damage. Having your house on fire and the fire department respond is, in itself, terrifying for many. Indeed, the process of airing out the smoke, cleaning up the water damage, dealing with the insurance claims and replacing furniture and carpets, and arranging for workers would also be very disruptive. For other people the repair process is simple and the losses are not significant. Sadly, some items like photos or heirlooms (equivalent to memories in the brain) will never be replaced.

The second mechanism for COVID-19 to cause brain damage is *via* inflammation. This occurs when COVID-19 replication inside cells causes the immune system to activate its alarm warning system *via* what is referred to as a cytokine storm. While this is part of a vigorous immune response that is necessary for the body's survival, it can have a number of effects which are detrimental to the brain. In the above metaphor, sometimes the water the fire department uses to put out the fire causes more damage than the fire itself; not because the fire department is incompetent, but because it is not possible to direct the water specifically enough to the source of the flames, or because the fire has spread into the insulation in the walls when they arrive.

One effect of inflammation is that it increases the permeability of the blood-brain barrier, which normally protects the delicate brain from toxins in the blood that do not bother other organs. This occurs in a number of diseases like H1N1 influenza or COVID-19 where there is sometimes an overproduction of pro-inflammatory molecules which can result in disruption of the signaling between brain cells (neurons). In addition, the inflammatory response changes the chemistry of the hypothalamic-pituitary axis, which controls a number of critically important hormones such as cortisol. Finally, the pro-inflammatory molecules can cause problems with the clotting mechanisms of the blood, leading to blood clots (and strokes) in the delicate blood vessels that supply the neurons with oxygen and nutrients and remove waste materials.

This process is very similar to that which occurs in delirium; this is why it is difficult or potentially impossible to separate the psychotic symptoms of delirium from the development of a primary mental disorder – other than by looking to see if a person's psychotic symptoms persist and if the symptoms are stable. If they are short-lived and the symptoms wax and wane in character and intensity (they are hallucinating different voices that come and go, and are often fragmented), they were likely experiencing a prolonged delirium. If the symptoms continue indefinitely and remain stable (for instance, auditory hallucinations of the same persistent male voice), they have most likely developed a psychotic disorder.

Other Medical and Neurological Conditions

Almost any previous brain trauma or brain disorder (such as Huntington's disease, Parkinson's disease, multiple sclerosis) can increase the risk of COVID-19-associated psychosis.

COVID-19 is also associated with a higher risk of seizures in patients with epilepsy and in patients without previously known epilepsy. This can be due to non-adherence to antiepileptic medication due to illness, rarely due to the antiepileptic medications themselves, or more commonly due to psychosis during the post-seizure recovery phase and last for up to a week (postictal psychosis). It is typically self-limiting unless further seizures occur but patients can experience psychotic symptoms in the hours and days after an epileptic attack.

Many other disorders can also contribute to the risk of psychosis including cancers, autoimmune disorders like systemic lupus erythematosus, genetic metabolic disorders, hormone disorders like thyroid problems, or sleep disorders like obstructive sleep apnea.

COVID-19-related Isolation

Social isolation can be a vulnerability for psychosis because it eliminates the reality testing that occurs when we share ideas with family, friends, coworkers, and even strangers. Not only might our friends tell us what they think: "Lighting your BBQ with jet fuel is a terrible idea, Chris," their nonverbal reactions also give us a lot of information and reinforcement about how we live (they laugh when we are teasing, or cry or look hurt if we are rude). People who live alone and have no social contact often lose cues around hygiene, appearance, or connection with their community. That is one of the reasons that faith is protective for people, as is having close friends and family members. They provide a rhythm and structure for how we engage in the world.

Social isolation is often an indicator of how someone is doing, as well as a cause of mental illness. This means that people who are socially isolated may have some issues that drive them to stay away from people – they are paranoid that people are out to get them, or they are suffering from prolonged depression, or they have experienced serious or repetitive assault or trauma, particularly from people who were supposed to provide safety, such as family or teachers. Consequently, the fear of getting close to people becomes a significant factor in their avoidance. Social isolation in these examples is related to traits of mental illnesses and vulnerability for a mental disorder. In addition, the continued social isolation can reinforce the traits (paranoia, depressed mood, or hypervigilance and fear), which then can cause more social isolation and create a downward spiral. Another factor that can be a cause and a contributor to social isolation is substance use, and alcohol dependence in particular.

The elderly are particularly vulnerable to social isolation. Loss of friends and family and/or the loss of a spouse or partner can drive someone into hopelessness. This can also lead to a sense of futility around human interactions, particularly if they feel out of touch or inept with culture, language, technology, and fashion. Or if they feel scared for their safety. This is accentuated when there is cognitive impairment from early dementia or the effects of long-term alcohol or cannabis usage.

When you add COVID-19 to this mix, the above vulnerabilities associated with social isolation can be dramatically accentuated. Elderly COVID-19 patients may be separated from familiar objects (such as photographs) and familiar smells (such as their favorite foods). Additionally, they may be forced to depend on others or to adapt to a different schedule, disrupting routines where they once ate when hungry and went to bed later. While these changes may appear minor, they can significantly disrupt sleep, or create a sense of helplessness, regression, and hopelessness. This can progress to despair, clinical depression, and/or sleep fragmentation, which are all risk factors for psychosis.

People in social isolation with alcohol dependence or nicotine dependence, or high levels of daily cannabis usage, who get COVID-19 and are hospitalized can be subject to withdrawal symptoms as noted above. Those with previous dementia or cognitive impairment are much more susceptible to delirium from the neuroinflammatory response of the body to a COVID-19 infection.

Trauma

Another group of people who have a significant vulnerability to COVID-19-associated psychosis are those who have experienced psychological trauma during their developmental years, particularly in childhood and adolescence. The changes that occur in the brain during these formative periods render them not only more susceptible to side effects but also more prone to experiencing more intense side effects compared to people without such traumatic experiences.

Adverse childhood experiences (ACE) include sexual, physical, and emotional abuse, and/or neglect. All children and adolescents experience some emotional abuse or neglect as part of their life experience, and they may be struck or get in fights. However, experiences like enduring repeated physical punishment with a belt, causing bruises, or a pipe, causing broken bones, can create a sense of hypervigilance and insecurity. This is accentuated when the abuse is irregular and more related to the parent or adult's mood or alcohol usage, rather than the actions of the child or adolescent. The same is true for neglect – which is why it is so important to recognize and treat post-partum depression and to support parents with addiction into recovery. Sexual abuse is particularly destructive, as the perpetrator often blames their victim, "I cannot help myself, you are so pretty/special/a tease," or pretends it did not happen, or was normal. Oftentimes, the abuser insists that their actions need to be kept as a secret from others. This leads to internal conflicts in the abuse victim, which alter brain chemistry and brain circuitry during development, as it causes confusion in the child or adolescent. When they are older and realize what happened to them, the trauma is often compounded by shame, which can be a highly destructive and destabilizing emotional system in the brain. Childhood abuse takes an even darker turn when the child's experiences are not believed. When victims feel dismissed, it can leave them adrift, diminishing their sense of emotional control and safety. This heightened vulnerability can pave the way for dissociative psychosis symptoms. The impact intensifies under stress, such as during a COVID-19 illness or recovery, bringing forth these symptoms, even if the original abuse occurred many years ago. Moreover, if these symptoms existed before the COVID-19 illness, they may present with increased intensity.

Multiple studies underscore the impact of ACE on predicting both physical and mental health outcomes. For instance, research among Syrian refugees demonstrated that ACE could better predict PTSD symptoms, including psychotic symptoms, compared to measures of exposure to war or refugee experiences (Karam et al. 2019). Similarly, a study involving US military veterans found that exposure to ACE was more predictive of poor mental and general health outcomes than their experience in military service (Hein et al. 2020). This trend persists in the context of COVID-19 patients. A recent study focusing on children and adolescents revealed that those with a history of childhood trauma were 1.54–3.49 times more likely to experience "psychotic-like experiences" compared to those without such trauma (Wang et al. 2023).

A pattern of ACE leads to hypervigilance, which is not a magical or imagined mental state; instead, it is a reflection of the person's autonomic nervous system. This includes the sympathetic (flight or fight system and adrenaline) and the parasympathetic system (which is one of the oldest nervous system pathways in terms of the evolution of the brain) and balances the effects of the sympathetic system (for instance, calming you down after a fright). The parasympathetic system also manages digestion and many aspects of breathing. The autonomic system is not part of our consciousness, but it controls and connects with every organ in the body and has an impact on every movement and action we take, as well as many emotions we have – it is the basis of the expression "I feel it in my gut."

An autonomic system on alert therefore can make us eagle-eyed for threats and give us acute hearing and contribute to attentional awareness for anticipating problems that might occur when we are scared or feel threatened. However, it can also make us too vigilant (hypervigilant) and edgy, jumpy, and quite exhausted from being on high alert at all times. These symptoms can cause not only our organs to be dysfunctional, but can also cause our brain to misinterpret normal bodily neuron feedback as an alarm signal, triggering feedback and immune responses which then perpetuate the end-organ dysfunction. A hypervigilant autonomic system also can contribute to dissociative psychosis experiences.

Individuals with dysregulated and hypervigilant autonomic nervous systems may experience a more severe course of illness and prolonged recovery when confronted by COVID-19, especially in comparison to those without ACE (Taylor et al. 2022). This heightened vulnerability leads to dysregulated or overreactive immune and hormone responses.

Moreover, individuals with dissociative symptoms face a higher risk of developing these disorders during the recovery phase from COVID-19. These dysregulations, coupled with the associated dissociative symptoms, contribute to what are

Table 7.3 Functional disorders linked to autonomic hypervigilance and dysregulation.

Chronic fatigue syndrome

Irritable bowel syndrome

Fibromyalgia (chronic muscle pain associated with tension)

Globus (swallowing dysfunction)

Tinnitus (ringing in the ears)

Palpitations and noncardiac chest pain

Chronic pain conditions

Functional neurologic disorders

Secondary migraines and headache syndromes

termed functional disorders. These disorders are undeniably real, far from being mere figments of the patient's imagination. Functional disorders often stem from a dysregulation of the autonomic nervous system, coupled with an accompanying overresponse from the immune system. The subsequent impact on organs can be extensive, affecting the metabolism of the body at a systemic level and influencing the cellular energy regulation system. These disorders are listed in Table 7.3.

Long COVID

Long COVID, which we will discuss more in the next chapter, is an immune-modulated functional disorder of the autonomic nervous system. It can be worsened by psychotic symptoms (positive, negative, or dissociative symptoms), and it can also generate dissociative psychotic symptoms in people with vulnerabilities discussed above. These include alcohol/drug misuse, social isolation, other medical or psychiatric illnesses, or previous severe ACE or adult PTSD. All of these can contribute to dysfunctional signaling of the autonomic nervous system and primary psychotic disorders or dissociative psychotic disorders, where the elephant and rider lose communication. This can lead to staring spells and blanking out, or losing time while performing rote activities. These dissociations are often triggered by the COVID-19 experience and/or by people/places that trigger the psychotic/frozen/dysregulated/drained state in people who have had prior traumatic experiences.

Thus, adverse childhood and adolescent experiences are a significant risk factor and vulnerability for both the development of COVID-19-associated psychosis and Long COVID-associated dissociative symptoms. In other words, recovery from COVID-19 likely contributes to (triggers) dissociative psychosis symptoms in hypervigilant people with dysregulated nervous systems. But these dissociative symptoms, through their impact in dysregulating the autonomic nervous system, may also worsen and extend the duration of Long COVID.

Complications of COVID-19 Psychosis

Patients with medical illnesses that contribute to psychosis are at higher risk of a complex of disorders that include catatonia, neuroleptic malignant syndrome (NMS, also referred to as malignant catatonia), and malignant hyperthermia (typically only seen in patients with surgical anesthesia, but also a risk in the intensive care unit environment).

These are complicated disorders associated with severe dysfunction of the brain chemistry that are associated with sleep disorders and muscle dysfunction, among other functions. The hallmark of catatonia is negativism, whereby patients appear to be refusing care or food or medication, mutism (refusing to speak), refusal to follow commands, stiffness of limbs, staring, and odd and repetitive movements and behaviors, which are sometimes seen as childlike.

NMS is very rare but life-threatening when it occurs. It is associated with a massively dysfunctional brain chemistry response to medication (typically antipsychotic medication) and/or an inflammatory cascade (from illness or massive overuse of muscles). Patients with psychotic disorders who are being treated with antipsychotic medications, and who also have COVID-19, have a higher risk of developing NMS. NMS has also been associated with COVID-19 in severely ill patients who end up in the ICU.

The symptoms of NMS include very high fever (typically greater than 39 °C), stiff, almost unmovable arms and legs (often described as being like "lead pipes"), along with muscle pain and a lack of urine output. In the hospital, the hallmark is a massive elevation of creatine kinase, which often is higher than laboratory instruments can read; this chemical is an enzyme that is released when muscles break down. If untreated, it can cause kidney failure and death.

Safety

Due to the physical and social isolation brought on by COVID-19, the risk of suicide is heightened in vulnerable individuals, particularly those experiencing symptoms of psychosis. If you are concerned that a friend or family member is experiencing psychosis, first ask whether they feel safe. This should be asked even if people are disorganized or not making a lot of sense in what they are saying. People who report they are suicidal or unsafe should be taken to professional medical care immediately (such as the emergency room), or you should contact a local mental health crisis team, or call emergency services. We will review how to manage safety concerns in more detail in Chapter 9.

In-hospital, patients who are suicidal should not be left alone until they are assessed by a mental health professional. People who are overwhelmed by real or imagined threats, and who feel hopeless, are of particular concern. Even if someone is not fully aware of their psychotic and thought-disordered state, they can still sense the fear, confusion, and potential disgust from others toward their behavior. They may believe that they have nothing to live for, or they may be overwhelmed by fear or suffering and see no hope of resolution – a state referred to as a "foreshortened future."

People who are intoxicated, using alcohol or drugs, or receiving medications such as steroids or benzodiazepines, are also at elevated risk of completing suicide while psychotic. Both medical or recreational neuroactive drugs can reduce their inhibition and can lead to impulsive and destructive acts.

The standard risks of suicidal behavior apply to patients with psychosis and/or COVID-19. People at increased risk for suicide include those with a history of suicide attempts, those grieving the loss of a close family member, partner, or friend to suicide, people with depression or other mental illnesses, people with a history of trauma or abuse, and people with criminal/legal problems or facing financial/job/relationship conflicts, leading to heightened feelings of isolation or hopelessness. Additionally, patients with progressive/severe medical illnesses or neurodegenerative disorders who get COVID-19 are at higher risk of suicide.

In addition to ensuring that the person with psychosis is safe, you can ask about the safety of others. While people with mental illness are less likely to cause violence than the general population, people with psychosis experiencing persecutory delusions can lash out if they mistake another person's actions as threatening. This is especially true if they feel they are in danger – such as being under threat or pursued by entities like aliens, intelligence agencies (CIA, NSA, FBI, or KGB/FSB and the like), or criminal organizations such as the mafia. When it is possible and safe, it is important to take away guns and other weapons from people experiencing these types of delusional or paranoid beliefs. Additionally, you can make sure they do not have access to motor vehicles. If you find yourself uncertain about the safety of others, it is better to err on the side of caution and promptly contact emergency mental health services.

As previously discussed in the chapter, individuals experiencing auditory hallucinations or intrusive thoughts telling them to perform specific actions are often described as having "command hallucinations." If these voices or thoughts direct them to hurt themselves or others, it poses a major risk to both the individual suffering from psychosis and those around them. In such cases, seek immediate assistance or call emergency services.

Treatment of COVID-19-associated Psychosis

The primary focus of treatment is to preserve the patient's life, to support their breathing and the work of the heart if seriously ill, as well as to ensure appropriate nutrition and sleep. The infection should be treated directly where appropriate, especially if there are important neuropsychiatric risk factors and vulnerabilities.

Medications

The medical management of COVID-19-associated psychosis for positive symptoms like delusions and hallucinations, which are the most common psychotic symptoms in COVID-19, involves the use of antipsychotic medications, sometimes referred to as neuroleptics. These medications function by blocking dopamine receptors. The choice of medication is typically guided by considerations such as side effects, potential drug interactions, and the clinician's familiarity with antipsychotic medications. The key point is that antipsychotic medications can reduce delusions and hallucinations, which can lead people to lash out or disrupt their medical care. But the focus has to be on treating and addressing the underlying cause of these symptoms. Antipsychotic medications only serve as a temporary solution, a medical band-aid on the psychotic symptoms.

Antipsychotic medications do not treat COVID-19 itself or stop the body's inflammatory response from triggering the symptoms. But they can settle patients' response enough to allow them to receive good medical care, creating an environment conducive to diagnosing and addressing the underlying issues.

The negative symptoms of psychosis discussed above, such as apathy and a lack of pleasure, often respond poorly to most antipsychotic medications, except clozapine, which consistently demonstrates unique efficacy across various studies. Additionally, in many studies, clozapine has been associated with dramatically extended life expectancy compared to other antipsychotic medications. Despite its efficacy, clozapine is underused due to the serious side effects that require careful monitoring, such as the white blood cell count and a risk of fatal constipation.

Clozapine is typically avoided when an individual has an infection or is in the process of recovery due to its potential to reduce white blood cells, which are the frontline troops of the immune response. Furthermore, as clozapine is associated with fatal constipation of the large bowel (responsible for water absorption), patients with COVID-19 may face an elevated risk of bowel complications. However, stopping the clozapine in a patient with COVID-19 can precipitate severe psychosis stemming from both the underlying psychotic disorder and the body's inflammatory response to COVID-19. Therefore, close monitoring is essential for patients on clozapine who develop COVID-19.

For all antipsychotics used to treat psychotic symptoms in COVID-19, regular reevaluation, typically every two to four weeks, is critical. This ongoing assessment is essential to determine whether the medication is still needed or if dose adjustments are required. As noted above, most patients (72% in one study) will see resolution of psychotic symptoms within six months (Moccia et al. 2023). Antipsychotic medications have side effects, and their use should not be continued indefinitely without careful consideration. Side effects can vary significantly based on the choice of medication, doses, and the health of the person receiving them. For a list of antipsychotic side effects, see Chapter 12.

Managing COVID-19-associated psychosis in special populations, like the elderly, is discussed above, as this will primarily be related to delirium. In pregnant and lactating women, treatment may involve changing the dose, with a preference for medications that do not readily cross the placenta or enter breastmilk. Given the physiological stressors already present in pregnant women, including hormonal and circulatory changes, they may be at higher risk of experiencing COVID-19-associated psychosis symptoms. Pregnant and postpartum women may face an increased risk return home to isolation, particularly if their child's nocturnal disruptions lead to severe sleep deprivation. The risk is particularly noteworthy for postpartum women, who are already at risk for postpartum depression and psychosis. The impact can be further heightened if they have, or are recovering from, COVID-19. These issues are further explored in Chapter 10.

Non-pharmacological Measures

These include nutrition support and good fluid replacement (chicken soup, vegetable broth, and miso soup really are good for you when ill.) While they will not directly treat psychotic symptoms, they can improve a person's overall condition and reduce factors that might stress the brain or contribute to delirium. In addition, maintaining regular contact with others is essential to avoid isolation. As we discussed earlier in the chapter, psychological support helps with reality testing. For patients in COVID-19 isolation wards, having access to familiar foods, clothes, or pictures of loved ones, including pets, becomes a crucial aspect of grounding and can help in the prevention of psychosis and delirium.

It is especially important for the elderly and people with cognitive impairment to have regular reorientation. You can tell them the day and date, where they are, where the bathroom is, how to get help, and how long they have been in the hospital. It is also important to remind people with cognitive impairment why they are there and what the plan for their care is. When a person is experiencing psychosis in a hospital, it helps when each new person who enters the room introduces themselves. It is preferable for clinicians, staff, and family members to sit rather than stand, as this reduces autonomic hypervigilance and the fight or flight system of the patient when compared to a person towering over them. It is important for clinicians and family to keep track of the patient's bowel movements, as the body's inflammatory response takes a lot of water and nutrients and can cause constipation. Severe constipation and other effects of dehydration can be a risk for psychotic symptoms in the context of delirium.

Patients with psychotic symptoms with a history of previous ACE, PTSD, or other mental illnesses like depression may benefit from psychological counseling or psychotherapy. This is especially true if the patient has insight around their psychotic symptoms, or if the symptoms are dissociative in nature. Addressing psychotic symptoms, especially dissociative symptoms, during recovery will very likely improve and speed up outcomes. Psychotherapists in this setting should focus on the "whole person" and integrate mind and body symptoms, rather than focusing purely on mental experiences.

A 72-year-old man was brought to the emergency room by ambulance with high fever and disorientation. Police had been called after a customer noticed a man collapsed outside a liquor store. The patient had a longstanding diagnosis of schizophrenia dating back 45 years and had recently been on olanzapine 20 mg per day. Notably, he had several admissions in the past year for alcohol intoxication and related falls. In the three days preceding admission, he developed a cough, fever, and loss of appetite. By the day of admission, he was barely able to walk due to muscle pains all over his body. On arrival, he was very confused and disoriented. He had a high fever of 40 °C, tremors in his upper limbs, and severe muscle stiffness all over his body. He was sweating, had a very fast heart rate of 142/min, and an elevated blood pressure of 178/102 mmHg. Laboratory tests in the emergency room revealed a very high creatine kinase > 20 000 IU/L, and complete blood count was remarkable for an elevated white blood cell of 18 000/mm³. All of these abnormal results were concerning for brain chemistry in disarray.

The man's COVID-19 antigen test was positive. Chest X-ray, urine analysis, and blood culture showed no abnormalities. His blood alcohol level was 0 and his urine toxicology screen showed no recreational drugs. His symptoms and blood tests clearly met the diagnostic criteria for NMS, which was related to receiving the antipsychotic medication in the context of COVID-19. Olanzapine was discontinued, and he was admitted to the intensive care unit for management with massive infusion of fluids to protect his kidneys. Lead-pipe rigidity (muscle stiffness) improved four days after admission. On the tenth day of hospitalization, his creatine kinase level decreased to 1902 IU/L, and he was able to walk.

Conclusion

Psychosis associated with COVID-19 is likely due to a range of factors that cause people to lose touch with reality. Most COVID-19-related psychosis is not caused by the virus itself, but instead is due to the body's immune response to the virus, preexisting or previously undiagnosed mental illness, recreational drugs and drug withdrawal, and sometimes side effects of medications used to support patients who are severely ill with COVID-19. In most patients, psychotic symptoms will not be due to any single factor, but will be a collection of issues that contribute to the brain not being able to function effectively.

The most common symptoms of psychosis in COVID-19 patients are delusions and hallucinations, and in most of these patients, the symptoms will resolve within six months of viral infection. In patients who find the symptoms distressing, or when psychosis affects their safety or ability to function, antipsychotic medications may be effective treatments.

In addition to the typical symptoms of psychosis, COVID-19 may be associated with dissociative psychotic symptoms, particularly in people with ACE (trauma). These symptoms exist on a spectrum from normal experiences to incapacitating. Severe dissociative psychotic symptoms may contribute to the development of Long COVID and may prevent full recovery from COVID-19. Addressing these symptoms with psychotherapy may improve a person's recovery and outcome.

Learning Points

- Experiencing psychotic symptoms *does not* mean you necessarily have a psychotic disorder. Some symptoms are common to the human experience or may be a reflection of stress. Persistent symptoms, or ones that impair safety or disrupt the ability to function in relationships, work, or in the community are more likely to represent a disorder requiring treatment.
- Psychosis that occurs during or after infection with COVID-19 is generally not due to the COVID-19 virus attacking the brain. Stress (like having a viral illness) may bring out an underlying mental disorder. Inflammation as part of the body's response to an infection (not just COVID-19) may cause delirium.
- Isolation due to having COVID-19 or separation from family or caregivers can reduce protective mechanisms and impair reality testing.
- People with preexisting vulnerabilities are more susceptible to COVID-19 psychosis: These include the elderly, people with preexisting mental illness, or people who develop depression while sick or recovering from COVID-19. People with medical conditions that affect the brain, and those who regularly use alcohol or recreational drugs are also at higher risk for psychosis when they are ill.

- People with preexisting Adverse Childhood Experiences or PTSD may be more likely to suffer dissociative psychosis during COVID-19 or during recovery.
- When psychotic symptoms, such as delusions or hallucinations, cause significant distress, treatment with antipsychotic medications can help reduce these symptoms and make the person feel safer.
- Psychotherapy may help to reduce symptoms and speed up recovery from COVID-19 infection in people with psychotic symptoms, particularly dissociative symptoms.

References

Brown, A., Begg, M., Gravenstein, S. et al. (2004). Serologic evidence of prenatal influenza in the etiology of schizophrenia. *Archives of General Psychiatry* 61 (8): 774–780. https://doi.org/10.1001/archpsyc.61.8.774.

Brown, E., Gray, R., Lo, M., S.L. et al. (2020). The potential impact of COVID-19 on psychosis: a rapid review of contemporary epidemic and pandemic research. *Schizophrenia Research* 222: 79–87. https://doi.org/10.1016/j.schres.2020.05.005.

Fiorentini, A., Cantù, F., Crisanti, C. et al. (2021). Substance-induced psychoses: an updated literature review. *Frontiers in Psychiatry.* https://doi.org/10.3389/fpsyt.2021.694863.

Hein, T.C., Muz, B., Ahmadi-Montecalvo, H., and Smith, T. (2020). Associations among ACEs, health behavior, and veteran health by service era. *American Journal of Health Behavior* 44: 876–892. https://doi.org/10.5993/AJHB.44.6.11.

Karam, E., Fayyad, J., Farhat, C. et al. (2019). Role of childhood adversities and environmental sensitivity in the development of post-traumatic stress disorder in war-exposed Syrian refugee children and adolescents. *The British Journal of Psychiatry* 214: 354–360. https://doi.org/10.1192/bjp.2018.272.

Khan, A., Levy, P., DeHorn, S. et al. (2008). Predictors of mortality in patients with delirium tremens. *Academic Emergency Medicine* (8): 788–790. https://doi.org/10.1111/j.1553-2712.2008.00187.x.

Marshall, M. (2023). How Covid-19 affects the brain. *New Scientist* 257 (3424): 14–15. https://doi.org/10.1016/S0262-4079(23)00189-6.

Mednick, S., Machon, R., Huttunen, M., and Bonett, D. (1988). Adult schizophrenia following prenatal exposure to an influenza epidemic. *Archives of General Psychiatry* 2: 189–192. https://doi.org/10.1001/archpsyc.1988.01800260109013.

Menninger, K. (1919). Psychoses associated with influenza: I. General data: statistical analysis. *JAMA* 72 (4): 235–241. https://doi.org/10.1001/jama.1919.02610040001001.

Menninger, K. (1926). Influenza and schizophrenia: an analysis of post-influenzal "dementia praecox," as of 1918, and five years later: further studies of the psychiatric aspects of influenza. *The American Journal of Psychiatry* 5: 469–529. https://doi.org/10.1176/ajp.82.4.469.

Moccia, L., Kotzalidis, G.D., Bartolucci, G. et al. (2023). COVID-19 and new-onset psychosis: a comprehensive review. *Journal of Personalized Medicine* 1: 104. https://doi.org/10.3390/jpm13010104.

Sass, L.A. (1994). Civilized madness: schizophrenia, self-consciousness and the modern mind. *History of the Human Sciences* 7 (2): 83–120. https://doi.org/10.1177/095269519400700206.

Smith, C.M., Gilbert, E.B., Riordan, P.A. et al. (2021). COVID-19-associated psychosis: a systematic review of case reports. *General Hospital Psychiatry* 73: 84–100. https://doi.org/10.1016/j.genhosppsych.2021.10.003.

Taquet, M., Geddes, J.R., Husain, M. et al. (2021). 6-month neurological and psychiatric outcomes in 236 379 survivors of COVID-19-19: a retrospective cohort study using electronic health records. *Lancet Psychiatry* 8: 416–427. https://doi.org/10.1016/S2215-0366(21)00084-5.

Taylor, K.S., Steptoe, A., and Iob, E. (2022). The relationship of adverse childhood experiences, hair cortisol, C-reactive protein, and polygenic susceptibility with older adults' psychological distress during the COVID-19 pandemic. *Molecular Psychiatry.* https://doi.org/10.1038/s41380-022-01805-2.

Tyson, B., Shahein, A., Erdodi, L. et al. (2022). Delirium as a presenting symptom of COVID-19. *Cognitive and Behavioral Neurology* 2: 123–129. https://doi.org/10.1097/WNN.0000000000000305.

Wang, D., Zhou, L., Zhou, L., and Chen, C. (2023). Psychotic-like experiences during COVID-19 lockdown among adolescents: prevalence, risk and protective factors. *Schizophrenia Research* 252: 309–316. https://doi.org/10.1016/j.schres.2023.01.027.

Warrington, T. and Bostwick, J. (2006). Psychiatric adverse effects of corticosteroids. *Mayo Clinic Proceedings* 81 (10): 1361–1367. https://doi.org/10.4065/81.10.1361.

8

Post COVID-19 Condition

Jennifer Hulme

Department of Family and Community Medicine, University of Toronto, Toronto ON, M5G 1V7 Canada

This is my personal story, edited from my essay for University Health Network (UHN) News, which was first published in January 2024.

"In April 2022, another COVID wave was sweeping Toronto. It was the sixth since the March 2020 declaration of a pandemic due to the spread of the coronavirus.

Restrictions and mask mandates in schools had been lifted after a decidedly unpopular delay in return to school during the previous COVID wave in January. Children under five had yet to have access to COVID vaccines and classrooms remained poorly ventilated in older schools.

At the time, I was working on the frontline of potential COVID exposure – in the UHN Emergency Department (ED) and at the COVID recovery site for people experiencing homelessness, where every single resident at the hotel was isolated with the disease.

But like many, I did not get COVID at work. I got it from my junior kindergarten-aged son after kissing him goodnight in between the stairway banisters.

My son and I dutifully isolated together upstairs, away from my husband, who was working long hours every day at the hospital caring for COVID patients. We had the usual flu-like symptoms of alternating fever, chills, congestion, and severe fatigue; the only alarming symptom for me was migrating joint pain, which traveled around my body for several days before fading into the background.

It wasn't long before I realized how lucky we were that my husband escaped infection, because soon, he would have to do absolutely everything.

At the time, I remember feeling lucky to be fully vaccinated, and anticipated a full recovery. I returned to work on day 11 after testing positive for COVID, fatigued, but otherwise fine. I was training for a 10-km run, and on day 16 tried to go for a jog. I could not get down the street. I walked home.

"That's odd." I thought, believing it was just a premature return to sport. I worked two overnight shifts in the ED that weekend. By day 21, I was suddenly, terrifyingly, sick with something that felt altogether very new. That's when my life changed forever.

After that, Long COVID took over my life. My symptoms seemed endless.

I was mostly bed bound with relentless post-exertional malaise (PEM), fatigue, cognitive impairment, memory loss, headaches, pulsatile tinnitus – which is a constant whooshing in the ear, and a disturbing sensitivity to sound called hyperacusis. I lost hearing in one ear and developed constant ringing in it.

I was breathless at rest. I could not remember my address. I went off work and onto disability. I secretly dreamed of losing a limb – at least then someone could tell me what was wrong and try to help me. Instead, I looked pale but "fine" while barely being able to walk.

The symptoms encroached on every aspect of my identity – mother, active, and social person, a physician, researcher. I embarked on a desperate quest for answers; submerged in a sea of Reddit anecdotes and scientific papers, I explored every hypothesis, and every medication and supplement on the market out of pure desperation.

Early on, I squeezed my way into the Long COVID clinic at UHN. Just having some validation and a diagnosis was helpful. I learned that I had a combination of Long COVID phenotypes, or groupings.

The first is the brutal cocktail of severe fatigue, brain fog and PEM – which is the worsening of symptoms after physical, mental, or emotional effort. This is known as myalgic encephalomyelitis, or the misnomer chronic fatigue syndrome, termed "ME/CFS" for short.

It's a disruption in the energy metabolism at a cellular level that's akin to a smartphone running out of battery much faster than the latest model. Staying within my "energy envelope" became the center of my being.

The second phenotype is related to autonomic dysfunction, with increased heart rate, lightheadedness, dizziness when standing, shortness of breath, headaches, nausea, and other gastrointestinal symptoms. The Canadian postural orthostatic tachycardia syndrome (POTS) guidelines are helpful, and trialing medications can be a game changer. I wish I had started ivabradine sooner.

The third phenotype is dominated by allergic-type symptoms, including rashes, headaches, worsening asthma, joint pain, or abdominal pain, nausea or diarrhea made worse with specific types of foods. This grouping is thought to be related to mast cell activation.

Slowly there emerged small victories. I felt very lucky to get access to hyperbaric oxygen therapy (HBOT). Because I suffered from sudden hearing loss, I qualified for HBOT funded by provincial health insurance. Within five sessions, my hearing came back in my left ear, tinnitus, and pulsatile tinnitus – extremely distressing symptoms – completely resolved. And there is early evidence that HBOT could help long haulers with fatigue, cognition, and brain functioning.

I've also been lucky to participate in the <u>Reclaim Trial</u>, where I benefited from the medication offered.

After a long and difficult road, I'm now grateful to be able to work again and for the good hours and good days, which are more frequent.

Many people ask me what I want the public and physicians to know about Long COVID. I think the first is that "the tests are not normal" – we are just not ordering the right tests. Every study of long haulers shows unbelievable pathology: immune dysregulation, mitochondrial dysfunction, neuroinflammation, brain damage, vascular damage, gut dysbiosis, poor perfusion of the brain, lungs, and other organs. We just do not have an easily accessible biomarker yet.

The second thing is that while there are no approved treatments for Long COVID yet, there IS hope, and there are treatments that help! Antihistamines, antidepressants for neuroinflammation, aggressive treatment of autonomic dysfunction, or POTS, resting and pacing for PEM – these things can help.

The third is that the best way to prevent Long COVID is to avoid getting COVID. I use CAN95 masks, nasal sprays, high-efficiency particulate air (HEPA) filters, and boosters. And, if you do get COVID, have a plan to enroll in CanTreatCOVID to contribute to the science on Long COVID secondary prevention.

And finally, we need a rapid acceleration of double-blinded, placebo-controlled, randomized clinical trials. Of the trials that are ongoing right now, only 12 of them are looking at pharmaceutical treatment of Long COVID. This is in part because we do not fully understand the root cause of post-viral illness – whether this is persistent virus, viral debris, reactivation of latent viruses, gut dysbiosis – and what is driving all of the downstream effects of end organ, vascular damage and microclotting. Until then, I hope everyone with Long COVID is seen, supported and heard."

Introduction

This chapter has been written to help you better understand the current knowledge on Long COVID pathology and treatments. Every detail will not be covered, but I will guide you through the most common syndromes seen in Long COVID, shedding light on the possible causes based on the science to date. Additionally, I will explore some treatments that can massively improve the quality of life for some people.

Where Can You Go for Reliable Information on Long COVID?

There are already a number of good sources of information on Long COVID for patients. TLC Sessions podcast is a great resource, run by two Long COVID sufferers, both journalists, to follow the science as it emerges with the biggest brains and up-to-the-minute information with weekly interviews. Documentary filmmaker Gez Medenger and immunologist Danny Altmann have written an approachable, comprehensive Long COVID Handbook to help understand, manage, and treat Long COVID. I have used some of the same headings from TLC Handbook to help structure this chapter; I cannot imagine a better, more accessible way to learn about the condition.

What Is Long COVID?

When someone develops post-COVID syndrome, they are often so sick and disoriented, it is hard to make sense of what is happening. Similarly, their physician, who is often not trained to diagnose post-viral illnesses, may also have difficulty discerning what is what and feel overwhelmed with the number of systemic symptoms. There are over 200 symptoms associated with Long COVID, and once we review the underlying pathology below, you will understand why one person may have severe fatigue and depression, while another has heart palpitations and shortness of breath. Another person may have all of these symptoms, and a new rash and sore throat every time they eat. We can start by organizing clusters of symptoms into "phenotypes," or groupings, based on the different ways that COVID-19 can affect our physiology.

The first grouping, which I describe above, comprises a significant decline in pre-illness activity level, PEM, unrefreshing sleep, cognitive impairment, and/or difficulty being upright, recognized as "ME/CFS" (Centers for Disease Control and Prevention 2021). This disruption in the energy metabolism at the cellular level might evoke memories of your college biology class. You may or may not recall that nicotinamide adenine dinucleotide (NAD+) is needed to make energy in the form of adenosine triphosphate (ATP). In this condition, there is a likely depletion of NAD+, although we still do not fully understand the mechanics behind why or how this happens.

The second phenotype encompasses the manifestations of autonomic dysfunction and results in orthostatic intolerance, which means that symptoms get better when you lie down. Blood pooling in the legs causes increased heart rate, lightheadedness, dizziness when standing, shortness of breath, feelings of "anxiety," headaches, nausea, and other gastrointestinal symptoms (Raj et al. 2020). POTS is defined in adults as an increase in heart rate by 30 beats per minute (bpm) when standing. However, many people suffering from Long COVID, also referred to as long-haulers, have some variation of this and still suffer from POTS symptoms. For example, their heart rate may rise by 20 bpm most of the time when standing, but they feel better when lying down, all while being disabled by their symptoms.

The third grouping is thought to be related to mast cell activation syndrome, called MCAS, with an up-regulated histamine response similar to that seen in people with asthma, eczema, and food and dust allergies. Indeed, having a history of allergy appears to elevate your risk for MCAS.

Pain syndromes are also present in post-COVID condition. Fibromyalgia is well-defined but poorly understood as a post-viral pain syndrome; people dealing with Long COVID and other post-viral illnesses describe pain in a number of different ways. The diversity in pain perception is thought to be due to small fiber neuropathy. There are also a number of neurological symptoms in post-COVID conditions that remain poorly understood, but consistent between patients (Davis et al. 2023; Zhou et al. 2023).

There are other symptoms that do not fit neatly into these categories, which are likely caused by the direct damage from the virus itself, and/or the lack of oxygen getting to tissues from vascular damage. These include loss of taste and smell, sensorineural hearing loss, tinnitus and pulsatile tinnitus, and of course new-onset depression and anxiety covered in other chapters of this book. These may be due to direct damage to parts of the brain responsible for pleasure, smelling, and taste, as well as the damage to vessels and inflammatory "cascades" set off by the severe acute respiratory syndrome coronavirus 2 (SARS-CoV-2) virus.

Why Is this Happening?

This is *The Question* driving researchers worldwide: What is the underlying cause of Long COVID? To quote a recent article by National Public Radio (NPR), "If Long COVID were a crime scene, authorities would have no shortage of leads" (Stone 2023). We have overwhelming evidence of problems with every organ, the immune system, and vessels, but we do not yet understand the driving root cause to target therapies and find a cure. Research to date points to evidence of immune dysregulation, autoimmunity, viral debris, viral persistence, reactivation of latent viruses, and direct organ damage caused by the COVID virus – or more likely – a combination of all of these.

Epstein-Barr Virus (EBV) and Human Herpes Virus-6 (HHV-6) Reactivation

There is growing evidence that people with Long COVID are more likely to have reactivation of either Epstein-Barr virus (EBV), human herpes virus-6 (HHV-6), or both (Zubchenko et al. 2022; Peluso et al. 2022). Is this a symptom of immune dysfunction, i.e. the immune system is no longer able to keep these latent viruses in check, or is it the actual cause of immune dysregulation? This mechanism likely plays a significant role in conditions such as chronic fatigue syndrome

(CFS)/myalgic encephalomyelitis (ME) (Seton et al. 2024). This would provide an elegant and unifying explanation for the overlap in post-viral syndromes. However, the findings of SARS-CoV-2 viral debris and growing evidence for viral persistence make this story incomplete.

Viral Debris

Some studies suggest viral debris as a potential driver of Long COVID. Even in the absence of live virus, the production of autoantibodies may keep the immune system persistently engaged in clearing nonexistent threats. Studies detecting viral proteins in the gut and spike antigens in people with Long COVID support this idea (Zollner et al. 2022). Excitingly, medications like monoclonal antibodies (mABs) have the potential to mop up viral debris.

Viral Persistence

There is growing evidence of live virus detected in various tissues, including the lungs and brains of animals, and more recently, in human brains through autopsy results. Long-term shedding of SARS-CoV-2 ribonucleic acid (RNA) in feces and detectable viral RNA in blood samples also hint at persistent infection. To begin to understand the pathology of Long COVID, it is important to first recognize that the virus binds to the angiotensin-converting enzyme-2 (ACE2) receptor, present widely throughout the body, which helps to explain why the virus has been detected everywhere (Stein et al. 2022). The virus may be hiding in certain sanctuaries, making biopsies challenging, and making us rely on autopsy studies (Proal et al. 2023). The autopsy studies are compelling; the COVID-19 virus was found in over 30 different cell types, in tissues throughout the body, and in all of the major organs. In one case, there was genetic material from the virus in a person who died more than 200 days after contracting COVID-19.

The Microbiome Puzzle

The role of the microbiome is likely really important, and still unclear. Laboratory scientists have found that people with neurological symptoms with Long COVID have perturbations of their gut microbiota. One research group showed that gut dysbiosis and the loss of ACE2 in the gut after COVID-19 infection causes the production of metabolites that cause cognitive dysfunction, like phenylacetic acid (Gheblawi et al. 2023). Another group transplanted the microbiota of Long COVID patients with and without neurological symptoms into mice with sterile intestines. In various tests, mice in the former group performed worse than those in the latter. They also found that the more severe the Long COVID symptoms, the more a patient's blood contained a protein indicating greater permeability of the intestinal barrier – in other words, a leaky gut, which can disrupt the functioning of the immune system, predisposing them to an autoimmune response (Mendes de Almeida et al. 2023). "We do not think this intestinal dysbiosis is the only player in this mechanism," said Dr. Falcone in an interview. "We think viral persistence also plays a role. It is probably the combination of the two that contributes to the sustained inflammation."

Immune Dysfunction

Recent data from prominent immunologists working on Long COVID illustrate that the immune system in Long COVID patients looks like an immune system constantly in battle (Yin et al. 2024). Cytotoxic T cells are elevated, and the presence of exhausted T cells prompts many questions. There are also activated T cells where they should not be: in the gut, lung, lymph nodes, spinal cord, and brain stem. Is this a response to persistent SARS-CoV-2 infection, fragments of the virus lingering in the body, or reactivation of other viruses like EBV and herpes HHV6? Or is this a form of autoimmunity? This dysregulated immune response extends to body sites such as the gut and the mouth, which may in and of itself disrupt the microbiome and perpetuate a pro-inflammatory state.

Viral persistence or reactivated viruses may also sustain ongoing inflammation sensed by the vagus nerve, driving some of the autonomic nervous system symptoms. Microglia, the immune cells in the brain, appear to be activated by persistent SARS-CoV-2, contributing to neuroinflammation and the notorious brain fog that plague so many people with Long COVID.

Pathological Manifestations of Long COVID

We now know quite a bit about what is abnormal in Long COVID patients: we have found poor oxygen transfer through peripheral blood vessels, poor blood flow to the brain, metabolic issues, energy deficits specifically related to the mitochondria, microclotting, hypoperfusion, inflammation of blood vessel linings, abnormal inflammatory function, mast cell activation, various forms of autoimmunity, small fiber neuropathy, and overactive immune cells in the central nervous system leading to brain inflammation (See Figure 8.1). Additionally, there is direct damage attributed to SARS-CoV-2 itself, potentially contributing to some Long COVID symptoms, especially in individuals severely affected or hospitalized with the virus.

When you hear about "medically unexplained symptoms" – it is often inaccurate. We now have a very clear explanation for why people with post-viral syndromes are sick.

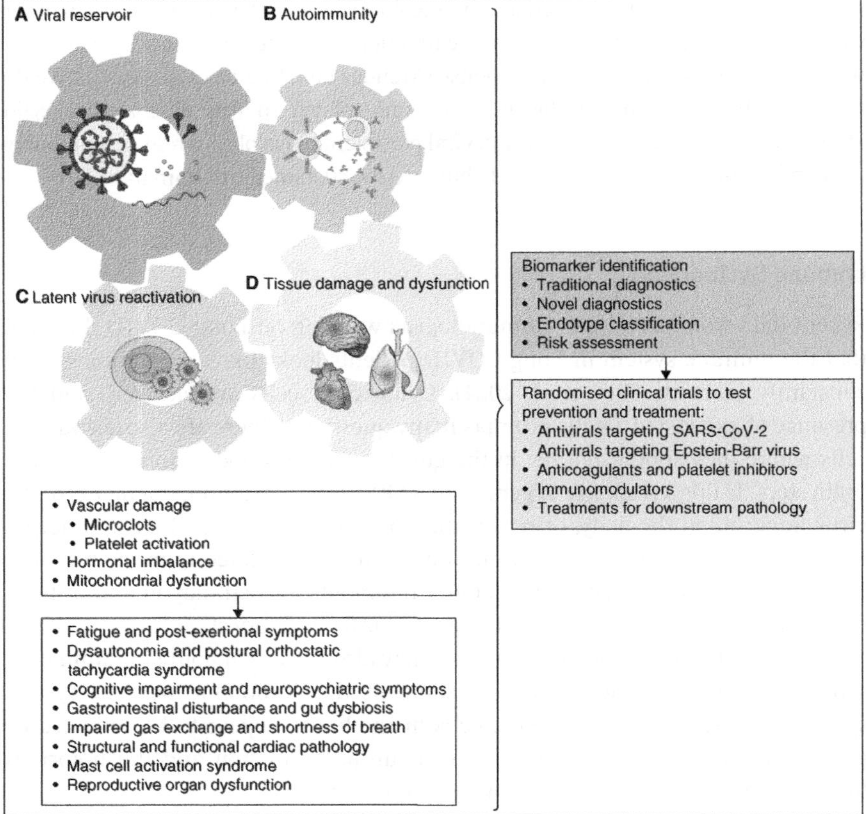

Figure 8.1 Pathophysiological Changes in Long COVID.

To begin to understand the pathology of Long COVID in particular, it is important to first recognize that the virus binds to the ACE2 receptors, which are in every organ of the body, including the lining of blood vessels. COVID-19 looks more like a vasculitis than an upper respiratory tract infection like the flu. The virus sets off a chain reaction, inducing vessel damage, heightened inflammation, platelet activation, and compromised oxygen extraction from the blood – a cycle marked by clotting and inflammation.

Let us look at some of the specific abnormalities that have been found in long-haulers, that act as clues as to what is driving Long COVID symptoms.

Microclots

Long-haulers seem to have hyperactive platelets and microclots in their blood in larger quantities than those without Long COVID. There is a significantly increased risk of blood clots, pulmonary embolisms, heart attacks, and strokes in the year following a COVID-19 infection, even in previously healthy people. While this is likely due to endothelial dysfunction, i.e. vascular inflammation, from COVID-19, it may also be partly attributed to hyperactive platelets and the presence of tiny, resistant microclots in the plasma. These microclots appear to block capillary beds, leading to reduced oxygen delivery to various tissues, which we see as poor perfusion and oxygen delivery to the lungs and brains of Long COVID patients.

Cerebral Hypoperfusion and Neuroinflammation

Brain fog, severe fatigue, and cognitive impairment are some of the most prominent symptoms of Long COVID. People with Long COVID describe the feeling as if there is insufficient blood in their brain to function properly, and they describe that their brain feels swollen. It turns out that both of these things are true! People with Long COVID may feel unsafe driving and have to stop. They may forget their own address, which feels terrifying.

Multiple studies have shown reduced blood flow in the brains of people with Long COVID even after a very mild infection. Specifically, there is decreased brain activity in areas associated with memory, emotional regulation, autonomic function, and motor skills. This is potentially due to the virus's affinity for the ACE2 receptor on blood capillary-surrounding cells. Vascular damage and microclotting likely reduce oxygen delivery in the brain. POTS is also well established to decrease brain perfusion.

Neurological symptoms and depression are also caused in part by brain inflammation and glial cell damage, particularly in the areas of the brain responsible for pleasure (Braga et al. 2023). Microglia are the immune cells of the brain that are constantly activated by persistent COVID-19 virus, driving neuroinflammation and brain fog.

Mitochondrial Dysfunction

Since having Long COVID, I have never thought so much about the mitochondria. Yet they are the engines, or powerhouses of the cell, and critical to our functioning. We now have evidence that people with Long COVID have mitochondrial dysfunction, paralleling the pathology and symptoms observed in ME/CFS. We know from CFS research that any type of physiological stress can reduce cellular energy in the form of ATP from mitochondria, resulting in what is called a PEM "crash."

A recent study showed that Long COVID patients had lower exercise capacity, local and systemic metabolic disturbances, severe exercise-induced myopathy, and amyloid deposits in their muscles – which worsened after inducing a PEM crash (Appelman et al. 2024).

Metabolic Dysfunction

Scientists are exploring various hypotheses to understand how SARS-CoV-2 affects metabolism. One of the hypotheses is that the post-COVID gut is unable to absorb tryptophan. This leads to the depletion of NAD+, the molecule crucial for energy production, and triggers a chain reaction. The body is forced to break down more tryptophan, resulting in insufficient levels, and subsequently increasing the production of inflammatory cytokines. The cascade may contribute to autonomic dysfunction, cognitive dysfunction, platelet aggregation, and problems with allergy and histamine regulation. Which came first, the chicken or the egg? We still do not fully understand.

Mast Cell Activation Syndrome (MCAS)

MCAS almost certainly plays a role in some Long COVID symptoms, leading to chronic migraines, headaches, intestinal problems, fibromyalgia, and psychiatric symptoms like anxiety and depression. Mast cells are the cells that cause the big "explosions" in response to serious allergies, and they may be activated by a number of different mechanisms: directly by the COVID-19 virus itself, by inflammatory cytokines, or through autoantibodies that react directly with mast cell receptors.

Inflammation

The inflammatory response in Long COVID is characterized by specific cytokine profiles. Viral RNA fragments have been found in nonclassical monocytes, the immune system's "garbage collectors." This contributes to an inflammatory milieu, marked by pro-inflammatory cytokines. This has implications for microglia and astrocytes, contributing to a spectrum of neurological symptoms. Of note, many long-haulers spend money out of pocket to get their cytokine levels tested, as these are not blood tests that are available to the average doctor or patient. Some physicians and patients are using these cytokine profiles "off-label" to determine clinical response to Miraviroc, described below.

Autoantibodies

COVID-19 can induce autoantibodies in some people, particularly in hospitalized patients. Autoantibodies are when the immune system attacks its own host instead of a virus or bacterial invader, causing a whole host of diseases and symptoms, depending on the target. Notably, many people with Long COVID develop autoantibodies to G protein-coupled receptors, which have a well-established link to neurological symptoms such as POTS. It is worth noting that my physician colleagues in North America do not seem to have access to this as a laboratory test, but it is used in France to help with the diagnosis of POTS, where physicians are more comfortable and familiar with the diagnosis and treatments for dysautonomia.

Direct Organ Damage

Contrary to conventional thinking that organ damage primarily occurs in severe COVID-19 cases, even those with mild acute infections show evidence of direct organ damage. Brain samples from humans and mice post-COVID-19 infection demonstrate neuroinflammation, microglial reactivation, and decreased oligo-dendrocytes. Additionally, people with Long COVID have reductions in gray matter thickness and total brain size.

How Is Long COVID Diagnosed?

Healthcare professionals are seeing more and more Long COVID, and therefore are increasingly in a better position to help their patients, despite the complex web of symptoms – ranging from allergic-type manifestations to metabolic and autonomic dysfunction, often accompanied by neurological symptoms or pain. Getting a diagnosis of the "phenotypes" of Long COVID like POTS, MCAS, and ME/CFS provides the basis for disability applications, accommodations, and workplace support. The World Health Organization (WHO) offers a broad working definition for Long COVID, emphasizing the importance of the patient's history over COVID-19 polymerase chain reaction (PCR) testing, which is becoming increasingly scarce. This is crucial for long-haulers, in the absence of a reliable test or biomarker, who need a community of support, validation from their families and workplaces, access to disability support, and access to treatments to support their recovery.

When Should You See Your Doctor?

Cara is a 29-year-old ICU nurse, who has struggled with severe fatigue since her bout of COVID-19 infection a few months ago. Worried about the possibility of Long COVID, she decided to consult her primary care doctor. An initial investigation and physical exam unveiled dysautonomia, as her heart rate increased 30 bpm on the Active Stand test, which measures changes in heart rate lying down and standing up. She was diagnosed with POTS. Her doctor explained that starting treatment could significantly enhance her quality of life. In particular, she mentioned that medications like Ivabradine and beta blockers, along with interventions like abdominal and leg compression, and water and salt adjustments, can be transformative. Given Cara's PEM, her doctor also screened her for ME/CFS. Cara's doctor explained that it was important for her to learn how to rest and pace, and to try different off-label treatments.

For those grappling with new depression, anxiety, and suicidality, getting medical help is critical. Every death by suicide due to Long COVID is avoidable, and a tragedy. Clinical trials are exploring the efficacy of selective serotonin reuptake inhibitors (SSRIs) for Long COVID brain fog. SSRIs may also reduce neuroinflammation, independent of the serotonin pathway. I have a friend who fully recovered after two years of being unable to work with brain fog from Long COVID. Given the evidence of very low serotonin levels in Long COVID patients, and the high prevalence of depression and suicidality, a trial of an SSRI is a no-brainer (Bird 2023).

Most patients will feel frustrated with the process and pace of getting medical care for their Long COVID symptoms. I can tell you as a physician, we have little to no training in post-viral illnesses, but I think this is going to change very quickly as the population suffering from Long COVID increases. I am personally involved in multiple efforts to improve training and guidelines for primary care, physicians, and specialists alike. Patients will not accept any less of us.

The other elephant in the room is the testing that patients are seeking out on their own and paying out-of-pocket. This includes testing for microclots using fluorescence microscopy. Patients need to be believed, and assessed, for POTS, PEM, MCAS, and pain syndromes. Until there is an accessible biomarker that is reliable, the inane focus on testing is incredibly problematic, because patients are paying a lot of money for tests that do not change how they feel, their treatments, or improve their quality of life.

Who Is at Risk for Long COVID?

Anyone with Long COVID has asked these questions: Why me? Is there something I could have done differently? Why does COVID-19 "look" like a cold in some people and disable others? (I say "look" because COVID-19 has proven itself to be a silent killer causing strokes, heart attacks, rheumatologic, and autoimmune disease, even months and years later.) Every time an article comes out about who is at the highest risk of developing Long COVID, I find it very unhelpful; being female is hardly a modifiable risk factor. Children and teens can and do go on to develop Long COVID (Lopez-Leon et al. 2022; Zheng et al. 2023). Most of the people I know with Long COVID were very fit – and even considered themselves athletes – before they became disabled. When you Google Long COVID and Olympians: athletes may even be at higher risk because they have more ACE-2 receptors on their larger muscle mass. So instead, let us focus on prevention.

How Do I Prevent Getting Long COVID If or When I Get Infected with COVID-19?

The best way to prevent Long COVID is to avoid getting infected by COVID-19 in the first place. As we know, this is no easy feat. We are working on systematic reviews of the evidence for each of these interventions, but it is safe to say that mechanical ventilation systems, coupled with natural ventilation strategies, such as opening windows, and a combination of both, can enhance air exchange and reduce viral particle concentration indoors. The integration of HEPA and minimum efficiency reporting value (MERV) air filtration systems help filter out potentially infectious particles. In-room or portable air filters, like HEPA, Corsi-Rosenthal, or other effective filtration methods, can further contribute to creating safer indoor environments. Implementation of UV technologies, encompassing far-wavelength and upper-room UV-C, may add an additional layer of protection by mitigating the presence of airborne viruses.

In terms of individual-level interventions, I recommend the comfortable CAN95 and KN95 masks, which can protect you at work, in crowded settings, while shopping at grocery stores, and so forth. Vaccination is your friend – in addition to preventing hospitalization and death from COVID-19, it prevents Long COVID by 15–40% depending on the study (keeping in mind the variability of all of these studies which are, by definition, retrospective) (Byambasuren et al. 2023; Watanabe et al. 2023). Complementary measures like saline nasal rinses, oral gargling with neti pots or saltwater, and mouthwash gargling with compounds like CPC, hydrogen peroxide, or alcohol-based solutions provide additional tools to reduce viral load and transmission (Baxter et al. 2022). The jury is still out in terms of evidence, but I also use nasal sprays that use nitric oxide and carrageenan to reduce viral load in the nose before and after exposure to people at work and in my social life.

I am involved in the only randomized trial that I know of looking at whether Paxlovid reduces Long COVID, called CanTreatCOVID. From the retrospective studies we do have, Paxlovid was associated with a 25% reduction in the risk of Long COVID (Xie et al. 2022), but we really need a randomized trial to know for sure how helpful it is in an otherwise healthy population. Metformin, a medication commonly used in the management of diabetes, has been shown to reduce the risk of Long COVID by 40–60% (Bramante et al. 2022). Prophylactic doses of antiplatelet agents, specifically aspirin (ASA), are often taken based on what we know about platelet activation. People with Long COVID will avoid exertion for up to a month after getting infected with COVID-19 again, but we do not know if 'radical rest' is effective. Anectodally, many of us went for a run two weeks after acute COVID-19, and never ran again. An anti-inflammatory diet may help, but we do not yet know for sure. Some people with Long COVID fast – using electrolytes or broth – when we become infected with COVID-19 again, based on the principal of autophagy described below. However, this is hard to do if you are taking metformin and Paxlovid, which have some gastrointestinal side effects, so you can try a "fasting mimicking diet" while acutely sick. CanTreatCOVID is also trialing a combined antioxidant therapy (300 µg selenium, 40 mg zinc, 45 mg lycopene, and 1.5 g vitamin C) for the prevention of hospitalization and Long COVID. I personally also take N-acetylcysteine (NAC), green tea extract, nattokinase, Omega-3 fatty acids, and a few other supplements in the hopes of reducing the harms from acute COVID-19 infections, but there is not concrete evidence for these.

What Treatments Are Available for Long COVID?

At the time that this goes to press, there are zero – count it, zero – FDA-approved treatments for Long COVID. When it comes to self-management strategies and medical treatments for Long COVID, many long-haulers have tried them all. The first question you may wonder about is "What worked for you?" Long COVID patients are desperate, and sick, and I can share with you what I have tried as a desperate and sick person who was weighing the risks and benefits of treatments as they went along. These are outlined below and in Table 8.1. My criteria for trying something is that it is safe; many treatments may not work for you, but I can share what has worked for me.

Self-management Strategies for Long COVID

Rest and Sleep

Long-haulers often find themselves grappling with the complexities of sleep disturbances, ranging from unrefreshing sleep to insomnia. These challenges may stem from disruptions in the hypothalamic-pituitary-adrenal axis and bottomed-out serotonin levels, vital components of our sleep-wake cycle. Of note, this also happens to people with concussions, or mild traumatic brain injury. Even a slight sleep deficit can have profound effects on long-haulers – we have no "bounce," or resilience. Some people have found melatonin, 5-HT, and in the case of headaches and pain syndromes, amitriptyline and gabapentin helpful for sleep.

Resting and Pacing: The Energy Envelope

PEM, a hallmark of Long COVID and ME/CFS, brings about crushing fatigue, a compelling need to rest, and cognitive impairment from minimal physical, emotional, or intellectual effort. It is akin to a smartphone running out of battery much faster than the latest model. When experiencing PEM, the phone battery is ever smaller and can only be fully recharged after prolonged and complete rest. What does that mean? The person's capacity to generate ATP is decreased, and they need a hard reset – full, uncompromising rest (physical, emotional, cognitive) until the person is at their symptom baseline for several days, allowing them to bring their capacity for energy production back to the highest level possible.

Discovering and staying within one's energy envelope becomes the center of one's being. Wearable technology, such as smartwatches and rings, can be useful tools to

Table 8.1 Long COVID treatments currently being used "off-label" by Long COVID patients.

Treatment	Rationale	Strength of evidence
Self-management		
Rest and sleep	Sleep disturbances from interruption of the HPA axis, low serotonin	Strong evidence from the concussion literature
Resting and pacing: the energy envelope	Manage post-exertional malaise; monitor with smartwatches, visible app	Strong evidence from ME/CFS literature
Diet	Diets may help with gut dysbiosis and reduce insulin resistance; intermittent and prolonged fasting for autophagy and immunomodulation; low-histamine diet for some	Limited evidence
Breathwork	Improve autonomic dysfunction through breathwork techniques	Limited evidence
Postural orthostatic tachycardia syndrome (POTS) management	Hydration, salt intake, compression stockings, Q-collar, vagal nerve stimulator	Low to moderate but strongly recommended by experts
Infrared sauna and cold-water plunge	Stimulate growth hormone disrupted in post-viral illness	Limited to case series
Medical management and pharmacologic		
Antihistamines	Modulate dysregulated mast cells and T cell function	Emerging
Hyperbaric oxygen therapy (HBOT)	Improve oxygen delivery to microvasculature, stimulate new blood flow to underperfused areas	Emerging, case series, and single center randomized controlled trial (RCTs)
POTS pharmacologic treatments	Ivabradine, beta blockers, midodrine, and other medications – use POTS guidelines – to improve brain perfusion and reduce tachycardia	Low-moderate evidence but recommended by experts
Nattokinase	Anecdotal reports suggest potential benefits in microclots	Limited
ASA (aspirin)	Address microclots and endothelial dysfunction	Limited
Anticoagulation	Triple anticoagulant therapy with ASA, clopidogrel, and apixaban to reduce microclot burden, indirectly improve immune dysfunction	Limited, reduced microclot burden in a poor-quality study

(Continued)

Table 8.1 (Continued)

Treatment	Rationale	Strength of evidence
Colchicine	Treat post-COVID pericarditis; potential antiplatelet properties	Limited
Niacin	Improve metabolic function; precursor of NAD+	Limited
Maraviroc	Target CC chemokine receptor 5 (CCR5) receptors to disrupt monocytic-endothelial-platelet axis	Limited
Paxlovid	Antiviral drug used in acute COVID-19; ongoing trials for Long COVID	Limited
Antivirals	Reduce serum levels of reactivated Epstein-Barr virus (EBV), human herpes virus 6 (HHV-6), human herpes virus 7 (HHV-7)	Low evidence from myalgic encephalomyelitis, or chronic fatigue syndrome (ME/CFS) literature
SSRIs, antidepressants	Regulate serotonin levels; decrease in neuroinflammation	Moderate evidence for depression or anxiety in Long COVID, emerging evidence for brain fog
Guanfacine (combined with N-acetylcysteine (NAC))	Guanfacine strengthens neural network connectivity, shown to improve cognition in patients with encephalomyelitis. NAC is an antioxidant. Both may reduce neuroinflammation by protecting mitochondria and deactivating microglia.	Low evidence from case series
Corticosteroids	Immunosuppressant and anti-inflammatory; potential pain relief	Limited
Low dose naltrexone	Immunosuppressant and anti-inflammatory; potential pain relief	Low evidence from ME/CFS literature
Probiotics	Address gut dysbiosis; potential impact on neuroinflammation	Low evidence
Nicotine replacement	Nicotine helps stimulate memory and cognition by activating proteins that help with neuronal communication	Low evidence from case series
Stellate ganglion block, vagal nerve stimulation	Address dysautonomia by blocking sympathetic nerve activity or stimulating vagus nerve	Low evidence from case series
Other supplements	Omega-3 fatty acids, NAC, magnesium threonate, Coenzyme Q10 (CoQ10), vitamin D3 and K2, creatine, taurine	Limited

quantify and manage activity levels as well as monitor biometrics like resting heart rate and heart rate variability to avoid crashes. I am familiar with the "Training Today" and "Visible" apps, which are tools to monitor heart rate variability (HRV) for avoiding crashes. The challenge lies in adapting daily activities into manageable portions and avoiding the enthusiasm that comes with a "good day" to pack everything into a day, especially during periods of feeling well. For some people, a good day means taking a shower; PEM is a brutal, debilitating symptom, and resting and pacing is just hard. Multiple ME/CFS and Long COVID websites including "Long COVID Physio" describe how to pace safely.

If you are counseled to start graded exercise therapy (GET) and cognitive behavioral therapy (CBT) for PEM, run in the opposite direction; this is based on a since discredited study, and can make PEM worse (Vink and Vink-Niese 2018; Ahmed et al. 2020). You may come across the term "structured pacing" from a small study (Parker et al. 2023), which describes improved outcomes after fixed incremental increases in activity. However, the Centers for Disease Control and Prevention (CDC), WHO, and other expert bodies specify that activities that exacerbate symptoms of PEM can result in long-term consequences, and should be avoided (WHO Regional Office for Europe 2021). If you are not limited by PEM, by all means, engage in rehabilitation designed for deconditioning; POTS gets better with progressive exercises performed lying down, for example. Many patients find Long COVID physical therapy helpful to simultaneously help manage the complexity of symptom-guided rehabilitation for ME/CFS and POTS.

Diet

While scientific evidence on dietary interventions for Long COVID remains limited, most long-haulers have experimented with every diet under the sun. A high-fiber diet, known for its anti-inflammatory properties, is considered beneficial for autoimmune inflammatory conditions. Fasting practices, such as intermittent and prolonged fasting, are popular in grassroots Long COVID communities. Fasting may promote autophagy, aiding in the removal of viral remnants or persistent virus. Fasting may also serve as an immune "reset" to help with immune dysfunction. For those with MCAS, a low-histamine diet has been reported to be very helpful by patients in patient-led research, and may be worth trying.

Breathwork

Autonomic dysfunction in Long COVID responds to breathwork. The work of Dr. Boon Lim is a valuable resource. This does not imply that Long COVID patients are merely anxious; instead, it acknowledges strong medical evidence that we can help influence our autonomic nervous system by using evidence-based breathwork techniques.

Infrared Sauna and Cold-water Plunge

There is growing evidence for these forms of treatments, which may stimulate growth hormone that is disrupted in post-viral illness (Soejima et al. 2015). I do both of these things. Perhaps one of the most frustrating experiences is that both of these treatments can trigger a "crash" in people who have exceeded their energy envelope. This can happen if the plunge is too cold for too long, or in a sauna that is too hot for too long – likely all part of the mitochondrial exhaustion of ME/CFS.

POTS Management

Although not every long-hauler meets the official criteria for POTS, a significant percentage experience some form of dysautonomia. Understanding and managing POTS symptoms can result in substantial improvements in quality of life. I recommend reading the Canadian POTS Guidelines, which include: increase fluid intake to 3–4l of water a day; eat as much salt as you can possibly take in (10g!); use compression stockings or tights; use an abdominal binder as tight as you can tolerate; try breath work; try autonomic conditioning exercises while lying down if you can tolerate it. It is also recommended to take recumbent breaks, lying down for five minutes, every hour if possible.

We need to talk about the role of rehabilitation and exercise, because it is strongly recommended for people with POTS. However, *GET should be avoided for people with PEM*. A lot of medical harm was done when a poor-quality study led to exercise being recommended for people with PEM and ME/CFS. Their batteries ran out of energy, and they were never able to restart. In a study of 477 people living with Long COVID, 75% reported functional deterioration after following recommendations to exercise (Wright et al. 2022).

The Stellate Ganglion Block gained a lot of interest after a case series of two Long COVID patients was published (Liu and Duricka 2022). The vagus nerve is what controls the body's parasympathetic nervous system, which is not working properly in most long-haulers. There is also good evidence for using a vagus nerve stimulator in POTS; I use a TENS machine connected to ear clips (Stavrakis et al. 2023).

Medical Treatments for Long COVID

POTS Medications

Pharmacologic treatments for POTS aim to increase blood flow to the brain by increasing blood volume, and reducing high heart rate upon standing, allowing the heart to fill properly. Commonly used medications include fludrocortisone, a mineralocorticoid that helps increase blood volume and blood pressure; midodrine, a vasoconstrictor that raises blood pressure; beta-blockers, such as propranolol or metoprolol, which reduce heart rate; and ivabradine, a medication that selectively inhibits the current in the sinoatrial node, lowering heart rate without affecting blood pressure. While observational studies and clinical experience support the use of these medications, there is a need for more rigorous randomized controlled trials to establish the optimal pharmacologic approach for POTS, considering both efficacy and potential side effects. Ivabradine can be magic for some people, including me.

Antihistamines

Observational studies suggest that antihistamines can be helpful for long-haulers. A combination of H1 and H2 blockers reportedly led to gradual symptom improvement, except for dysautonomia in one study (Glynne et al. 2022); I feel they were helpful for the first year of Long COVID for me. In addition to helping dampen down dysregulated mast cells, antihistamines might also function as T cell modulators, aligning with abnormal T cell function observed in long-haulers. You can also try Quercetin, an over-the-counter supplement meant to help stabilize mast cells.

Vascular Therapies: Hyperbaric Oxygen Therapy (HBOT)

It is helpful to think of Long COVID as a microvascular and endothelial disease that causes difficulty getting oxygen to tissues in the microvasculature. I feel very lucky to have had access to HBOT. So, what is the evidence for this expensive and time-intensive intervention? We have data to suggest that this treatment results in significant improvement in fatigue, cognition, and brain functioning (specifically, verbal and executive function and information processing) (Zilberman-Itskovich et al. 2022).

Preventing and Treating Microclots: Aphoresis, Nattokinase, Antiplatelet Agents (ASA, Plavix), Anticoagulants, Colchicine

Apheresis

Apheresis is an invasive procedure to remove and spin down blood, removing the elements of blood that may be contributing to microclots. We cannot ignore the anecdotes that people have gotten significant benefit from this procedure, but I worry about desperately sick people facing the high cost and lack of evidence (Davies 2022). A recent promising study showed significant benefit in terms of clinical markers of immune dysfunction (Achleitner et al. 2023).

Nattokinase

Long COVID patients often turn to nattokinase, an enzyme derived from fermented soybeans, due to anecdotal reports suggesting potential benefits in addressing immune dysfunction and improving symptoms associated with micro-clots and vascular issues. We do not know if it works, but there does not seem to be much harm except to your pocketbook.

Aspirin

People with Long COVID may use aspirin, based on the presence of microclots and endothelial dysfunction. While the evidence is still limited, it is worth taking in the spirit of stroke and heart attack prevention, given the vascular nature of COVID-19 and theoretical benefit to reducing the burden of platelet aggregation.

Anticoagulation

"Triple anticoagulant therapy" is used off-label. There is a small study that found that two medications, ASA and clopidogrel, and an anticoagulant, apixaban, reduced the microclot burden for 24 long-haulers who also reported improvement in their symptoms (Kell et al. 2022). This was a poor-quality study, and the risks of triple therapy in terms of serious bleeds may outweigh the benefits. This requires much more study before being used by patients, and I do not recommend this.

Colchicine

Some Long COVID clinics have experience with colchicine to treat post-COVID pericarditis, which makes a lot of sense as a standard treatment for inflammation of the lining of the heart. Those same people then reported that they felt better overall, and the thinking is that perhaps colchicine, which is a type of anti-inflammatory, may have antiplatelet properties. There was, however, no evidence that colchicine helped people with severe acute COVID-19.

Metabolic Function: Niacin

In patient-led research, niacin was found to improve Long COVID symptoms. It is a relatively benign supplement. In its nicotinic acid form, it is a precursor of NAD+, which we need to make cellular energy. The unpleasant "flushing" from niacin can be mitigated by taking aspirin beforehand. From personal experience, the flushing sensation can be enjoyable (except for that one time that I thought I was going to explode).

Viral Persistence and Immune Disruption

Maraviroc

Online communities have been sharing anecdotes of improvement with Maraviroc, an antiretroviral drug for human immunodeficiency virus (HIV). In a small study of people with elevated cytokine levels, in combination with pravastatin, a statin medication, patients reported improvement in multiple symptoms, along with improvement in vascular biomarkers associated with Long COVID severity (Patterson et al. 2023). I know of one person who has recovered on Maraviroc, and their physician follows their cytokine levels as a marker of clinical response. They are lucky to have that doctor willing to work with them! However, the cost is very high and further study is needed.

Paxlovid

There are several trials ongoing (Table 8.2), looking to study whether a longer treatment course with Paxlovid, which is the antiviral drug used to treat acute COVID-19, may be helpful in Long COVID. I suspect that if there are live viral reservoirs, that they are well hidden, beyond the reach of this antiviral.

Nicotine

A 2023 case series reported rapid and significant improvements lasting up to three months in four patients who used nicotine patches for the treatment of Long COVID (Leitzke 2023). The author proposes that nicotine, which has a very high affinity for nicotinic acetylcholine receptors (nAChRs), might displace the SAR-CoV-2 virus from neural pathways and therefore help with cholinergic signal transmission that is impaired in Long COVID. Harms include the high cost of patches and temporary side effects including nausea, palpitations, and difficulty sleeping. Even in the absence of persistent COVID-19 virus, nicotine may help stimulate memory and cognition by activating proteins that help with neuronal communication. Like many of these off-label treatments, I can share that I found nicotine very helpful for brain fog, but it has not been a "cure" for me personally. You can find patient-developed protocols under #thenicotine-test on Twitter/X.

Reactivation of Latent Viruses

Based on limited trials for ME/CFS patients, some Long COVID patients have tried antivirals with anecdotal improvement in their symptoms. When you look at the research, the trials were able to reduce EBV, HHV-6, and HHV-7 levels in ME/CFS patients, and patients reported improvements in symptoms. However, antivirals were not a cure; these viruses stay dormant in reservoirs, and in people with immune dysfunction, they love to come out and replicate (Seton et al. 2024). Antivirals have a good safety record and are well tolerated, but are taken for six months or longer in ME/CFS studies. This fits into the category of maybe worth trying.

Table 8.2 Upcoming placebo controlled Long COVID trials (from clinicaltrials.gov).

Treatment	Rationale in Long COVID recovery
Baricitinib	Baricitinib is a Janus kinase (JAK) inhibitor with immunomodulatory properties. It is used for the treatment of rheumatoid arthritis (RA), alopecia areata, and acute COVID-19 for hospitalized patients.
Pycnogenol	Antioxidative, anti-inflammatory and antiproliferative effects and has been shown to improve vascular endothelial function
Cordyceps	Cordyceps is a fungus with purported anti-inflammatory and immunomodulatory effects
Vorioxetine (selective serotonin reuptake inhibitors (SSRI) with established pro-cognitive properties)	It may improve cognition through modulatory effects on cellular and cytokine systems.
Ampligen® (rintatolimod)	Ampligen is an experimental immunomodulator. The trial seeks to understand its role in modulating the immune response in Long COVID patients.
Paxlovid	Treat persistent viral infection and/or overactive immune response and
Fluvoxamine	selective serotonin reuptake inhibitor (SSRI) (FDA-approved for obsessive-compulsive disorder (OCD)) that also activates the sigma-1 receptor (an immunomodulatory receptor). The trial aims to explore its potential anti-inflammatory effects and symptom improvement in Long COVID.
Ibudilast	Ibudilast is an anti-inflammatory drug.
Pentoxifylline	Pentoxifylline helps red blood cells reach tissues more easily, and has anti-inflammatory properties.
Amantadine	Amantadine is an antiviral and anti-Parkinsonian drug. The trial aims to explore its antiviral properties in Long COVID.
Human umbilical cord blood (RegeneCyte) Infusion	Cord blood contains various stem cells with potential regenerative properties. The trial aims to explore the regenerative potential in Long COVID.
Metformin	Metformin is an antidiabetic drug with anti-inflammatory properties. The trial aims to assess its potential in modulating inflammation and metabolic dysfunction in Long COVID.
BC 007	BC 007 is thought to bind and neutralize autoantibodies directed against G-protein coupled receptors (GPCRs) which have a role in ME/CFS and POTS.

Table 8.2 (Continued)

Treatment	Rationale in Long COVID recovery
RSLV-132	RSLV-132 is an immunomodulatory compound, designed to digest the ribonucleic acid contained in autoantibodies and immune complexes and thereby render them biologically inert.
Testofen (a specialized extract of *Trigonella foenum-graecum* (Fenugreek) seed)	Testofen is being investigated for its potential hormonal and anti-inflammatory effects in Long COVID.
LAU-7b	LAU-7b is an anti-inflammatory compound and an antiviral.
Ivabradine	Ivabradine is a heart medication. The trial aims to explore its potential in managing symptoms related to heart rate and autonomic dysfunction in Long COVID.
AER002 monoclonal antibodies (mABs)	Monoclonal antibodies are being investigated for their potential in neutralizing the virus and reducing symptoms in Long COVID.
Oxaloacetate	Oxaloacetate is a compound involved in cellular metabolism. The trial aims to explore its potential in modulating metabolic dysfunction in Long COVID.
Larazotide (AT1001)	For pediatric patients with Long COVID. Larazotide is being investigated for its potential in modulating gut barrier function and inflammation in Long COVID. Used to treat multisystem inflammatory syndrome in children (MIS-C), a complication of COVID-19 in children
Probiotics	Probiotics are being explored for their potential in modulating gut microbiota and immune response in Long COVID.
Low-dose naltrexone	From ME/CFS and Fibromyalgia literature, it may help reduce pain and inflammation and improve well-being and immune function.
Nitrate/nitric oxide	Nitric oxide (NO) is a signaling molecule that contributes to numerous physiological functions, including enhanced skeletal muscle mitochondrial respiration, vasodilatory, and anti-inflammatory effects.
Ensitrelvir	Antiviral to treat viral persistence
Histamine receptor blockers	Modulate immune response and dampen down mast cell activation syndrome (MCAS).
Steroids: methyprednisolone	Methylprednisolone is a well-known immunosuppressant used for multiple diseases of (suspected) autoimmune etiology.

(Continued)

Table 8.2 (Continued)

Treatment	Rationale in Long COVID recovery
Growth hormone therapy	Patients with abnormal growth hormone secretion, as measured by glucagon stimulation test, with Long COVID or concussion, may benefit.
Non-pharmacologic studies	
Inhaled hydroxy gas – a mixture of hydrogen and oxygen	Inhaling a mixture of hydrogen and oxygen is being explored for its potential antioxidant and anti-inflammatory effects.
Auricular transcutaneous vagus nerve stimulation	Stimulation of the vagus nerve, especially through the auricular (ear) approach, is being investigated for its potential in modulating autonomic function, reducing inflammation, and improving symptoms in Long COVID.
Transcranial direct current stimulation (tDCS)	tDCS involves applying a low electrical current to the brain. It is being explored for its potential in modulating neural activity and cognitive function, aiming to address cognitive symptoms associated with Long COVID.
Stellate ganglion blocks	Stellate ganglion blocks involve injecting anesthetic near the stellate ganglion to block sympathetic nerve activity. This procedure is being investigated for its potential in modulating autonomic function and alleviating symptoms related to dysautonomia in Long COVID.
Transcutaneous vagus nerve stimulation (tVNS)	Similar to auricular stimulation, transcutaneous vagus nerve stimulation involves applying a mild electrical current to the skin to stimulate the vagus nerve. It is being explored for its potential in modulating autonomic function and reducing inflammation in Long COVID.
Paced breathing with heart rate variability biofeedback	Paced breathing, combined with heart rate variability biofeedback, modulates the autonomic nervous system. It aims to improve heart rate variability, potentially benefiting symptoms related to dysautonomia in Long COVID.
Hyperbaric oxygen therapy for Long COVID syndrome (HOT-LoCO)	Enhance oxygen delivery to tissues, and improve endothelial dysfunction.

Neuroinflammation and Cognition: SSRIs, Guanfacine, and NAC

SSRIs are usually prescribed for anxiety and depression, and they are thought to work by regulating serotonin levels. The trials that are currently looking at vortioxetine for brain fog are still underway. Anyone who is experiencing a mood disorder or brain fog in the context of Long COVID may benefit from an SSRI, given the increasing evidence of bottomed out serotonin levels, and the thought that SSRIs can decrease neuroinflammation through a separate pathway.

A case series found that combined treatment with guanfacine and the antioxidant, NAC reduced the brain fog from Long COVID in 8 out of 12 patients (Fesharaki-Zadeh et al. 2023) Four patients discontinued therapy, two for unspecified reasons and two due to hypotension or dizziness. The researchers chose guanfacine, as it strengthens network connectivity and is anti-inflammatory; it has been shown to improve cognition in patients with encephalomyelitis. NAC is an antioxidant that protects mitochondria by increasing levels of the antioxidant, glutathione. The two agents may also reduce neuroinflammation by protecting mitochondria and deactivating microglia. This case series received a lot of press, but as of now, it is not being studied further. I take NAC daily based on my comfort with the medication and potential benefits.

Immunomodulators and Anti-inflammatories: Corticosteroids, Low-dose Naltrexone

Steroids

Corticosteroids are a big hammer. They act as an immunosuppressant and anti-inflammatory. The public became very familiar with dexamethasone because it was shown to be effective in severe acute COVID-19. However, there are many side effects both with short-term and long-term use of corticosteroids. Some people with Long COVID report benefits from using them, but this seems to be those who have new rheumatologic symptoms, and benefits are not usually sustained.

Low-dose Naltrexone

Naltrexone is medication clinicians routinely use for alcohol use disorder, as it blocks the euphoria from stimulation of the opioid receptors in the brain. Interestingly, there is evidence for its use in ME/CFS and for Long COVID at very low doses, where it can function as a painkiller and anti-inflammatory (NCT05430152 2022). In my personal experience, it seemed to help for a few weeks and then its benefit wore off. However, some people with ME/CFS and Long COVID report sustained benefit (O'Kelly et al. 2022). It is absolutely worth trying.

Gut Dysbiosis: Probiotics

Probiotics, specifically LV 299, have gained a lot of attention within TLC community. It is worth trying if you are motivated by the findings of gut dysbiosis and the growing evidence for how it may contribute to neuroinflammation (Alenazy et al. 2022). In short: no evidence yet – all vibe (NCT05080244 2021).

Other Supplements

All of us have kitchens overflowing with supplements, worth hundreds, if not, thousands of dollars. There is very little evidence for any supplements, and there is little hope of getting clarity on what might be helpful. This is because there is limited funding for this type of research, and the incremental benefits may be too small to measure in a randomized controlled trial. However, based on my understanding of physiology and with the support of my Long COVID dietician and physical therapist, I recommend trying omega-3 fatty acids, NAC, magnesium threonate, coenzyme Q10, vitamin D3, and vitamin K2. You can also try creatine monohydrate, which comes in a powder format, and taurine. A recent study showed that taurine levels were bottomed-out in long-haul patients (Wang et al. 2023).

What Does the Future of Long COVID Prevention, Diagnosis, and Treatment Look Like?

Without question, this is one of the major public health challenges of our lifetimes. Look around you. There is a global labor shortage, attributed to "quiet quitting," and suddenly "nobody wants to work anymore." Meanwhile, health economists are pointing out that up to 1 in 10 people have Long COVID, affecting their ability to work, and long-term disability applications are at an all-time high (Kuang et al. 2023).

So, what can we do? My hope is that we get better sterilizing immunity from intranasal vaccines (Iwasaki and Putrino 2023). We can also work together to clean our indoor air – which benefits children in school, and people at work, in so many ways! We can learn how to use the individual tools at our disposal, like nasal sprays and masks, to prevent transmission of COVID-19 until we have durable protection from its long-term effects. I also hope we generate great evidence to help us know what to do when we DO get infected with COVID-19. For now, I recommend traveling with metformin, along with a personal HEPA filter, masks, and nasal sprays.

Of the 250+ trials that are ongoing right now, too few of them are actually looking at pharmaceutical treatment of Long COVID (Table 8.2). This is in part because we do not fully understand the root cause of post-viral illness. Some of the most exciting therapies are those that include antivirals and neutralizing mABs that go after viral reservoirs (Henrich 2024). I have been lucky to participate in one of the trials and notice great benefit from the medication. I am grateful for this research, and I hope that we see a rapid acceleration for this type of double-blinded, placebo-controlled, randomized clinical trial.

Conclusion

A Long COVID diagnosis relies on symptoms that are otherwise unexplained after a COVID-19 infection. A timely diagnosis is crucial for offering appropriate support and interventions for individuals experiencing Long COVID. Prevent COVID-19 infections by managing indoor air quality, and utilizing individual tools like masks, vaccination, and nasal sprays. When you get COVID-19, consider using metformin, nasal rinses, and the rest; follow the emerging science on Paxlovid, aspirin, fasting, and antioxidant therapies for Long COVID prevention. Other medical treatments include antihistamines, SSRIs to reduce neuroinflammation, and HBOT. Self-management strategies include resting and pacing, dietary changes, probiotics, fasting, and breathwork.

Learning Points
<ul><li>Long COVID groupings, or phenotypes, include POTS, MCAS, and ME/CFS, which are post-viral conditions that can also be caused by EBV and other viruses.</li><li>There are many abnormalities in the blood of people with Long COVID – elevated exhausted T cells, inflammatory cytokines, vascular transformation biomarkers like vascular endothelial growth factor (VEGF), and poor brain, lung, and tissue blood flow and oxygen exchange. But we do not yet have a reliable, affordable blood test, or biomarker.</li><li>Healthcare professionals play a vital role in assessment, diagnosis, and treatments – both on and off label – and support with disability applications and workplace accommodations.</li><li>Long COVID patients and healthcare professionals are deeply invested in learning about treatment strategies. No FDA-approved treatments exist for Long COVID, so patients are seeking out self-management and medical interventions to address viral persistence, microclots, gut dysbiosis, and neuroinflammation.</li><li>POTS treatment can significantly improve quality of life, including salt and fluids, abdominal compression, transcutaneous vagus nerve stimulation (t-VNS), and prescribed medications like ivabradine.</li><li>The future of Long COVID research is to identify the root causes of post-viral illness and explore pharmaceutical treatments that target viral reservoirs and debris with mABs, and neutralize autoantibodies that likely drive ME/CFS and POTS. Other treatments are antioxidative, anti-inflammatory, and antiproliferative, and aim to help "downstream" by regulating the immune system and helping with repair of the vascular endothelium (Table 8.2).</li></ul>

References

Achleitner, M., Steenblock, C., Dänhardt, J. et al. (2023). Clinical improvement of long-COVID is associated with reduction in autoantibodies, lipids, and inflammation following therapeutic apheresis. *Molecular Psychiatry* 28 (7): https://doi.org/10.1038/s41380-023-02084-1.

Ahmed, S.A., Mewes, J.C., and Vrijhoef, H.J.M. (2020). Assessment of the scientific rigour of randomized controlled trials on the effectiveness of cognitive behavioural therapy and graded exercise therapy for patients with myalgic encephalomyelitis/chronic fatigue syndrome: a systematic review. *Journal of Health Psychology* 25 (2): https://doi.org/10.1177/1359105319847261.

Alenazy, M.F., Aljohar, H.I., Alruwaili, A.R. et al. (2022). Gut microbiota dynamics in relation to long-COVID-19 syndrome: role of probiotics to combat psychiatric complications. *Metabolites* 12 ((10): https://doi.org/10.3390/metabo12100912.

Appelman, B., Charlton, B.T., Goulding, R.P. et al. (2024). Muscle abnormalities worsen after post-exertional malaise in long COVID. *Nature Communications* 15 (1): 17. https://doi.org/10.1038/s41467-023-44432-3.

Baxter, A.L., Schwartz, K.R., Johnson, R.W. et al. (2022). Rapid initiation of nasal saline irrigation to reduce severity in high-risk COVID+ outpatients. *Ear, Nose, and Throat Journal.* https://doi.org/10.1177/01455613221123737.

Bird, L. (2023). Low serotonin linked to long COVID. *Nature Reviews Immunology* 23 (12): 784. https://doi.org/10.1038/s41577-023-00966-7.

Braga, J., Lepra, M., Kish, S.J. et al. (2023). Neuroinflammation after COVID-19 with persistent depressive and cognitive symptoms. *JAMA Psychiatry* 80 (8): 787–795. https://doi.org/10.1001/jamapsychiatry.2023.1321.

Bramante, C.T., Buse, J.B., Liebovitz, D. et al. (2022). Outpatient treatment of Covid-19 with metformin, ivermectin, and fluvoxamine and the development of Long Covid over 10-month follow-up. *medRxiv : The Preprint Server for Health Sciences.* https://doi.org/10.1101/2022.12.21.22283753.

Byambasuren, O., Stehlik, P., Clark, J. et al. (2023). Effect of covid-19 vaccination on long covid: systematic review. *BMJ Medicine* 2 (1): https://doi.org/10.1136/bmjmed-2022-000385.

Centers for Disease Control and Prevention (2021). IOM 2015 Diagnostic Criteria | Diagnosis | Healthcare Providers | Myalgic Encephalomyelitis/Chronic Fatigue Syndrome (ME/CFS) | CDC. https://www.cdc.gov/me-cfs/hcp/diagnosis/iom-2015-diagnostic-criteria-1.html.

Davies, M. (2022). Long covid patients travel abroad for expensive and experimental "blood washing.". *The BMJ.* https://doi.org/10.1136/bmj.o1671.

Davis, H.E., McCorkell, L., Vogel, J.M., and Topol, E.J. (2023). Long COVID: major findings, mechanisms and recommendations. *Nature Reviews. Microbiology* 21 (3): 133–146. https://doi.org/10.1038/s41579-022-00846-2.

Fesharaki-Zadeh, A., Lowe, N., and Arnsten, A.F.T. (2023). Clinical experience with the α2A-adrenoceptor agonist, guanfacine, and N-acetylcysteine for the treatment of cognitive deficits in "Long-COVID19." *Neuroimmunology Reports* 3: https://doi.org/10.1016/j.nerep.2022.100154.

Gheblawi, M., Wang, F., Basu, R. et al. (2023). Abstract 13173: loss of ACE2 in a diabetic obese setting exacerbates cardiovascular dysfunction in the setting of gut Dysbiosis. *Circulation* 148 (Suppl_1): https://doi.org/10.1161/circ.148.suppl_1.13173.

Glynne, P., Tahmasebi, N., Gant, V., and Gupta, R. (2022). Long COVID following mild SARS-CoV-2 infection: characteristic T cell alterations and response to antihistamines. *Journal of Investigative Medicine* 70 (1): https://doi.org/10.1136/jim-2021-002051.

Henrich, T.P.M. (2024). Placebo-controlled, randomized trial of Ensitrelvir (S-217622) for viral persistence and inflammation in people experiencing long COVID (PREVAIL-LC). https://Clinicaltrials.Ucsf.Edu/Trial/NCT06161688 (accessed 16 July 2024).

Iwasaki, A. and Putrino, D. (2023). Why we need a deeper understanding of the pathophysiology of long COVID. *The Lancet Infectious Diseases* 23 (4): https://doi.org/10.1016/S1473-3099(23)00053-1.

Kell, D.B., Laubscher, G.J., and Pretorius, E. (2022). A central role for amyloid fibrin microclots in long COVID/PASC: origins and therapeutic implications. *Biochemical Journal* 479 (4): https://doi.org/10.1042/BCJ20220016.

Kuang, S., Earl, S., Clarke, J. et al. (2023). Experiences of Canadians with long-term symptoms following COVID-19. https://www150.statcan.gc.ca/n1/en/pub/75-006-x/2023001/article/00015-eng.pdf?st=COf7tEVC (accessed 16 July 2024).

Leitzke, M. (2023). Is the post-COVID-19 syndrome a severe impairment of acetylcholine-orchestrated neuromodulation that responds to nicotine administration? *Bioelectronic Medicine* 9 (1): 2. https://doi.org/10.1186/s42234-023-00104-7.

Liu, L.D. and Duricka, D.L. (2022). Stellate ganglion block reduces symptoms of Long COVID: a case series. *Journal of Neuroimmunology* 362: https://doi.org/10.1016/j.jneuroim.2021.577784.

Lopez-Leon, S., Wegman-Ostrosky, T., Ayuzo del Valle, N.C. et al. (2022). Long-COVID in children and adolescents: a systematic review and meta-analyses. *Scientific Reports* 12 (1): https://doi.org/10.1038/s41598-022-13495-5.

Mendes de Almeida, V., Engel, D.F., Ricci, M.F. et al. (2023). Gut microbiota from patients with COVID-19 cause alterations in mice that resemble post-COVID symptoms. *Gut Microbes* 15 (2): https://doi.org/10.1080/19490976.2023.2249146.

NCT05080244 (2021). Evaluation of the efficacy of probiotics to reduce the occurrence of long COVID. https://Clinicaltrials.Gov/Show/NCT05080244 (accessed 16 July 2024).

NCT05430152 (2022). Low-dose naltrexone for post-COVID fatigue syndrome. https://Clinicaltrials.Gov/Show/NCT05430152 (accessed 16 July 2024).

O'Kelly, B., Vidal, L., McHugh, T. et al. (2022). Safety and efficacy of low dose naltrexone in a long covid cohort; an interventional pre-post study. *Brain, Behavior, and Immunity – Health* 24: https://doi.org/10.1016/j.bbih.2022.100485.

Parker, M., Sawant, H.B., Flannery, T. et al. (2023). Effect of using a structured pacing protocol on post-exertional symptom exacerbation and health status in a longitudinal cohort with the post-COVID-19 syndrome. *Journal of Medical Virology* 95 (1): https://doi.org/10.1002/jmv.28373.

Patterson, B.K., Yogendra, R., Guevara-Coto, J. et al. (2023). Case series: maraviroc and pravastatin as a therapeutic option to treat long COVID/post-acute sequelae of COVID (PASC). *Frontiers in Medicine* 10: 1122529. https://doi.org/10.3389/fmed.2023.1122529.

Peluso, M.J., Deveau, T.-M., Munter, S.E. et al. (2022). Impact of pre-existing chronic viral infection and reactivation on the development of long COVID. *medRxiv: The Preprint Server for Health Sciences*. 2022.06.21.22276660. https://doi.org/10.1101/2022.06.21.22276660.

Proal, A.D., VanElzakker, M.B., Aleman, S. et al. (2023). SARS-CoV-2 reservoir in post-acute sequelae of COVID-19 (PASC). *Nature Immunology* 24 (10): 1616–1627. https://doi.org/10.1038/s41590-023-01601-2.

Raj, S.R., Guzman, J.C., Harvey, P. et al. (2020). Canadian cardiovascular society position statement on postural orthostatic tachycardia syndrome (POTS) and related disorders of chronic orthostatic intolerance. *Canadian Journal of Cardiology* 36 (3): https://doi.org/10.1016/j.cjca.2019.12.024.

Seton, K.A., Espejo-Oltra, J.A., Giménez-Orenga, K. et al. (2024). Advancing research and treatment: an overview of clinical trials in myalgic encephalomyelitis/chronic fatigue syndrome (ME/CFS) and future perspectives. *Journal of Clinical Medicine* 13 (2): 325. https://doi.org/10.3390/jcm13020325.

Soejima, Y., Munemoto, T., Masuda, A. et al. (2015). Effects of Waon therapy on chronic fatigue syndrome: a pilot study. *Internal Medicine* 54 (3): 333–338. https://doi.org/10.2169/internalmedicine.54.3042.

Stavrakis, S., Cai, X., Morris, L. et al. (2023). LB-456640-4 noninvasive vagus nerve stimulation in postural tachycardia syndrome: a randomized clinical trial. *Heart Rhythm* 20 (7): https://doi.org/10.1016/j.hrthm.2023.04.051.

Stein, S.R., Ramelli, S.C., Grazioli, A. et al. (2022). SARS-CoV-2 infection and persistence in the human body and brain at autopsy. *Nature* 612 (7941): https://doi.org/10.1038/s41586-022-05542-y.

Stone, W. (2023). Unraveling long COVID: here's what scientists who study the illness want to find out. *NPR* (September 2023).

Vink, M. and Vink-Niese, A. (2018). Graded exercise therapy for myalgic encephalomyelitis/chronic fatigue syndrome is not effective and unsafe. Re-analysis of a Cochrane review. *Health Psychology Open* 5 (2): https://doi.org/10.1177/2055102918805187.

Wang, K., Khoramjoo, M., Srinivasan, K. et al. (2023). Sequential multi-omics analysis identifies clinical phenotypes and predictive biomarkers for long COVID. *Cell Reports Medicine* 4 (11): 101254. https://doi.org/10.1016/j.xcrm.2023.101254.

Watanabe, A., Iwagami, M., Yasuhara, J. et al. (2023). Protective effect of COVID-19 vaccination against long COVID syndrome: a systematic review and meta-analysis. *Vaccine* 41 ((11): https://doi.org/10.1016/j.vaccine.2023.02.008.

WHO Regional Office for Europe (2021). *Support for Rehabilitation Self-management After COVID-19-Related Illness.* World Health Organization.

Wright, J., Astill, S.L., and Sivan, M. (2022). The relationship between physical activity and Long COVID: a cross-sectional study. *International Journal of Environmental Research and Public Health* 19 (9): https://doi.org/10.3390/ijerph19095093.

Xie, Y., Choi, T., and Al-Aly, Z. (2022). Nirmatrelvir and the risk of post-acute sequelae of COVID-19. *medRxiv.* https://www.medrxiv.org/content/10.1101/2022.11.03.22281783v1.

Yin, K., Peluso, M.J., Luo, X. et al. (2024). Long COVID manifests with T cell dysregulation, inflammation and an uncoordinated adaptive immune response to SARS-CoV-2. *Nature Immunology.* https://doi.org/10.1038/s41590-023-01724-6.

Zheng, Y.B., Zeng, N., Yuan, K. et al. (2023). Prevalence and risk factor for long COVID in children and adolescents: a meta-analysis and systematic review. *Journal of Infection and Public Health* 16 ((5): https://doi.org/10.1016/j.jiph.2023.03.005.

Zhou, T., Sawano, M., Arun, A.S. et al. (2023). Internal tremors and vibrations in long COVID: a cross-sectional study. *medRxiv.* 2023.06.19.23291598. https://doi.org/10.1101/2023.06.19.23291598.

Zilberman-Itskovich, S., Catalogna, M., Sasson, E. et al. (2022). Hyperbaric oxygen therapy improves neurocognitive functions and symptoms of post-COVID condition: randomized controlled trial. *Scientific Reports* 12 (1): 11252. https://doi.org/10.1038/s41598-022-15565-0.

Zollner, A., Koch, R., Jukic, A. et al. (2022). Postacute COVID-19 is characterized by gut viral antigen persistence in inflammatory bowel diseases. *Gastroenterology* 163 (2): 495–506.e8. https://doi.org/10.1053/j.gastro.2022.04.037.

Zubchenko, S., Kril, I., Nadizhko, O. et al. (2022). Herpesvirus infections and post-COVID-19 manifestations: a pilot observational study. *Rheumatology International* 42 (9): 1523–1530. https://doi.org/10.1007/s00296-022-05146-9.

9

Mental Health Crisis

Alison Rembisz[1] and Talya Shahal[2]

[1] Department of Psychiatry, Harvard South Shore, Brockton, MA, 02301, USA
[2] Veterans Administration Boston Healthcare System, Harvard Medical School, Boston, MA 02132, USA

John is a 50-year-old healthy man who lost his beloved wife to COVID-19 in the early months of the pandemic. The sudden loss of his life partner and the mother of his two teenage children left him devastated. Grief overwhelmed him, and in his attempts to cope, he turned to alcohol to numb the pain.

John's drinking escalated, and he began to rely more and more on alcohol to deal with his emotions. He would spend hours at the local bar, often coming home heavily intoxicated. His drinking started to affect his behavior at home.

While intoxicated, John's emotional pain turned into anger and frustration. He became agitated and verbally abusive, particularly toward his teenage children, Sarah and Daniel. He made threats, yelled at them, and sometimes threw belongings around the home. This created a hostile and unsafe environment for his children, who were already struggling to cope with the loss of their mother.

Sarah and Daniel, scared and deeply concerned for their father, confided in their aunt Betty about their situation. She recognized the urgency of the matter and the potential danger that John's behavior posed to the children. She knew they needed help.

Betty found helpful resources online offering advice on how to best support John and his family through this difficult time. She learned how to approach John about this sensitive issue and where he could receive treatment. With encouragement from his sister and children, John agreed to seek help. They drove together to a local mental health treatment facility that specialized in treating substance use and mental health disorders. John was evaluated by a psychiatrist who recommended treatment for John's mood symptoms as well as medically supervised treatment for alcohol withdrawal symptoms.

John spent the next week on a mental health unit. He met daily with his team of providers, and they collaboratively created an individualized plan for treating his alcohol use and his ongoing grief. Following his admission, John was discharged home, and participated in an intensive outpatient program in which he attended daily group and one-on-one counseling sessions. He was started on a daily medication that helped him maintain sobriety by reducing cravings for alcohol. Two months later, John graduated from the program equipped with a better understanding of the unhelpful thoughts and behaviors that contributed to his problematic alcohol use, along with skills to help him cope with the sudden loss of his wife. He was feeling better, was able to return to his beloved fishing hobby, and enjoyed spending more time with his children.

Introduction

The term *mental health crisis* describes a psychiatric emergency in which a person is severely distressed and not acting like themselves. In other words, their dysregulated behaviors may hinder their ability to care for themselves or function well in the community, posing a potential danger to themselves or others. Much like John in our introductory case, a mental health crisis can be triggered by overwhelming stress that impairs coping and problem-solving skills. A mental health crisis can occur regardless of whether someone has a preexisting mental health condition. It is a psychiatric emergency because the intense distress and impaired ability to cope can lead to agitation, aggression, and violence, significantly increasing the risk of harm.

Similar to any other health emergency, it is important to recognize when you or someone you care about is experiencing a mental health crisis, and seek help. However, behaviors during a mental health crisis can be unpredictable, catching loved ones off guard and leaving them unsure of how they can help. Knowing the warning signs of an impending crisis, understanding how to approach someone experiencing it, and being aware of available treatment options can be lifesaving. In this chapter we will explore mental health crises stemming from the COVID-19 pandemic, offering case examples that illustrate various causes of agitation and ways a crisis can present. We will also delve into risk factors, de-escalation strategies, and commonly used treatments for dangerous behaviors associated with psychiatric emergencies, such as agitation, aggression, violence, self-harm, and suicide. This chapter's goal is to provide practical and straightforward information that you can use to navigate these challenging situations.

Mental Health Crises as a Result of the COVID-19 Pandemic

Pandemics have been compared to natural disasters with similar large-scale impacts on mental health, and the COVID-19 pandemic is no exception. It brought illness, loss, grief, isolation, and financial instability, creating a perfect storm for mental health challenges. Each of these stressors alone are well-known precipitants of adverse mental health outcomes. However, the pandemic forced individuals, families, and communities to endure many, if not all, of these stressors simultaneously. In addition to unprecedented levels of internal and external stress, many people faced barriers to accessing mental healthcare due to pandemic disruptions and closures. As a result, patients experienced treatment delays and gaps in care.

While data on the mental health fallout from the pandemic vary, there is a consensus that psychiatric conditions surged compared to the pre-pandemic era. Symptoms of anxiety, depression, and post-traumatic stress disorder (PTSD) took the front seat. Early in the pandemic, people increased risky health behaviors such as smoking and drinking alcohol (Lindert et al. 2021, pp. iv31). In December of 2020, the Centers for Disease Control and Prevention (CDC) Health Alert Network issued an advisory due to a dramatic increase in drug overdose deaths across the United States, with the largest increase occurring from March 2020 to May 2020, aligning with the onset of the COVID-19 pandemic. The overdoses during this period involved synthetic opioids, including illicit fentanyl (Centers for Disease Prevention and Control 2020).

Furthermore, disaster-related stress and subsequent mental health consequences linger beyond the event itself. Although the federal COVID-19 Public Health Emergency ended on May 11, 2023, communities continue to grapple with ongoing unemployment and other trauma-related stressors, including survivor's guilt and moral injury. Moral injury is a term that describes the negative psychological impact that occurs when an individual commits or witnesses acts that violate their core values.

Psychosocial stress, substance use, and worsening mental health illnesses are risk factors that can lead to a mental health crisis. When individuals feel overwhelmed and struggle to cope with stress, they may experience heightened feelings of helplessness and hopelessness, increasing the risk of impulsive actions. This may manifest as aggression or violence directed toward oneself or others. Provisional data from the CDC indicate an increase in the number of deaths by suicide by 2.6% from 2021 to 2022 (Centers for Disease Prevention and Control 2024). Data from the WISQARS National Violent Death Reporting System also indicate a rise in homicide deaths, with the homicide death rate increasing by 1.55% from 2019 to 2020 (Centers for Disease Prevention and Control 2024).

Brain Circuitry, Neurotransmitters, and Hormones Involved in Aggressive Behavior

People react to stress and fear in a variety of ways. Some people may experience anxiety characterized by worries and physical symptoms, which we learned about in Chapter 6. In others, stress can lead to dangerous behaviors, such as aggression and violence. Why is this? Aggression is a behavior that can be observed in almost all animals, including humans. In our ancestors, anger and aggression were innate reactions to stress that were necessary for survival, similar to other life-sustaining behaviors like feeding and thirst. If you can imagine an early hunter-gatherer coming face to face with a lion, he had two options for survival: fight back or run away. In this situation, the brain perceives the threat and ramps up the appropriate *fight or flight* response, so the hunter can react accordingly. In the modern world, we still have the same hardwiring in our brains as our ancestors, but most of us do not worry about facing a lion. Instead, we encounter different forms of stress: work, relationships, trauma, and more recently, the COVID-19 pandemic. Although these are mostly *psychological* forms of stress, our brain and body react by ramping up the same *physical* fight or flight response.

Let's take a closer look at the regions of our brain that play a role in activating and suppressing aggressive behaviors. The *hypothalamus* is an area where aggression is activated, while the *prefrontal cortex* is an area of our brain known for managing impulsivity. Using a car as an analogy for aggressive behavior, the *hypothalamus* can be thought of as a gas pedal for activating aggression, while the *prefrontal cortex* can resemble applying the brakes – or inhibiting – aggression. A person with a healthy *prefrontal cortex* can stop themselves from acting out, while a person who has suffered damage to their *prefrontal cortex*, can be more impulsive and act on signals to behave aggressively. You can see examples of these conditions in Table 9.1.

Another region of the brain called the *amygdala* becomes active during fearful situations. It helps us recognize a threat. It is thought that the amygdala may play a role in aggression because an overactive amygdala can lead to excessive defensive behaviors. Put another way, someone with an overactive amygdala can misinterpret nonthreatening situations as a threat and may react with violence. The amygdala plays an important role in activating the fight or flight response when a stressor is encountered by activating the hypothalamic-pituitary-adrenal pathway (see Figure 9.1).

We see in Figure 9.1 that there are also neurotransmitters and hormones that play a role in aggressive behavior. *Cortisol, testosterone, and serotonin* facilitate signaling between the *amygdala, hypothalamus, and prefrontal cortex*, and their varying levels can predispose someone to becoming agitated, impulsive, and aggressive (Batrinos 2012).

Table 9.1 Agitation due to general medical conditions.

Cause	Conditions	Comments
Disorders of the nervous system	• Head trauma • Dementia • Seizure disorders • Stroke • Encephalopathy • Drug or alcohol intoxication or withdrawal	• Head trauma and dementias, particularly those affecting the frontotemporal region cause structural damage to regions integral in mediating aggressive behaviors • Patients with seizure disorders (particularly temporal seizures) may become agitated after the seizure • Strokes can result in damage to areas of the brain involved in aggression, agitation, and impulsivity • Encephalopathy is a brain disorder commonly caused by kidney or liver failure
Disorders of the endocrine system	• Thyroid disease • Adrenal disorders • Diabetes mellitus • Electrolyte imbalance	• The endocrine system is responsible for maintaining level of hormones that have effects on the brain • Dysfunction of the thyroid gland (thyroid hormone) and adrenal gland (cortisol, testosterone) can impair inhibition or activation of critical regions involved in mediating aggression • Both low and high blood sugar levels, often seen in Diabetes Mellitus, can cause agitation • Abnormal levels of critical electrolytes, such as sodium, calcium, and potassium, can cause agitation
Infections	• Respiratory infections • Infections of the brain • Urinary tract infections (UTIs) • Sexually transmitted infections (STIs)	• Infections of the respiratory tract such as COVID-19 and pneumonia can lead to hypoxia, which is a major cause of delirium • All infections have potential to cause delirium, especially encephalitis and UTIs • STIs (e.g. neurosyphilis) can directly affect the brain

Cortisol, also known as the *stress hormone*, earned this nickname due to its effects on the body when someone encounters a stressor. Imagine yourself in a stressful situation, such as giving a presentation to a large audience. What physical changes do you notice in your body? You may be very alert, you may start to sweat, your heart may beat rapidly, and perhaps your arms are a little shaky. These

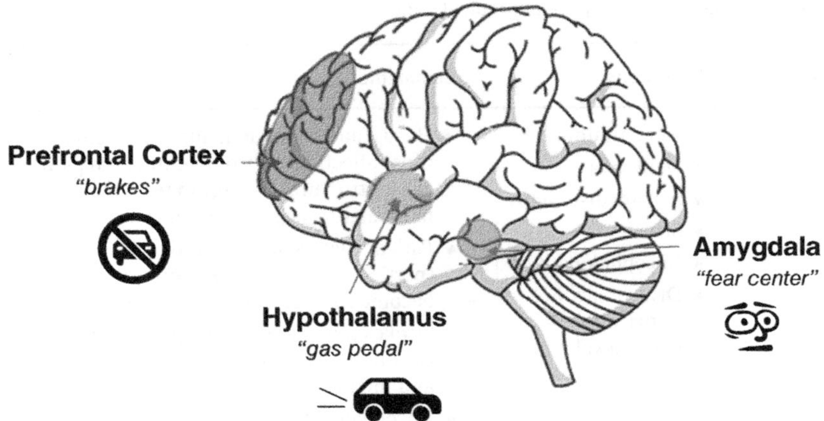

Figure 9.1 Regions of the brain involved in agitation, impulsivity, and aggression.

are all physical reactions to stress that occur due to the *amygdala* signaling to the *hypothalamus* to send out cortisol. Cortisol diverts the body's energy to prepare for a fight or flight response. At the same time, cortisol inhibits other bodily functions, such as the immune system and digestion, that are not as important in the moment a stressor is encountered.

Testosterone is typically the first hormone that comes to mind when you think of aggressive behavior, as male sex is an established risk factor for potential violence. However, similar to most chemicals that act in the brain and body, testosterone has many functions including sexual maturation, muscle development, and dominance behaviors. Its role in aggressive behavior is complex. That being said, we can see on imaging studies that testosterone activates the *amygdala* in adult males and works to enhance emotional reactivity leading to an aggressive response (Batrinos 2012). In one study comparing testosterone levels and violent crimes in inmates, researchers found that more aggressive inmates had higher levels of testosterone. However, they had also found similarly elevated levels of testosterone in nonaggressive inmates considered to be more socially dominant, further alluding to testosterone's complex role in aggression and social behavior (Ehrenkranz et al. 1974).

Serotonin is a neurotransmitter that is well known for its association with depression, but low serotonin levels are also correlated with impulsivity, which can lead to aggressive behavior. Practically, serotonin is difficult to measure, so most studies use a serotonin metabolite called 5-hydroxyindoleacetic acid (5-HIAA) that is found in the fluid surrounding the brain and spinal cord (the cerebrospinal fluid or CSF). Several studies have found that monkeys with low CSF levels of 5-HIAA are more likely to engage in risky interactions that escalate into unrestrained aggression with higher rates for injury. In other words, monkeys with low 5-HIAA are not constantly aggressive, but rather, they show poor impulse control and are more likely to put themselves in dangerous situations (Higley et al. 1996). Imaging studies in humans show that serotonin acts on the *prefrontal cortex* to inhibit impulsive behavior. Therefore, individuals with lower serotonin levels are more likely to act impulsively, which can lead to aggressive behavior (Batrinos 2012).

Medical and Psychiatric Illnesses as Risk Factors for Violent Behavior

Violence is not a medical or psychiatric disorder. Each person has a different response when they are under stress, and it is virtually impossible to predict whether someone will behave violently in a given situation. However, some medical and psychiatric conditions are more likely to cause agitation, aggression, and impulsivity. These conditions are considered risk factors for violent behavior.

Homeostasis is the body's ability to maintain a stable internal environment by regulating various physiological processes, ensuring conditions are optimal for survival and function. Disrupting homeostasis can lead to violent behavior, as it may affect the balance of neurochemicals and physiological functions, influencing emotional regulation and impulse control in a way that increases the risk of aggressive reactions. Considering the previous section's brief introduction to the complex brain and body pathways involved in mediating aggression, impulsivity, and agitation, you can begin to understand the multitude of medical and psychiatric conditions that can offset this delicate balance and predispose someone to behaving violently.

Infections, especially those affecting breathing like COVID-19, can trigger delirium, as you may recall from Chapter 4. We will review its role in violence later in this chapter.

Certain neurological conditions can affect impulse control and emotional regulation, potentially leading to violent behavior:

- Traumatic Brain Injury (TBI) can result in personality changes, impulsive behavior, and aggression.
- Frontal lobe damage can lead to impairment in decision-making and impulse control.
- Dementia can cause behavioral dysregulation, paranoia, and aggressive behavior.

Medical conditions leading to metabolic imbalances, such as hypoglycemia (low blood sugar) and hyperthyroidism, can result in symptoms like irritability, agitation, and, in rare cases, violent behavior when left untreated. Conditions affecting the adrenal glands, such as Addison's or Cushing's disease, can cause over- or under-production of cortisol, contributing to agitation. Brain injuries, such as Wernicke's encephalopathy (associated with vitamin B1 deficiency, often due to heavy alcohol use) and hepatic encephalopathy (resulting from liver dysfunction), can also be associated with agitation.

A few psychiatric disorders include aggressive behavior as part of their diagnostic criteria:

- Intermittent explosive disorder
- Conduct disorder
- Antisocial personality disorder
- Disruptive mood dysregulation disorder

People with these disorders are at higher risk for violence. However, many other mental health disorders also carry the risk of aggression as a complication of the illness.

According to the Diagnostic and Statistical Manual DSM-5 Handbook of Differential Diagnosis, substance-related disorders are the most frequent cause of aggressive behavior (First 2014). Substance use can impair judgment, lower inhibitions, and lead to aggressive or violent outbursts during both intoxication and withdrawal. Substances can also contribute to substance-induced mood disorders, or they may worsen the severity of other mental health conditions.

Additional psychiatric diagnoses that are associated with aggressive behavior include (First 2014):

- Developmental delays: Autism spectrum disorder and learning disabilities may decrease emotional regulation and cause increased impulsivity, leading to aggressive behavior in some instances.
- Trauma-related disorders, including PTSD. People with PTSD may experience irritability, anger, and potentially violent reactions, particularly when experiencing traumatic triggers.
- Bipolar disorder: During manic episodes, people with bipolar disorder may become agitated, impulsive, and at times, aggressive. They might pose a risk to themselves, or others due to impaired judgment.
- Schizophrenia. Individuals with schizophrenia may experience hallucinations or delusions that can lead to violent behavior. Many times, their reality testing is impaired.
- Personality disorders. Patients with certain personality disorders, such as antisocial personality disorder, may disregard the rights of others and engage in aggressive or violent acts without remorse.

Table 9.2 Medications associated with increased agitation.

Medication class	Examples
Steroids	• Prednisone • Dexamethasone
Hormones	• Thyroid hormones • Androgens (testosterone)
Psychiatric medications	• Lithium- causes agitation when blood levels are extremely high • Antipsychotics- in rare occasions, they might cause a paradoxical effect of worsening agitation instead of decreasing agitation • Antidepressants can increase irritability • Benzodiazepines–can cause a paradoxical effect, especially in older adults and in people with delirium; can worsen agitation instead of providing a calming and sedating effect • Stimulants (mixed amphetamine salts, methylphenidate)
Pain medications	• Opioids
Antiseizure medications (anticonvulsants)	• Lamotrigine • Levetiracetam

Additional factors related to medical and mental illnesses may increase a person's risk for agitation and violence. Whether prescribed or taken illicitly, certain medications can cause irritability or agitation, which may escalate to aggression or violence. Examples include steroids (such as prednisone) and hormones (thyroid hormones, androgens). For more examples, see Table 9.2.

Finally, individuals who are in pain or suffering from untreated medical conditions may become irritable and, in some cases, resort to violence as a way to express their distress.

Delirium

Mrs. Johnson is a 79-year-old woman who is admitted to the hospital with difficulty breathing due to COVID-19 pneumonia. She has a history of high blood pressure and type 2 diabetes. Prior to admission, she had been living independently in the community. In the hospital, she is placed in the COVID-19 isolation ward and started on oxygen therapy. On her third day in the hospital, Mrs. Johnson experiences more difficulty breathing, and she is transferred to the intensive care unit (ICU). She requires mechanical ventilation to support her breathing. Her family is informed about her critical condition, but they are unable to visit due to the strict isolation protocols.

On her fifth day of hospitalization, Mrs. Johnson's condition stabilizes. She is gradually weaned off the ventilator, and her oxygen levels improve. However, the medical staff begin to notice changes in her behavior. She is showing signs of delirium as she becomes increasingly agitated and disoriented, struggling to follow instructions. She becomes suspicious of the medical staff and accuses them of harming her. Nurses witness her tugging on her IV line and trying to leave her bed despite her fragile state. Following an incident where Mrs. Johnson threw a tray at the staff and accused them of poisoning her, her treatment team consults with an in-hospital psychiatrist to help manage her behaviors. The goal is to prevent harm to herself or others due to her confusion, paranoia, and impulsivity.

Mrs. Johnson's case outlines a classic example of delirium. As we learned in Chapter 4, delirium is a medical term used to describe a sudden state of fluctuating confusion accompanied by changes in thinking and behavior. Patients with COVID-19 are at risk of developing delirium, especially if they have a severe respiratory infection, such as pneumonia and acute respiratory distress syndrome (ARDS). Between 73% and 83% of patients requiring ICU level of care develop delirium (Beckwith et al. 2023). However, the ICU is not the only setting where delirium is encountered, and it can occur at home and other settings. It is important to know how to assess and manage symptoms of delirium, as it is commonly associated with increased morbidity and mortality, and can complicate a patient's hospital course.

Delirium manifests differently in individual patients. As you may recall, key symptoms include fluctuating cognitive impairment marked by confusion, disorientation, and difficulty maintaining attention or following directions. Other common signs include visual and auditory hallucinations, along with paranoid thoughts. Individuals experiencing delirium often exhibit unusual behavior, and, as in Mrs. Johnson's case, can easily become aggressive or agitated. All these symptoms can interfere with delivery of necessary care and can complicate a patient's hospital stay. Targeted interventions including both behavioral plans and medications can help mitigate disruptions caused by delirium, leading to improved outcomes. In cases of severe delirium, where there is a risk to oneself or others, as seen in Mrs. Johnson's case, a psychiatrist might be consulted to assist with treatment and management.

As we have discussed in prior chapters, delirium often occurs in patients with an underlying medical illness. The brain is susceptible to changes in functioning by various illnesses, just like other parts of the body. Older adults, patients who are severely ill, patients with preexisting cognitive impairment, and patients with prolonged hospital stays, especially in the ICU, are most vulnerable. Perhaps the most important risk factor for developing delirium is patients who have a past history of delirium. Infections like urinary tract infections (UTIs) or respiratory infections (pneumonia, COVID-19) are common causes of delirium. Other common causes that need to be taken into account include metabolic disturbances, substance intoxication or withdrawal, preexisting conditions, medications (especially when combined with other medications), sleep disturbances, and severe pain. Finally, patients can develop delirium after surgery, especially if they have other risk factors. Oftentimes there are multiple risk factors that lead to delirium. See Table 9.3 for the medical workup of delirium.

Delirium can manifest at various stages of the illness, sometimes before the underlying cause is known. For example, delirium has been described in COVID-19 patients that were otherwise symptom-free (Beckwith et al. 2023). Therefore, an important aspect of assessing delirium is conducting a full medical

Table 9.3 Medical workup for delirium.

Type of test	Examples
Laboratory tests	• Blood count (CBC): to check for anemia, infection, or other blood-related issues • Basic metabolic panel: to assess electrolyte imbalances and kidney function • Liver function tests • Thyroid function tests • Blood cultures • Urinalysis: to detect urinary tract infections or metabolic abnormalities • Toxicology screen: to rule-out substance induced delirium • Arterial blood gas (ABG): to assess oxygen and carbon dioxide levels, as well as acid-base balance • Lumbar puncture: in cases where central nervous system infections or other neurological conditions are suspected
Imaging studies	Depending on the clinical presentation and findings, imaging studies may be indicated, including: • Head CT (computed tomography): to rule out structural brain abnormalities such as tumors, bleeding, or strokes • Brain MRI (magnetic resonance imaging): more sensitive than CT, it can detect subtle structural brain abnormalities • Chest X-ray: to identify respiratory infections or other chest-related issues • Electroencephalogram (EEG): EEG may be useful in cases where nonconvulsive seizures or other electrical abnormalities are suspected as a cause of delirium

work-up to detect possible causes. In addition to a comprehensive history and physical exam, doctors suspecting delirium may order the following medical work-up to look for possible causes:

Mrs. Johnson is seen by the psychiatrist while the medical team conducts a work-up to rule out a new medical cause of her symptoms. She is diagnosed with delirium related to her severe COVID-19 illness.

Her treatment team initiates interventions to manage her delirium. They modify her environment to reduce sensory stimulation, provide frequent reorientation, and engage in communication strategies that are calming and reassuring. Her doctors prescribe an antipsychotic to treat the hallucinations and paranoia contributing to her agitation after numerous attempts at redirection are unsuccessful.

Mrs. Johnson's delirium gradually begins to improve with these interventions. She becomes less agitated and more cooperative with care. After a few days, she is again oriented to her surroundings. Her clinicians inform her family of her progress. Through virtual visits, family members are able to participate in her care and to provide emotional support.

Mrs. Johnson's condition improves, and she is successfully weaned off oxygen therapy. She is transferred to a general medical ward for further recovery. She is no longer agitated or confused, and her delirium is considered to have resolved. She no longer requires antipsychotics. She is now better able to participate in physical therapy, which helps her regain her physical strength.

In this case, Mrs. Johnson developed delirium as a complication of severe COVID-19 pneumonia. Her case is an example of how delirium can be triggered by various factors, including the severe illness itself, the isolation and stress associated with the pandemic, and perhaps even the medications used in her treatment.

Anticipating Agitation

Agitation is a term used to describe a state of extreme inner restlessness or heightened arousal and can present in a variety of ways. Agitation can occur suddenly or over time. It may present along a continuum of behavior: from subtle increases in activity to aggressive or violent behavior. People experiencing agitation may have excessive talking or movement, disruptive behavior, impulsivity, or problems with focusing. They may have difficulty sitting still, might pace, or they may wring their hands or clench their fists. We can anticipate agitation by identifying potential triggers and by recognizing warning signs of impending or escalating agitation.

It helps to understand the factors or situations that can lead to agitation and to proactively attempt to address or avoid triggers. If you or a loved one has had a prior episode of agitation, it can be helpful to keep an updated list of potential triggers, warning signs, and mitigation strategies that had previously been successful for reducing agitation. When speaking with clinicians, you can ask the following questions: "Is agitation a common symptom of [pertinent diagnosis]?" "Could my current/new medications cause agitation?" "What should I do first if agitation occurs?" "When is agitation considered an emergency?"

Agitation can surface without a medical reason or a preexisting psychiatric condition; it could just be due to a stressful circumstance. We all experience stress, and it is normal to feel overwhelmed from time to time. Anticipating agitation also means recognizing when stress is taking a toll on your mental well-being. Experiencing emotions like helplessness, hopelessness, persistent depression, irritability, anxiety, or an uptick in substance use are indicators that your mental health may be slipping, and it is important to tell your doctor or mental health professional. Addressing symptoms early is key to prevent symptoms from escalating.

The next few sections will provide further details on de-escalation and management strategies for managing agitation. Agitation does not always lead to violent behavior, but we should always treat it as a warning sign. If you can recognize when someone is in an agitated state, initiating de-escalating strategies early may help prevent them from harming themselves or others, which might cause deep feelings of shame and remorse later on.

How to Talk to an Agitated Person

Regardless of the underlying cause, agitation is a sign of a mental health crisis and requires immediate intervention. The first, and most important, intervention is to first try communicating with the agitated person. This may seem intimidating at first, as the person experiencing agitation may struggle to think or communicate clearly. They may have difficulty expressing their needs, and they may not hear you initially. We hope this section can make you feel more comfortable, as we will review helpful strategies to effectively communicate with a person who is agitated (Table 9.4). Effective communication can have an immediate impact on de-escalating the situation.

There are 10 components of effective verbal de-escalation (Richmond et al. 2012):

1) Respect personal space.
2) Do not be provocative.
3) Establish verbal contact.
4) Be concise.
5) Identify wants and feelings.
6) Listen closely and empathically to what the patient is saying.

Table 9.4 Helpful communication skills with an agitated person.

Approach	Communication	Example statements	Avoid
Ask what they need	Maintain a calm tone and express support and concern to establish trust.	"I can see that you are upset, help me understand what is going on."	Telling them to "calm down," which can increase agitation
Be nonconfrontational, yet straightforward	Convey respect and use concise and simple language.	"I want to help."	Arguing
Listen with your full attention	Respond empathically and validate emotions.	"I can see that this is important to you."	Interrupting
Attempt to come to a mutual understanding	Inspire hope and offer choices to empower the agitated person.	"Would you rather take some time to yourself, or do you want me to stay with you?"	Telling them what to do

7) Agree or agree to disagree.
8) Set clear limits.
9) Offer choices and optimism.
10) Debrief the patient and surroundings.

First, maintain your own safety and the safety of others. Keep a safe distance from the agitated individual. Many resources recommend a "two-arms-length-rule," or standing at least twice your arm length from the individual. Place yourself closest to the doorway or to an alternative exit (to have an escape route). If you are feeling unsafe, call for help. If you are worried about violence, do not hesitate to call 911.

A purposeful demonstration of calmness and composure can help to de-escalate the patient. Here are a few tips to improve nonverbal communication:

- Maintain a nondominant body posture such as standing slightly to the side of the person rather than directly in front of them.
- Keep hands relaxed and in view.
- Avoid sudden movements or excessive gesturing.
- Avoid touching someone when they are agitated.
- Maintain empathic and nonjudgmental facial expressions and body language.

Sometimes de-escalation involves setting limits. Do not tolerate a violation of your boundaries or other unacceptable behavior. You can say, "I want to help, but

I will not tolerate violence and aggression" or "I expect you to treat me with respect." Always take threatening statements or behaviors seriously. If you feel unsafe, remove yourself from the situation.

De-escalation Techniques

De-escalation describes techniques used to reduce agitation and to maintain the safety of the patient and others. De-escalation emphasizes a noncoercive, patient-centered approach to help the individual manage their distress and regain control of their behavior. The previous section outlined strategies for communicating with an agitated person, which is an important first step in de-escalation. Table 9.5 lists additional techniques commonly used to de-escalate agitation.

Medication and Restraint Use in Managing Agitation

Agitation may persist even with effective use of de-escalation techniques. Many times, agitation stands out as the primary symptom, and it needs swift management with medication and/or restraint so that safety is maintained and other necessary interventions can be made. Let's delve into an example with the following case:

Mr. Smith is a 65-year-old male with chronic obstructive pulmonary disease (COPD), hypertension, and diabetes. His health had been relatively stable until a few days ago when his cough became more severe, it became harder for him to breathe, and he lost his sense of smell. Over the next day, he started to feel dizzy and weak, then anxious and restless. He began pacing around the house. His wife noticed he was confused and did not seem to make sense when speaking with her. She immediately called 911 and redirected him with calming behaviors and reassurance until help arrived.

On the way to the hospital, Mr. Smith's condition worsened. The confined ambulance space and difficulty breathing made him feel anxious and agitated. Recognizing Mr. Smith's low oxygen levels, paramedics attempted to provide him with oxygen, but in his agitated and confused state, he became combative and hostile. By the time he arrived to the emergency room, he threatened doctors and nurses and was attempting to punch at staff. The emergency department medical staff attempted verbal de-escalation, but he was too confused. Concerned about his safety, staff had to restrain him in order to administer an antipsychotic injection to calm him down. Within a few minutes, he was able to calm down and rest, and clinicians were then able to administer oxygen and perform a physical exam.

Once Mr. Smith calmed down, staff immediately removed his restraints. Mr. Smith tested positive for COVID-19. He was hospitalized to treat his breathing difficulties. He was placed on one-on-one observation status to monitor his agitation. He continued to

Table 9.5 De-escalation techniques.

De-escalation technique	Examples	Rationale
Modify the environment	• Reduce noise and bright lights. • Move the person to a different setting when possible (go for a walk, get out of the car). • Be on the lookout for anything the person can potentially use as a weapon and remove it.	• A calm and quiet place can minimize distractions and facilitate de-escalation.
Behavioral redirection	• Redirect the individual's focus to a less distressing topic or activity.	• Can reduce anxiety and help the individual maintain safety
Offer calming activities	• Mindfulness or deep breathing • Calling family or friends • Journaling • Coloring • Engaging in exercise	• Can help reduce physical symptoms of agitation, such as shortness of breath or a rapid heartbeat
Provide options	• Provide the individual with a choice between acceptable options. • Offer activities that align with the person's interests. • Ask them what works best for them in these types of situations.	• Helps to regain a sense of control • Oftentimes, people with agitation are aware of strategies that calm them down

be confused and agitated and required additional doses of antipsychotic medications. Within the next few days, he was more cooperative with care, accepted treatment such as oxygen, and his oxygen levels improved. As a result, his confusion and agitation significantly improved. He was able to participate in his medical care and made a full recovery.

This case demonstrates how breathing problems and low oxygen levels in COVID-19 can lead to agitation. By promptly recognizing the underlying cause and providing medications and restraints to ensure his safety, Mr. Smith's team ensured that he was able to receive the medical care he needed to recover without further delays.

It can be jarring to witness a loved one in restraints, and medications to treat agitation may be unfamiliar. The goal of the next two sections is to provide clarity on ways agitation may be managed in the hospital setting, including the use of medications and restraints when necessary.

Medications to Treat Agitation

During the COVID-19 pandemic, lockdown measures deterred patients with milder symptoms of illness from presenting for care. Therefore, emergency departments saw increased levels of agitation due to increased severity of illness on presentation. Much like Mr. Smith in our case example, agitation in the setting of respiratory distress and delirium was a common presentation for COVID-19 patients with severe illness. Patients presenting for emergent psychiatric care were also more likely to be agitated due to psychosocial factors associated with the pandemic, such as challenges accessing social services, mental health units, substance use treatment centers, and homeless shelters. Agitation in all of these cases requires prompt treatment so that further assessment and care can be provided. This section will review medications commonly used to manage agitation in the hospital setting.

There are multiple medication classes that can assist with treating agitation, and medications can be administered in multiple forms (oral, intravenous or IV, intramuscular or IM, and even in a transdermal patch form). The nature of the agitation, the patient's willingness and ability to participate in treatment, and the urgency of the situation are taken into account when clinicians decide which medications to use.

- *Antipsychotic medications*: Antipsychotics, such as haloperidol, risperidone, olanzapine, or quetiapine, can help manage agitation in conditions like schizophrenia, bipolar disorder, or delirium – particularly when hallucinations or delusions cause agitation. Some antipsychotics, such as haloperidol and olanzapine, can be given in IV or IM forms, making them good options in emergency situations if the patient is unwilling to accept oral medication. Antipsychotics can occasionally treat severe agitation associated with dementia-related psychosis, usually after a person has tried behavioral interventions or other medications first. This is because antipsychotics carry a Food and Drug Administration

(FDA) black box warning: they increase mortality 1.6- to 1.7-fold in patients with dementia-related psychosis (Curry et al. 2023). Antipsychotics may also affect heart rhythm; doctors use an electrocardiogram (EKG) to monitor this side effect.

- *Benzodiazepines*: Benzodiazepines like lorazepam or diazepam are typically chosen to manage agitation in cases of alcohol or benzodiazepine withdrawal, acute stimulant intoxication, or when the cause of agitation is not known. Patients can take lorazepam in an oral, IV, or IM formulation. Benzodiazepines are generally not given in cases of agitation due to delirium, and they may also contribute to a person's risk for delirium, especially older adults. Benzodiazepines can make it harder to breathe, especially in people with lung diseases or in those under the influence of alcohol or opioids (Curry et al. 2023).
- *Sedative-hypnotic (sleep) medications*: Medications like trazodone and melatonin can help manage agitation by promoting sleep. Disrupted sleep-wake cycles are common in agitated patients, particularly those with delirium and dementia (Chen et al. 2021). Patients with impaired cognition are also prone to *sundowning*, which is a term that describes a pattern of recurring agitation, usually in the early or late evening. If patients are in a care facility or hospital, this may occur around shift changes for staff. Trazodone is commonly used to address anxiety and agitation related to sundowning. Trazodone may also affect heart rhythm and low blood pressure; doctors monitor blood pressure and use an EKG to monitor these side effects.
- *Mood stabilizers*: For individuals with bipolar disorder, mood stabilizers such as lithium or valproic acid may help reduce agitation during manic or hypomanic episodes. Valproic acid, also known as Depakote, is also often utilized in managing agitation in the setting of a traumatic brain injury or delirium. Valproic acid can be given as a pill or by disintegrating *sprinkles*, as well as by IV. Of note, valproic acid does not have the same effects on the heart as antipsychotics, Selective Serotonin Reuptake Inhibitors (SSRIs), or trazodone, but it can affect the liver and the platelets, which are monitored closely during the treatment. Both valproic acid levels and lithium levels are monitored during treatment to avoid extremely high levels that can be toxic.
- *Antidepressants*: Antidepressants like SSRIs may be used to manage agitation when it is associated with underlying depression, anxiety, or dementia. Trazodone and SSRIs are types of antidepressants that might be useful in patients with dementia with behavioral disturbances (Gerlach and Kales 2018). It is particularly common for these patients to become agitated in the evening (this is known as sundowning). This frequently impacts their care and has the potential to negatively impact their surroundings.
- *Antianxiety medications*: Anxiolytics such as buspirone, gabapentin, hydroxyzine, and clonidine (either oral or as a transdermal patch) may be prescribed to relieve anxiety-related agitation.

The Use of Restraints in Hospitals

Occasionally, a person experiencing a mental health crisis will continue to escalate and pose a risk to themselves or others despite using behavioral interventions and medications. In these cases, seclusion and/or restraints may be necessary to ensure the safety of the patient and others around them.

- *Seclusion* is the confinement of a patient alone in a room or area from which the patient is physically prevented from leaving. Seclusion can be locked or unlocked.
- *A restraint* is any manual method, physical or mechanical device, material, or equipment that immobilizes or reduces the ability of a patient to move his or her arms, legs, body, or head freely.

The need to use restraint or seclusion can be distressing for patients, loved ones, and clinicians alike. This being the case, clinicians attempt to avoid restraint and seclusion whenever possible. Unfortunately, they are sometimes needed. When using seclusion and restraint, clinicians choose the least restrictive form to maintain the physical and psychological safety of the patient and others.

Seclusion is considered a type of restraint, but it is less restrictive than physically immobilizing a person. It is often used in agitated patients when they pose a risk to others, but not to themselves. Patients in seclusion are often somewhat cooperative, but despite de-escalation efforts and medication use, they may still make threats of aggression or violence. Seclusion is usually a separate room or area that is designed to limit external stimuli and is void of extra equipment or furniture. There is always at least one staff member who monitors the secluded patient.

If a patient cannot demonstrate the ability to remain safe in seclusion, or if they pose an imminent risk of harming themselves and others, then the use of physical restraints may be necessary. There are several types of physical restraints.

Soft medical restraints are most often used in patients with delirium, dementia, or other forms of cognitive impairment that interfere with care. When patients are confused, delirious, and agitated, this can lead to combative or outright aggressive behavior. This may include swinging at staff, or kicking clinicians while they try to provide necessary care. As previously discussed, hallucinations and paranoia can co-occur with confusion, and these may also lead to patients pulling on IV lines or EKG leads. These behaviors not only interrupt important points of care, but are also dangerous for the patient and others. If scratching and pulling continue to be a concern despite limited limb mobility, clinicians will often recommend soft cloth restraints with or without cotton mittens to limit the dangers associated with pulling at lines and scratching.

Leather restraints are generally reserved for more aggressive patients that are actively violent despite efforts to use less restrictive means. The positioning of the restraints can vary. The restraints may be applied to a chair with the patient in a seated position or to a bed with the patient lying down. Four-point restraining involves securing each limb, whereas two-point restraints secure the opposite arm and leg, reducing the risk of injury while still immobilizing the patient. Finally, five-point restraints may be necessary to prevent a patient from pulling on cuffs and causing bodily harm. This can involve securing the chest or head to the chair or bed with a strap.

The Joint Commission (Crisis Prevention Institute 2011) provides up-to-date guidelines and standards for restraints and seclusion. These include:

1) A physician or licensed practitioner must see and evaluate the patient within one hour of initiating intervention.
2) Seclusion or restraint can only be used when clinically justified and after consideration of alternative treatment options.
3) Seclusion and restraints must have time-limited orders: Four hours for adults (older than 17 years), two hours for adolescents (9–17 years), one hour for patients younger than 9 years.
4) Patients must have continuous monitoring with periodic evaluation with the intent to discontinue intervention at the earliest possible time.
5) A face-to-face reevaluation must be performed before each renewal of initial time-limited orders.
6) Clinical leadership (i.e. the medical director) must be notified after 12 hours of continuous seclusion or restraint and every 24 hours thereafter.
7) With the patient's informed consent, family should be notified promptly when seclusion or restraint is initiated.
8) Debriefing with patient and staff should be performed after intervention has been discontinued.

(Crisis Prevention Institute, 2011).

Self-harm and Suicide

Self-harm and suicide are real risks in individuals experiencing a mental health crisis. Thoughts about suicide and suicidal behavior are considered psychiatric emergencies. *Suicidal ideation*, a term encompassing thoughts about ending one's own life, can range from passive thoughts about death, such as, "It would be easier if I were dead," to more active contemplation, including planning the details of a potential suicide attempt. Suicidal behavior involves acting on these thoughts and can range from planning a suicide attempt to taking concrete steps like writing a suicide note or obtaining lethal means. The CDC defines suicide as death resulting from injuring oneself with the intent to die. A suicide attempt occurs when someone harms themselves with the intent to die, but their actions do not result in death (Crosby et al. 2011).

An international meta-analysis combined various studies on suicide rates before and after the advent of the COVID-19 pandemic. The authors revealed a notable increase in suicidal ideation and attempts across diverse populations since the onset of the pandemic. The findings also indicated that suicide deaths are likely to rise as the enduring mental health impacts of the pandemic unfold (Yan et al. 2023). The rise in suicidal ideation and behavior can be attributed to the pandemic's exacerbation of risk factors associated with suicide. Factors such as isolation, domestic conflicts, financial loss, heightened symptoms of anxiety and depression, and preexisting mental health conditions were identified as intensified risk factors for suicide attempts during the COVID-19 pandemic (Yan et al. 2023).

The World Health Organization (WHO) considers a *history of prior suicide attempt(s)* as the most robust predictive factor of suicide (World Health Organization 2014). In addition to this, Table 9.6 outlines other critical risk factors for suicide, as well as protective factors against suicide.

Similar to our discussion about risk factors for violence, most people at elevated risk for suicide will not experience suicidal thoughts or act on their thoughts. Still, it is important to recognize warning signs:

- Individuals becoming increasingly withdrawn or isolated
- Talking about being a burden
- Feelings of hopelessness or worthlessness
- Increased substance use
- Looking for a way to access lethal means
- Extreme mood swings
- Talking or posting in social media about wanting to die
- Giving away possessions
- Planning for suicide

If you or a loved one are experiencing a mental health crisis, which can include thoughts about suicide, emergent help is often necessary. In many countries, there are suicide and crisis numbers to call. In the US, you can reach the National Suicide and Crisis Lifeline by calling or texting the number "988." The Lifeline provides confidential support to anyone in a suicidal crisis or in emotional distress. Veterans may press "1" after dialing "988" for veteran-specific care. Other options for emergency services include dialing "911" or presenting to the nearest emergency room for evaluation and treatment.

Table 9.6 Suicide risk factors and protective factors.

Risk factors for suicide	Protective factors against suicide
• Access to weapons, especially firearms • Mental and physical illness • Substance use • Male sex • White and American Indians/Alaskan Natives ethnicities • Age over 70 • Veterans • Isolation and/or lack of social support • Pain	• Strong sense of social support • Engagement in mental health and medical care • Help-seeking behavior • Future-oriented thoughts (e.g. a sense of hope) • Lack of access to lethal means • Married status • Responsibility for children • Employment

Conclusion

In wrapping up our exploration of mental health crises, it is essential to grasp the gravity of the term and the potential dangers it signifies. A mental health crisis unfolds when an individual deviates significantly from their usual demeanor, displaying distressing behaviors such as agitation, aggression, violence, or even suicidal tendencies. Unfortunately, preliminary data indicate a surge in violence and suicide since the advent of the COVID-19 pandemic, underscoring the urgency of addressing this issue head-on.

Although much has changed since the beginning of the COVID-19 pandemic, there continues to be ongoing uncertainty about new variants and shifting public guidelines. As such, we continue to encounter many stressors associated with COVID-19. In essence, this chapter serves as a guide, emphasizing not only the recognition of mental health crises but also the importance of timely intervention and support. By understanding the complexities of these crises and the tools at our disposal, we empower ourselves and our communities to navigate the challenges and emerge stronger in the aftermath.

Learning Points

- The term *mental health crisis* describes a psychiatric emergency in which a person is severely distressed and not acting like themselves. They may be agitated, aggressive, violent, or suicidal, posing a potential danger to themselves or others. Preliminary data suggests an increase in violence and suicide since the onset of the COVID-19 pandemic.

- There are many medical and psychiatric conditions that serve as risk factors for agitation, or aggressive behavior. Among these, substance-related disorders, including intoxication and withdrawal from substances, are highlighted as a frequent cause of aggressive behavior.
- Substance use has increased since the onset of the COVID-19 pandemic.
- Delirium is a state of confusion with changes in thinking and behavior; it signifies an underlying medical issue. An individual with delirium is at increased risk of becoming agitated, which may lead to aggressive behavior.
- Risk factors for violence include a personal history of violence, family history of violence, history of trauma or abuse, impulsivity, and increased stress. Common stressors that were exacerbated by the COVID-19 pandemic include financial instability, loss, illness, housing instability, and grief.
- Agitation is a term used to describe a state of extreme inner restlessness or heightened arousal and can present in a variety of ways. Anticipating agitation by identifying triggers and initiating coping strategies early on can help prevent escalation into crisis.
- De-escalation techniques are used to calm an agitated person and to help them regain a sense of control. An important first step in de-escalating an agitated person is communicating with them in a calming, respectful, and empathic manner. Additional strategies include moving to a more calming setting, removing upsetting triggers, focusing on a calming activity, or calling a friend or family member.
- In addition to de-escalation techniques, medications can help reduce agitation. There are many different classes of medications that can address the various underlying causes of agitation when necessary.
- Seclusion and/or restraints may be necessary to ensure the safety of an agitated individual and others around them if the risk of violence is imminent, or if agitation is interfering with provision of medical care.
- Suicidal ideation and behavior, heightened during the COVID-19 pandemic, is a psychiatric emergency. Warning signs include withdrawal, expressions of hopelessness, and planning for suicide.
- National suicide and crisis numbers can be a lifeline during a mental health crisis.

References

Batrinos, M.L. (2012). Testosterone and aggressive behavior in man. *International Journal of Endocrinology and Metabolism* 10 (3): 563–568. https://doi.org/10.5812/ijem.3661.

Beckwith, N., Probert, J., Rosenbaum, B.L. et al. (2023). Demographic features, physical examination findings, and medication use in hospitalized, delirious patients with and without COVID-19 infection: a retrospective study. *Journal of the Academy of Consultation-Liaison Psychiatry* 64 (1): 35–44. https://doi.org/10.1016/j.jaclp.2022.07.010.

Centers for Disease Control and Prevention (2020). Health Alert Network CDCHAN-00438. https://archive.cdc.gov/emergency_cdc_gov/han/2020/han00438.asp (accessed 16 July 2024).

Centers for Disease Control and Prevention (2024). Suicide data and statistics. https://www.cdc.gov/suicide/facts/data.html?CDC_AAref_Val=https://www.cdc.gov/suicide/suicide-data-statistics.html.

Centers for Disease Control and Prevention (2024). Violence prevention. https://www.cdc.gov/violence-prevention/index.html.

Chen, A., Copeli, F., Metzger, E. et al. (2021). The psychopharmacology algorithm project at the Harvard South Shore Program: an update on management of behavioral and psychological symptoms in dementia. *Psychiatry Research* 295: 113641. https://doi.org/10.1016/j.psychres.2020.113641.

Crisis Prevention Institute, Milwaukee, USA (2011). Joint Commission Standards on Restraint and Seclusion/Nonviolent Crisis Intervention Training Program. https://www.crisisprevention.com/CPI/media/Media/Resources/alignments/Joint-Commission-Restraint-Seclusion-Alignment-2011.pdf (accessed 16 July 2024).

Crosby, A., Ortega, L., and Melanson, C. (2011). *Self-Directed Violence Surveillance: Uniform Definitions and Recommended Data Elements (Version 1.0)*. Atlanta, GA: Centers for Disease Control and Prevention, National Center for Injury Prevention and Control.

Curry, A., Malas, N., Mroczkowski, M. et al. (2023). Updates in the assessment and management of agitation. *Focus* 21 (1): 35–45. https://doi.org/https://doi.org/10.1176/appi.focus.20220064.

Ehrenkranz, J., Bliss, E., and Sheard, M.H. (1974). Plasma testosterone: correlation with aggressive behavior and social dominance in man. *Psychosomatic Medicine* 36 (6): 469–475. https://doi.org/10.1097/00006842-197411000-00002.

First, M.B. (2014). *DSM-5 Handbook of Differential Diagnoses*. Arlington, VA: American Psychiatric Publishing https://doi.org/10.1176/appi.books.9781585629992.

Gerlach, L.B. and Kales, H.C. (2018). Managing behavioral and psychological symptoms of dementia. *The Psychiatric Clinics of North America* 41 (1): 127–139. https://doi.org/10.1016/j.psc.2017.10.010.

Higley, J.D., Mehlman, P.T., Higley, S.B. et al. (1996). Excessive mortality in young free-ranging male nonhuman primates with low cerebrospinal fluid 5-hydroxyindoleacetic acid concentrations. *Archives of General Psychiatry* 53 (6): 537–543. https://doi.org/10.1001/archpsyc.1996.0183006008301.

Lindert, J., Jakubauskiene, M., and Bilsen, J. (2021). The COVID-19 distater and mental health-assessing, responding, and recovering. *European Journal of Public Health* 9(31) (Supplement_4): iv31–iv35. https://doi.org/10.1093/eurpub/ckab153.

Richmond, J.S., Berlin, J.S., Fishkind, A.B. et al. (2012). Verbal de-escalation of the agitated patient: consensus statement of the American Association for Emergency Psychiatry Project BETA de-escalation workgroup. *The Western Journal of Emergency Medicine* 13 (1): 17–25. https://doi.org/10.5811/westjem.2011.9.6864.

World Health Organization (2014). Preventing suicide: a global imperative. www.who.int (accessed 16 July 2024).

Yan, Y., Hou, J., Li, Q., and Yu, N.X. (2023). Suicide before and during the COVID-19 pandemic: a systematic review with meta-analysis. *International Journal of Environmental Research and Public Health* 20 (4): 3346. https://doi.org/10.3390/ijerph20043346.

10

Maternal Mental Health After COVID-19

Megan Shedd[1] and Susan Hatters-Friedman[2]

[1] Department of Psychiatry, University Hospitals/Case Western Reserve University, Cleveland, OH, 44106, USA
[2] Department of Psychiatry, Case Western Reserve University, Cleveland, OH, 44106, USA

Introduction

Pregnancy and the postpartum period are vulnerable times for maternal mental health, and poor maternal mental health is associated with a variety of adverse outcomes related to birth, infant well-being, and family well-being. On a global scale, during the COVID-19 pandemic the mental health of pregnant and postpartum people has worsened. Since the World Health Organization (WHO) declared the COVID-19 an international public health emergency in January 2020 (and subsequently a global pandemic in March 2020), there has been unprecedented disruption in the social and economic fabric of entire populations, manifested by widespread social isolation, job loss, financial insecurity, increased childcare burdens, and reduced access to healthcare. This disruption has led to extensive and highly visible morbidity and mortality. A disproportionate impact has been felt by the most vulnerable groups, including the elderly, individuals with chronic medical conditions, ethnic and racial minorities, those from lower income households, and the focus of this chapter, *pregnant and postpartum people.*

Several questions have surfaced amidst fears about the effects of COVID-19 on people traversing the journey through the perinatal period, from pregnancy through birth, to raising a newborn infant: Are pregnant people more susceptible to acquiring COVID-19 infection after an exposure? Does COVID-19 infection result in detrimental impacts to maternal mental health? What effect does COVID-19 infection during pregnancy have on the health of their baby? These questions, and many more, have preoccupied many mothers and their loved ones in the center of the COVID-19 pandemic. Now, at the time of writing this book chapter, the approach to

COVID-19 among governments and populations has shifted. In the United States, the Centers for Disease Control and Prevention (CDC) ended the Public Health Emergency in May of 2023, ushering in a new framework for how we think about COVID-19. In the aftermath, we must accept that COVID-19 is here to stay as an endemic infection with seasonal fluctuations, affecting much of the population for years to come. Many pregnant or postpartum individuals will be forced to navigate these vulnerable periods with the reality of the new COVID-19 era on their minds. Moreover, in light of emerging research on the long-term physical and mental health consequences of Long COVID, COVID-19 infection can no longer be considered simply a respiratory illness, but instead, a systemic inflammatory illness that has the potential to affect major organs in the body, including the brain.

Being exposed to the COVID-19 virus or acquiring COVID-19 infection during pregnancy or in the postpartum period is a highly stressful experience, especially in the setting of rapidly changing information and overwhelming misinformation about the general and mental health consequences of the COVID-19 virus. The purpose of this chapter is to help the reader wade through this dynamic information landscape to answer many of these anxiety-provoking questions. We also intend for this chapter to serve as a guide for pregnant and postpartum people who are struggling with their mental health due the impact of COVID-19 infection in themselves or in a family member. The first portion of this chapter will assist the reader in understanding the basics of psychiatric disorders that are commonly encountered in the perinatal period, including their typical symptom presentations, their impact on pregnancy outcomes and fetal health, and the most common pharmacological and non-pharmacologic treatment approaches to promote maternal mental well-being. We will then segue into describing the impact that COVID-19 has had on maternal mental health, alerting pregnant and postpartum readers to the mental health changes they might expect after experiencing COVID-19 infection in the perinatal period, and helping readers understand how to combat any COVID-related mental health problems impacting mothers. We will describe the complex interplay of the direct effects of the COVID-19 virus and the indirect impact of pandemic-related stressors on maternal mental health, highlighting the importance of prevention efforts in acquiring COVID-19 infection and the promotion of social connectedness in fostering mental health resiliency during the critical perinatal period.

Overview of Maternal Mental Health

What Is Perinatal Depression?

Perinatal depression describes clinically significant depression occurring during pregnancy or in the postpartum period. The postpartum period generally encompasses up to one year following the birth of the baby. As discussed in Chapter 5, clinical depression is not just one symptom, but a combination of symptoms that together can affect every aspect of life. In general, people with clinical depression can experience persistent negative feelings and thoughts, diminished ability to feel positive emotions, anxiety, reduced energy and motivation, sleep and appetite disturbance, and trouble concentrating and thinking clearly. They might replay negative thoughts over and over in their head, a phenomenon called rumination. They might carry immense guilt or feel like a burden to their partners, friends, and family. In more severe cases, people with depression have thoughts of dying and ending their own life, or they might lose grasp of reality, a phenomenon called psychosis. Moreover, the symptoms of clinical depression are severe enough to impact functioning, either at home, in your social life, or at work or school. For example, this might manifest as a decline in work performance, leaving the house less often, isolating from friends, forgetting to follow through on major obligations, neglecting personal hygiene or chores, and getting annoyed easily with partners or loved ones.

It is important to recognize that depression is not a monolithic condition. One mother's experience of depression may look very different from another. Some mothers may remain in bed most of the day, sleep excessively, and feel empty, while others may experience significant restlessness, inability to fall asleep even when tired, and intense irritability and crying spells. Similarly, from an outsider's perspective, new or expecting mothers with depression can range from appearing slowed down, distant, and numb – to revved-up and emotional. In other situations, where mothers are suffering in silence and masking their symptoms, loved ones may fail to recognize the true extent of the mother's depression. Regardless of the way depression appears in new or expecting mothers, perinatal depression is a serious condition and should be treated as such. Like any serious medical condition during the perinatal period, depressed mothers need help in the form of evidence-based treatment and social support. Table 10.1 summarizes the signs and symptoms of depression in the perinatal period.

How Is Depression Unique in the Perinatal Period?

Pregnancy and childbirth are times of dramatic change – to the woman's physiology, to her body, and to her psyche. These changes often create a challenge for pregnant and postpartum mothers to determine which changes are normal, and which changes are atypical or excessive. Given that there is some overlap between the signs and symptoms of depression and the expected changes during pregnancy and postpartum (such as appetite and sleep), this can cause confusion in new and expecting mothers in understanding what these changes might represent and may cause some difficulty in diagnosis.

We know that shifts in anatomy, hormones, and social roles during pregnancy and the postpartum period can lead to some expected disruptions in appetite,

Table 10.1 Signs and symptoms of depression during the perinatal period.

Persistent negative feelings and thoughts	**Diminished ability to feel positive emotions**
Sadness	Lack of joy
Anger	Reduced sense of purpose
Guilt	Decreased satisfaction
Worthlessness	Lack of feelings of connectedness[a]
Hopelessness	Inability to feel gratitude
Apathy or emptiness	Inability to feel amusement
Replaying of negative self-talk	Less laughter
Anxious distress	**Reduced energy levels and drive**
Excessive worry	Fatigue
Intrusive thoughts[b]	Sluggishness
Inability to relax	Low libido
Indecisiveness	Low motivation
Muscle tension	Decreased self-care
Irritability	Reduced physical activity
Sleep disturbance	**Appetite changes**
Trouble falling or staying asleep	Eating too little
Early morning awakening	Weight loss
Sleeping too much	Eating too much
Reduced concentration	**Suicidality**
Mental fogginess	Thoughts about death or dying
Difficulty remembering things	Death wish
Careless mistakes	Thoughts or plans to end life
Inability to carry out daily tasks	Intent to end life

[a] May include difficulty feeling bonded to the fetus or the baby.
[b] Intrusive thoughts are often related to the pregnancy or baby's health.

energy levels, sleep, and sex drive. For instance, the changes in estrogen and progesterone levels during pregnancy promote increased appetite in preparation for increased calorie demands required for a growing fetus. In the postpartum period, breastfeeding and caring for a newborn also demand high energy reserve in the form of calories, resulting in the biological feedback to increase hunger cues prompting the replenishment of those used energy stores. Conversely, nausea associated with morning sickness, likely caused by increased levels of the placenta-produced pregnancy hormone, human chorionic gonadotropin (hCG), as well as indigestion and acid reflux caused by pressure the growing fetus places on the stomach, can lead to the opposite effect: *reduced* appetite during pregnancy. Furthermore, discomfort with a growing baby bump, late night feeds, and increased oxytocin levels (the hormone responsible for uterine contractions in pregnancy and promoting bonding with the baby) cause sleep fragmentation and reduced energy levels. Finally, with these surging sex hormones and disturbances to sleep and energy, compounded by uncomfortable physical symptoms and psychological adjustments to a rapidly changing body and the increased maternal demands, it is no surprise that decreased sex drive is a common experience among pregnant and postpartum women. All of these changes – while expected in the perinatal period – if present in excess or if paired with atypical changes to mood might be a signal to further assess for a mental health condition. Of course, defining *excessive* and *atypical* can be challenging for even the most knowledgeable mothers. That is why it is helpful to speak to a medical professional with tools to screen for perinatal depression and other commonly occurring perinatal mental health issues. Two commonly used questionnaires that an obstetrician or prenatal care clinician can give to screen for depression include the Patient Health Questionnaire-9 (PHQ-9) and the Edinburgh Postnatal Depression Scale (EPDS).

In addition to the challenges of distinguishing normal postpartum changes from the signs of clinical depression, there is a unique entity associated with childbirth called "baby blues" or "postpartum blues" that can mimic postpartum depression, further complicating the process of arriving at an accurate diagnosis for women struggling with mood changes in the postpartum period (Friedman and Resnick 2009). "Baby blues" is a syndrome characterized by some similar symptoms to depression – low mood, irritability, and mood swings. However, what differentiates "baby blues" from clinical depression is that it tends to resolve within two weeks from birth, and it *never* involves severe symptoms, such as suicidal thinking or psychosis. Understandably, "baby blues" can lead mothers to incorrectly believe that they are suffering from symptoms of depression. Furthermore, clinicians not versed in perinatal issues might misdiagnose postpartum depression in mothers with "baby blues," subjecting new mothers to the wrong treatment methods. Table 10.2 summarizes the overlapping and distinguishing symptoms between normal pregnancy changes, "baby blues," and postpartum depression.

As we have previously established, there are many considerations unique to the perinatal period when assessing a new or expecting mother for depression. While perinatal depression can certainly look very similar to depression occurring at other points in a woman's life, there are often distinctive features that may arise in pregnancy and postpartum. One of those distinct features is excessive worry about the health of the pregnancy or the baby. This might cause expecting mothers, for example, to constantly check the heartbeat of their baby with a fetal heart monitor or seek out multiple visits with their doctor when they feel a slight decrease in the

Table 10.2 Differentiating normal pregnancy changes, "baby blues", and postpartum depression.

	Normal pregnancy changes	"Baby Blues"	Postpartum depression
Mood	None or mild changes that are short-lived	Low mood, irritability, and mood swings that resolve within two weeks	Persistent low mood that lasts longer than two weeks
Sleep	Sleep deprivation Sleep is restorative	Sleep deprivation Mild insomnia Sleep is restorative	Sleep deprivation Moderate-to-severe insomnia Moderate-to-severe excessive sleeping Sleep is not restorative
Energy	Reduced energy levels related to increased caregiving demands and sleep deprivation	Reduced energy levels related to increased caregiving demands and sleep deprivation	Extreme fatigue out of proportion to level of caregiving demands or amount of sleep deprivation
Appetite	Increased hunger	Increased hunger	Reduced appetite that results in weight loss Increased hunger that results in weight gain
Suicidality or psychosis	Not present	Not present	May be present
Functioning	Not impaired	Not impaired	Impaired
Bonding	Not impaired	Not impaired	May be impaired

frequency of movements of the fetus. In postpartum mothers, it can cause women to be unable to nap when the baby is napping, because they feel compelled to check on the baby's breathing every minute. Often reassurance from their doctors about the health of the baby does not curb the worry, and checking continues, further exacerbating sleep and mood disturbances, creating a spiral of worsening symptoms. Another common symptom of depression, unique to pregnant and postpartum women, is reduced connectedness to the baby. In pregnancy, this can cause a woman to feel indifferent or ambivalent about the pregnancy, resulting in reductions in self-care and diminished motivation to receive prenatal care. In the postpartum period, reduced connectedness to the baby can lead to reduced pleasure in interacting with the infant, and reduced sensitivity to the infant's behavioral cues. Furthermore, depression may be especially impactful on new and expecting mothers and their loved ones, owing to the distinct phases of life that pregnancy and postpartum represent. During pregnancy, depression is closely associated with poor birth-related outcomes such as premature birth, preeclampsia, babies being born with low birth weight, and an increased likelihood of requiring a cesarean section delivery rather than a vaginal delivery. We also know that depression in mothers can negatively impact the health of the baby. Specifically, depression in the perinatal period has also been linked to psychological and cognitive developmental delays in the infant.

Who Is at Risk of Developing Perinatal Depression?

We know that the *single most predictive factor* of developing perinatal depression is having a history of depression in the past, with the postpartum representing a period of especially heightened vulnerability to developing depression. Among women with a history of depression, those who experience depression during pregnancy are at the highest risk of developing postpartum depression. Additionally, women with a history of depression who suddenly discontinue their antidepressant treatment when they discover they are pregnant face high rates of reemergence of clinical depression. Apart from a history of depression, there are several psychological and social factors that are known contributors to the development of depression during pregnancy and the postpartum period. Being exposed to stressful experiences during the perinatal period is a risk factor for developing depression. These stressors can include direct complications related to the pregnancy or delivery, such as a traumatic birthing experience, losing the fetus or newborn, a premature birth, and having to hospitalize the newborn in the neonatal intensive care unit (NICU). These stressors can also be related to life in general, such as having little-to-no social support from a significant other or from family members, having an insecure financial or work situation, or experiencing traumatic events. Early identification of risk factors for perinatal depression is crucial to implement proper screening and diagnostic evaluation to ensure timely treatment when warranted.

How Common Is Perinatal Depression?

When expecting mothers seek out prenatal care, they often learn the ins and outs of common medical conditions during pregnancy, such as gestational diabetes, pre-eclampsia, and preterm birth to name a few. However, an often-surprising fact for expecting mothers is that depression is *the most common complication of childbirth,* surpassing better-known perinatal conditions such as gestational diabetes, preeclampsia, and preterm birth. In the United States, the CDC estimates that 1 in 10 women are affected by depression in pregnancy, while 1 in 8 women suffer from postpartum depression (Centers for Disease Control and Prevention n.d.). A more recent study found that low- and middle-income countries have an even higher burden, with alarming estimates suggesting that up to 1 in 4 women are affected with depression during pregnancy or in the postpartum period (Mitchell et al. 2023). Perinatal and postpartum depression is often shrouded in mystery and a lack of awareness due to the stigma surrounding mental health, leading to hesitancy in openly discussing and sharing lived experiences.

Treatment of Perinatal Depression

Despite the alarming facts known about the risk factors and detrimental impact of perinatal depression, it remains largely underrecognized and undertreated, partly due to the stigma associated with seeking care during pregnancy or postpartum, as well as the difficulty in finding clinicians with expertise in diagnosing and treating mental health conditions in pregnant, postpartum, and breastfeeding mothers. Moreover, due to the paucity of high-quality research in populations of pregnant and postpartum women, there are often misunderstandings about the diagnosis and treatment of mental health conditions during the perinatal period. Since there are ethical concerns about subjecting pregnant and nursing mothers to clinical trials, much of the mental health research is drawn from observational studies, which have inherent limitations. It requires researchers to adjust for confounding factors and be astute in recognizing the limitations of the research methodology. Since much of the early research was flawed, many misconceptions persist, such as the belief that pregnancy protects women from developing depression or that certain antidepressants commonly used to treat depression cause congenital birth defects. Outdated knowledge among clinicians has led many women with preexisting depression to be advised by their trusted healthcare professionals to stop taking their antidepressants during pregnancy, often without a thorough discussion about the risks and benefits, which can have harmful consequences for both the mother and her baby.

Due to the variable presentation of depression in pregnancy and the unique considerations of providing treatment to pregnant, postpartum, or breastfeeding mothers, seeking out care from a medical professional with training and experience in reproductive mental health is strongly encouraged. Special care should be taken to identify the distressing symptoms, to map out the specific impact those specific symptoms are having on the mother's ability to function, and to develop a tailored treatment approach contextualized to the mother and her unique circumstances. The approach for treating depression in pregnancy and postpartum is a combination of non-pharmacologic and pharmacologic methods. The non-pharmacologic approaches, which include promoting quality sleep, psychotherapy, and light therapy, are generally the first approach in mild to moderate forms of perinatal depression, as they are not directly associated with risk of exposure to the fetus or nursing infant. Medications are additionally considered as a form of treatment. The primary medications used to treat depression during pregnancy and postpartum are antidepressants known as selective serotonin reuptake inhibitors (SSRIs). In certain instances of moderate to severe postpartum depression, a type of antidepressant neurosteroid (either brexanolone or zuranolone) might be offered to patients. While it can certainly be scary to take a medication in pregnancy or while breastfeeding, a great many mothers and families have been helped by medication, and we know from research and clinical practice that the risk of untreated mental health symptoms during pregnancy and postpartum is much greater than the risk of antidepressant exposure to the baby. In fact, the American College of Obstetrics and Gynecologists (ACOG) published recent clinical practice guidelines recommending treatment with both psychotherapy and antidepressant medication, including SSRIs and brexanolone, for depression in pregnancy, postpartum, and breastfeeding mothers. Furthermore, they recommended against discontinuing medications for mental health based solely on pregnancy or lactation status (American College of Obstetrics and Gynecologists 2023).

Peripartum Anxiety and Obsessive-Compulsive Symptoms

Perinatal anxiety and obsessive-compulsive symptoms are also exceedingly common in the perinatal period, and often occur together with perinatal depression. Anxiety symptoms include excessive worry, especially related to health of the pregnancy or the baby, inability to relax, restlessness, muscle tension, irritability, fatigue, difficulty concentrating, sleep disturbance, and panic attacks. Anxiety can manifest in the body through physical signs, such as trembling, fast heartbeat, shortness of breath, and excessive sweating.

Obsessive symptoms in the perinatal period generally take the form of intrusive thoughts, images, or impulses. These obsessions cause significant distress and may feel "off" or not in line with their values. In response to the distress caused by these obsessions, individuals develop behaviors in an attempt to reduce or neutralize the obsession. These repetitive behaviors, known as compulsions, serve to neutralize the obsession. New mothers with obsessive-compulsive symptoms often report obsessive thoughts about pathogens infecting the baby. As a result, the mother may give the baby frequent baths and change their clothes often. They will clean their home repeatedly and feel the impulse to continue to clean a surface, even after it has been sanitized multiple times. Another common complaint of mothers with obsessive-compulsive symptoms is intrusive fears about the baby's health. For example, they might develop a fear that their baby will stop breathing, leading them to compulsively check the infant's breathing throughout the day and night.

Some obsessive thoughts can invoke extreme distress and significant shame in the mother, specifically those that involve deliberate harm to the baby. Mothers will avoid their baby altogether out of fear of impulsively harming the baby. They often will hide these thoughts from their loved ones or from mental health clinicians for fear of having their baby removed from their custody or getting admitted to a psychiatric hospital. However, it is important to recognize that these thoughts are involuntary and do not reflect the true desires of the mother. Treatment for perinatal anxiety and obsessive-compulsive symptoms included psychotherapy as a first line. For obsessive-compulsive symptoms, therapy will often include exposing them to the obsessive triggers and helping them to resist the impulse to act on their compulsion. In instances of more severe manifestations of anxiety or obsessive-compulsive symptoms, treatment can also include SSRIs.

Postpartum Psychosis

Postpartum psychosis is a rare but serious mental health condition affecting mothers. It typically occurs in the first few weeks after delivery, though it can also occur later in the postpartum period. Psychosis is characterized by severe difficulties in thinking and accurately interpreting reality. Individuals experiencing psychosis may report hearing voices, experiencing delusional beliefs–fixed false beliefs that are inconsistent with their culture–and having unusual speech or thinking patterns. In postpartum psychosis, women often exhibit significant changes in mood and episodes of confusion (Friedman et al. 2019). They may behave in ways that do not make sense. Given the nature of psychosis, it is associated with significant functional impairment, and there is an elevated risk that the mother may inadvertently or deliberately harm herself or her baby (Friedman et al. 2019). For these reasons, postpartum psychosis is a psychiatric emergency, and individuals who have concerns that they are experiencing postpartum psychosis should call emergency services or go to the nearest emergency department for medical attention. The treatment for postpartum psychosis includes psychiatric hospitalization, treatment with antipsychotic or mood stabilizing medication, and extensive social support.

A Closer Look at Sleep Problems in the Postpartum Period

It is well-established that postpartum mothers taking care of their newborn babies have a harder time falling asleep and staying asleep. Common symptoms of poor-quality sleep include daytime sleepiness, irritability, poor concentration, slow thinking, and memory deficits. While it is certainly a challenging endeavor, promoting quality sleep in the postpartum period is one of the most important interventions for reducing the risk of postpartum depression and anxiety. As previously discussed, postpartum depression and anxiety can also cause significant sleep disruption. This creates a negative cycle between poor sleep quality and worsening mood that is often difficult to break. When thinking about sleep problems in the postpartum period, it is important to determine whether the sleep disturbance is caused by clinical depression, anxiety, or obsessive-compulsive symptoms, or another condition altogether. Sometimes, adequately treating the underlying depression or anxiety is sufficient to combat sleep disturbances; however, it is not uncommon for residual sleep issues to persist even when perinatal mood or anxiety symptoms appear to be improving.

Another commonly encountered mental health condition that can occur in the postpartum period is insomnia. Insomnia is a combination of symptoms that include problems falling asleep, problems staying asleep, or waking up earlier than expected. It is often caused by a combination of behavioral factors, such as distorted thoughts and anxiety about sleep and poor sleep routine, and by biological factors, such as genetics and hormonal changes. Insomnia can be managed first-line with a type of cognitive behavioral therapy (CBT) specifically developed for insomnia and second-line with medication. There are also some common physical conditions that occur in pregnancy that result in poor quality sleep. These include restless legs syndrome, periodic leg movement disorder, and obstructive sleep apnea. New and expecting mothers should also take notice that symptoms of these sleep conditions can worsen in pregnancy and the postpartum period. Restless legs syndrome and periodic limb movement disorder are disorders of movements. Restless legs syndrome generally manifests by discomfort in the lower extremities when trying to sleep accompanied by a frequent urge to move the legs. People with restless legs syndrome often struggle to find comfortable positions in bed, and their co-sleeping partners may notice frequent movements during the night. Periodic limb movement disorder is also characterized by frequent movements during sleep, but it does not carry the subjective discomfort in the lower extremities. In fact, individuals with periodic limb movement disorder may not realize they move their legs at all.

To combat postpartum sleep deprivation, we recommend that pregnant people develop a structured sleep plan in consultation with a medical or mental health professional before giving birth. This plan should take into account any preexisting barriers to quality sleep and incorporate reasonable interventions to promote quality sleep. Strategies may include equitable division of feeding and other newborn care duties with a partner, sleep hygiene and relaxation training, massage, exercise, and psychotherapy. Medical professionals can give the mother a "sleep prescription" to emphasize the importance of implementing the sleep plan and foster buy-in from the mother's support network. Using CBT techniques, therapists can help new and expecting mothers identify cognitive distortions, also known as mistakes in thinking, that lead to sleep impairment. A common cognitive barrier to good quality sleep often seen in mothers is the belief that their self-worth as a mother is tied to self-sacrifice, leading them to prioritize newborn care over their own well-being. This attitude can prevent them from requesting support from a partner or loved one out of fear of being perceived as a failure as a mother. Providing early education to expecting mothers and their partners can help them avoid or overcome this common cognitive pitfall.

Perinatal Mood and Anxiety Disorders Before and After COVID-19

The COVID-19 pandemic had a serious and unprecedented impact on maternal mental health worldwide. While low- and middle-income countries were disproportionately affected by COVID-19 infection, no country was immune to the fallout. At the onset of the pandemic and throughout its course, research from all over the globe sought to measure and quantify the extent of the impact. Many governments and non-governmental agencies, including educational institutions, employed massive surveillance efforts. The bulk of the evidence suggests that the prevalence of perinatal depression and anxiety increased following the onset of the COVID-19 pandemic. Researchers conducted a meta-analysis, pooling data from multiple high-quality small-scale studies to collectively analyze the results. This approach is advantageous because it allows researchers to identify trends in the data using larger sample sizes. In this meta-analysis, data from eight studies were combined, enabling the analysis of depression and anxiety symptoms among 7 750 pregnant and postpartum women in Turkey, Italy, China, Canada, and Greece. Depression symptoms were measured using the EPDS, and anxiety symptoms were measured by the State-Trait Anxiety Inventory. The researchers found that, compared to pre-pandemic levels, symptoms of both maternal anxiety and depression were higher during the pandemic (Hessami et al. 2022). In another larger meta-analysis, researchers examined 22 studies that included 15 098 participants before the COVID-19 pandemic and 11 836 participants during the COVID-19 pandemic. The participants spanned five continents, including Europe, North America, South America, Asia, and Africa. Researchers only included studies that had clearly defined criteria for diagnosing postpartum depression, such as the EPDS. Overall, when the pooled data were analyzed together, the COVID-19 pandemic was associated with an increased prevalence of postpartum depression (Zhang et al. 2023). Some studies have estimated that the prevalence of postpartum depression during the pandemic was 24%, compared to 17% before the pandemic (Lin et al. 2023).

In addition to the increased prevalence of depression and anxiety during pregnancy and the postpartum period, the pandemic also brought significant changes to the delivery of perinatal mental health services. This resulted in the exacerbation of preexisting treatment gaps in some cases, while also shifting the provision of in-person services to a telehealth model. In one study conducted in the United States, researchers analyzed claims data of approximately 2 million individuals covered by commercial insurance and Medicaid. They found that while postpartum mental health diagnoses increased during the COVID-19 pandemic, the provision of prescription drugs for treating postpartum mental health disorders decreased (Rokicki et al. 2022). This suggests that the healthcare system in the United States was unable to keep pace with the increased burden of perinatal mood and anxiety disorders during the COVID-19 pandemic. In a system that already struggles to recognize and adequately treat perinatal mental health disorders, the pandemic likely amplified the existing treatment gap. This was due to the pandemic's disruption of mental healthcare services, especially early in the pandemic, and pandemic-related job losses that made mental healthcare too expensive for many. While the provision of pharmacologic treatment for perinatal mood and anxiety disorders decreased among both commercial insurance and Medicaid recipients, the study found a slight increase in the provision of psychotherapy among those with commercial insurance (Rokicki et al. 2022). This increase likely reflects the widespread adoption of telehealth services due to social distancing and quarantining policies in the United States. However, this benefit of increased access to psychotherapy was not seen among lowerincome Medicaid recipients, (Rokicki et al. 2022) which may be due to barriers such as lower technology literacy or a limited number of telehealth clinicians who accept Medicaid.

Similarly, obsessive-compulsive disorders affecting the perinatal period have also risen during the COVID-19 pandemic. A study performed in the United States examined the prevalence of obsessive-compulsive symptoms in a large cohort of pregnant women during the early months of the COVID-19 pandemic. It showed that rates of obsessive-compulsive symptoms more than doubled in those early months of March and April of 2020 compared to rates observed in the pre-pandemic period (Mahaffey et al. 2022). The study revealed that factors which increased obsessive-compulsive symptoms included high pandemic-related stress, having suspected but undiagnosed COVID-19 infection, pandemic-related income loss, and limited outdoor access. These factors were hypothesized to be related to fears of contracting the virus, fears surrounding the impact of infection of on the fetus, scarcity of resources, and disruption to provision of prenatal care (Mahaffey et al. 2022). Moreover, demographic factors that predicted higher rates of obsessive-compulsive symptoms in pregnancy during the pandemic included first-time pregnancy, younger maternal age, and single relationship status. This suggests that the typical fears associated with new mothers, such as lack of experience with childbirth and newborn care, and the reduced social support among single mothers, were compounded by pandemic-related fears (Mahaffey et al. 2022).

Early in the pandemic, there were many factors that likely contributed to rising rates of perinatal mood and anxiety disorders, including fear of the COVID-19 virus in the setting of uncertainty about its health effects and lack of infection control measures. As the pandemic evolved, governments implemented large-scale efforts to prevent the spread of the COVID-19 virus by enacting social distancing and quarantine measures and shutting down schools and services that were deemed "non-essential." As a result of these efforts, there was a loss of social support, increased labor demands at home related to childrearing and education, job loss, financial insecurity, limited access to meaningful and recreational activities, and reduced access to mental healthcare services. These findings underscore the importance of COVID-19 infection prevention, access to mental healthcare, financial security, and social connectedness in promoting maternal mental health.

Impact of COVID-19 in the Perinatal Period

Understandably, a fear of any pregnant woman is to become ill with COVID-19 infection at some point during the pregnancy. We are regularly exposed to infectious pathogens, but in most people with healthy immune systems, these pathogens are eliminated before they can cause infection. However, during pregnancy, immunity is lowered. This is an adaptive response to prevent our immune system from mistaking the fetus as "foreign" and mounting an immune response that could harm the fetus. The trade-off is that pregnancy can sometimes leave women unable to mount an appropriate response to certain pathogens, making them more susceptible to infection. This dampened immune response can persist after a pregnant woman becomes infected with a pathogen, placing her at risk for more severe complications. For instance, we know that pregnant women are at increased risk of acquiring and experiencing more severe complications from the influenza virus due to the normal physiologic and immunologic changes in pregnancy. Therefore, it was a reasonable concern at the onset of the pandemic that COVID-19 infection could pose a similar risk to pregnant women, prompting significant research to determine if such a relationship exists.

An important question to answer is if pregnant women are more likely than their non-pregnant counterparts to develop a COVID-19 infection after an exposure. Answering this question could help pregnant women make informed decisions about weighing the risk and benefits of certain precautions, such as social distancing, self-isolation, and receiving the COVID-19 vaccine. Unfortunately, at the time of writing this chapter, there is not enough data to conclusively determine whether pregnancy increases susceptibility to acquiring COVID-19 infection after exposure to the virus. Another important question to examine is whether pregnant women are more likely to have severe symptoms or negative health outcomes if they become infected with COVID-19, as this information could help them make informed decisions about precautions and preventive measures. The CDC in the United States maintains the National Notifiable Diseases Surveillance System, which has been instrumental for tracking COVID-19-related data during the pandemic. Based on this surveillance data, the CDC was able to examine the risk of severe COVID-19 infection among pregnant women in the United States. During an approximately eight-month period (from January 22 to October 3) of 2022, the CDC identified 1.3 million women of reproductive age with laboratory results that confirmed COVID-19 infection. Among that group of women, the CDC was able to confirm that 461 825 were pregnant at the time of the COVID-19 infection. The data showed that 88% of these pregnant women with laboratory confirmed COVID-19 were exhibiting active symptoms (while the other 12% were asymptomatic). The researchers analyzed the data carefully, using the non-pregnant reproductive age women with COVID-19 as a control group and appropriately adjusting the data to control for common factors that could confuse the results, such as age, race, ethnicity, and other underlying medical conditions. They found that pregnant women with COVID-19 infection were more likely than non-pregnant women to be admitted to the intensive care unit (ICU), receive intubation, receive extracorporeal membrane oxygenation, and die from COVID-19 infection and its associated complications (Zambrano et al. 2020). The researchers hypothesized that biological changes associated with pregnancy, including decreased lung volume, changes to the pregnant person's immune system, and increased risk for blood clotting, were responsible for these negative outcomes (Zambrano et al. 2020). In another meta-analysis, which pooled and analyzed the data from multiple smaller-scale international studies, the researchers compared pregnancy outcomes between pregnant women with and without COVID-19 infection in several low- and high-income countries. They found that rates of premature birth, newborn admission to the NICU, and mortality among mothers and infants were higher in those with COVID-19 infection (Simbar et al. 2023). They also found that the risk of these poor outcomes was greater in lower-income countries compared to higher-income countries (Simbar et al. 2023). In order to determine which factors in pregnancy increased the risk of developing severe COVID-19 disease, researchers looked at a group of pregnant women infected with COVID-19 and split them into two groups, those without medical condition and those with co-occurring medical conditions. The study design was a large-scale meta-analysis that included data from multiple studies across the globe. The researchers found that pregnant women with the medical conditions of diabetes mellitus, hypertension, HIV infection, obesity, and anemia were at higher risk of developing severe complications from COVID-19 infection compared to pregnant women without these conditions (Smith et al. 2023). These findings suggest that pregnant women are a high-risk group for developing severe COVID-19 illness compared to their non-pregnant counterparts. While these findings are certainly concerning, the absolute risk of severe disease from a COVID-19 infection remains low, even among pregnant women. In other words, most women who do acquire COVID-19 infection during pregnancy have a mild course of symptoms. Another important point to consider when interpreting these data is that the reduced ability to treat severe COVID-19 infections early in the pandemic, due to a strained healthcare system during COVID surges, may have been a major driving factor for these results. As we have learned more about the virus and the rates of COVID-19 infection have decreased, we have become better equipped to treat severe COVID-19 infection. Nonetheless, since severe COVID-19 infection has the potential to cause devastating outcomes in pregnant women (not to mention the toll on mental health), prevention of COVID-19 should be a priority.

There are a host of infections that, if acquired during pregnancy, can infect the fetus and result in poor health outcomes in the infant. A number of these infections, for example, cytomegalovirus, are generally mild in the mother, but can result in serious birth defects. In the center of the uncertainty of the COVID-19 pandemic, there were reasonable concerns about the potential effects that COVID-19 infection acquired during pregnancy could have on the development of the fetus. While case reports have suggested that *in utero* transmission from mother to fetus can occur, data from multiple studies provide reassurance, indicating that direct transmission of COVID-19 from mother to fetus during pregnancy is likely a rare phenomenon (de Medeiros et al. 2022). A large-scale meta-analysis examining 70 different studies including a total of 10047 pregnant women from across the globe, was reassuring as it showed no evidence of COVID-19 in the placenta, umbilical cord, amniotic fluid, or breast milk (de Medeiros et al. 2022). This indicates that the likelihood of the fetus becoming directly infected with COVID-19 *in utero* is low, indicating an even lower likelihood of congenital anomalies associated with the virus. Early in the pandemic, it was observed that elective cesarean sections were high (Turan et al. 2020), likely related to the fears of transmitting the COVID-19 virus to the newborn during vaginal delivery. Many expecting mothers had questions surrounding the mode of delivering their baby. In the setting of uncertainty around the effects on the newborn and aggressive attempts to prevent transmission, many women with COVID-19 infection in labor were open to a cesarean section. More recent studies examining this phenomenon have found that there is no evidence that elective cesarean section delivery reduces the transmission of the virus to the infant. Therefore, COVID-19 infection alone without other clinical justification should not be a reason to pursue cesarean section delivery (Villar da Motta et al. 2023).

Pregnant women in the center of the COVID-19 pandemic have been faced with the question of how they should prevent COVID-19 infection. Some of the measures, like masking and handwashing, are relatively easy to implement and have very few downsides. On the other hand, measures that create social isolation during the perinatal period, a period that demands connectedness, is likely to create unintended mental health consequences. Many pregnant and postpartum women make this sacrifice by attending prenatal appointments by telehealth or not seeing extended family for months, all in the effort to protect their pregnancy and newborn. When the vaccine was first developed, there was significant uncertainty, and many women were concerned about how it might affect their pregnancy. Thankfully, the COVID-19 messenger ribonucleic acid (mRNA) vaccination in pregnancy is safe and effective for preventing COVID-19 infection. A meta-analysis examining the data from 23 studies including 117 552 vaccinated pregnant people showed that the vaccine was 89.5% effective. There were no increased risks of adverse outcomes among pregnant people vaccinated with the COVID-19 vaccine. Compared to unvaccinated pregnant people, rates of miscarriage, premature birth, pulmonary embolism, placental abruption, postpartum hemorrhage, ICU admission for the mother, low birth weight, NICU admission for the infant, and maternal death among pregnant people who received the COVID-19 vaccine were not significantly different (Prasad et al. 2022). In addition to being safe, the COVID-19 vaccine given to the mother in pregnancy passes protective antibodies to the baby *in utero* and through breastfeeding. Considering these benefits and weighing the potential for devastating outcomes related to severe COVID-19 infection in pregnancy, receiving vaccination for COVID-19 in pregnancy is recommended.

COVID-19 Pandemic-related Stress and Maternal Mental Health

High levels of maternal stress during pregnancy are associated with negative physical and behavioral consequences in the infant, with some of these effects persisting into childhood. The primary hypothesis explaining how maternal emotional stress impacts the fetus is through fetal programming. When the mother is exposed to environmental stressors, physiological changes occur that can be transmitted to the fetus *in utero*, especially during the early stages of brain and organ development, when the fetus is more susceptible to insults. The stress hormone cortisol likely plays a major role, while molecules that regulate inflammation, known as pro-inflammatory cytokines, might play a role to a lesser extent. In response to exposure to these molecules, the fetus attempts to adapt by reprogramming its biology, leading to more persistent downstream changes. In the postpartum period, high levels of maternal stress, similar to perinatal depression and anxiety, are also associated with reducing maternal bonding. Given the nature of these mechanisms, there was notable interest in understanding the effects of COVID-19 pandemic-related stress on the health of the infant. A study in Canada examined the relationship between pandemic-related stress and the birth outcomes of preterm birth and low birth weight during the COVID-19 pandemic among research participants. Reassuringly, they found no significant associations between stress and the risk of preterm birth or low birth weight (Gorgui et al. 2023). In another study, researchers launched the Maternal COVID-19-related Prenatal Exposure (MOM-COPE) project, which focused on studying pregnant and postpartum women in maternity units in northern Italy. The researchers examined the relationship between pandemic-related stress during pregnancy and the infant's ability to regulate emotions and self-soothe. Many mothers in the study had been exposed to stressful conditions during the pandemic, such as living in a high-contagion area or having a relative or friend require intensive care or die due to COVID-19 infection. The researchers hypothesized that pregnant mothers who experienced diminished emotional and psychological well-being during pregnancy and postpartum due to the pandemic would have infants with a fussy temperament or reduced ability to regulate their emotions. Indeed, they found that high levels of COVID-19 pandemic-related stress, combined with reduced social support, led to increased anxiety in new mothers, more parenting stress, and reduced maternal bonding with their baby. These factors, in turn, were associated with a negative impact on the infant's temperament and ability to self-soothe by the time they were three months old (Provenzi et al. 2023).

COVID-19-Specific Stressors in Maternal Mental Health

During the pandemic, pregnant women, mothers, and families faced an incredible increase in stressors. These included not only the direct impact of COVID-19 but also the stress from necessary protective measures such as lockdowns and hospital safety procedures, as well as additional financial and childcare stress (Friedman 2020). Pregnant women expecting baby showers, a celebration of their pregnancy with family and friends, no longer had the same sense of community. When giving birth, visiting restrictions were in place such that in addition to the laboring person, only one COVID-negative family member could be present. And even if mothers were fortunate enough to have a healthy baby and be discharged quickly, they often faced limited visitors and minimal home help because of lockdowns. Mothers struggled without adequate supports at home.

Further, if the baby had serious medical issues requiring admission to the NICU for treatment, It could be incredibly stressful for the family, even during the best of times (Friedman et al. 2011). During the pandemic, for safety reasons, often only one parent was allowed to visit the NICU. Mothers often feel guilt when their infant is sick, even when they have done everything right; these feelings of self-blame could become much worse during the pandemic.

Bonding with a critically ill infant, without the presence of other supportive people, could be especially fraught. Grieving the loss of a stillbirth baby is difficult at any time, but it was particularly hard during the pandemic, when support systems were more difficult to access, often couldn't be in person, and hospitals were understaffed.

Long COVID and Maternal Mental Health

The COVID-19 virus has the potential to cause prolonged symptoms that last beyond the acute infection stage of the illness. This phenomenon has been termed post-acute COVID-19 syndrome or Long COVID. While it appears that individuals with more severe COVID-19 infection are at higher risk of developing Long COVID, persistent symptoms can occur after both mild and severe COVID-19 infection. In addition to prolonged respiratory symptoms, such as shortness of breath, those with Long COVID can experience a variety of other physical and mental health symptoms, including fatigue, headaches, brain fog, problems sleeping, loss of taste and smell, body aches, depression, and anxiety. At this time, studies examining Long COVID in pregnant or postpartum women are limited. Of the studies that have been conducted, they suggest that individuals in the perinatal period can also develop Long COVID. In one study in the United States, researchers examined individuals who were pregnant or up to six weeks postpartum with known or suspected COVID-19 infection. They found that among pregnant women who tested positive for COVID-19, 25% had symptoms persist eight weeks after their symptoms began (Afshar et al. 2020). In another study evaluating the symptoms of Long COVID during pregnancy, researchers in Turkey compared a group of pregnant women with laboratory confirmed COVID-19 infection to a group of pregnant women without COVID-19. The researchers used a technique called matching, where each pregnant woman with COVID-19 infection was matched to a pregnant woman without COVID-19, but who had similar clinical features. For instance, if a woman with COVID-19 infection was in her twenties, pregnant with her first child, and smoked cigarettes, she would be matched with a pregnant woman with the same characteristics minus the COVID-19 infection. This technique helps researchers isolate the specific variable that they intend to study. They found that in the group with COVID-19 infection, there were significantly elevated rates of reported fatigue, joint pain, muscle aches, and loss of sense of smell four weeks after the COVID-19 infection (74%) compared to the control group (14%), suggesting that COVID-19 infection caused or worsened these symptoms in pregnant women. Furthermore, the more COVID-19 symptoms that were present at the onset of their infection, the higher the likelihood of developing persistent

COVID-19 symptoms (Kandemir et al. 2023). It is plausible that due to the significant physiologic and immunologic changes during the perinatal period, pregnant and postpartum people may be particularly susceptible to developing mental health symptoms or having an exacerbation of preexisting mental health symptoms after a COVID-19 infection.

Currently, there is no specific medication to treat Long COVID. Emphasis should be placed on prevention. The COVID-19 vaccine has been shown to lower the risk of developing Long COVID in those individuals who have a breakthrough infection after receiving the vaccine. Furthermore, the vaccine does not appear to worsen the symptoms of Long COVID in those who have already developed it (Ceban et al. 2023). The approach to treating depression, anxiety, fatigue, and sleep disturbance in the perinatal period due to Long COVID does not differ significantly from treating these problems in the absence of COVID-19 infection. Pregnant and postpartum people who are experiencing mental health symptoms from Long COVID should seek out care from a trusted mental health professional, ideally one who has experience in caring for individuals in the perinatal period. A treatment plan should be tailored to the individual. It should start with characterizing the symptoms of Long COVID and their impact on the woman's life with special consideration to the unique phase of life she is in as a new or expecting mother. Non-pharmacologic approaches, such as a "sleep prescription," psychotherapy, and low-impact physical activity, should be encouraged and maximized. In moderate to severe symptoms, medications like SSRIs can be considered. New and expecting mother can seek out Long COVID support groups in their local community or online.

Conclusion

Pregnancy and the postpartum period are important times to be aware of the risk of mental health issues, most commonly depression or anxiety, though psychosis is fortunately rare. Due to both COVID-19 itself and the protective measures taken during the pandemic, this period has seen an increased risk for pregnant people and mothers. The risks of untreated depression are serious and can include suicide or difficulty bonding with the baby. It is critical that people experiencing mental health symptoms during the perinatal period are aware of these symptoms and can access treatment, including psychological services and medication, when needed. Sleep is also critically important during this period to decrease risk and should be negotiated with social support when possible.

> **Learning Points**
>
> - Postpartum depression impacts mothers, their infants, and families. Postpartum depression is responsive to therapy and antidepressant medication, and women should seek treatment.
> - Postpartum anxiety can occur alongside postpartum depression or on its own.
> - Abnormal sleep is an important symptom of postpartum disorders. In addition, working on a plan with family members or other supports so that the new mother can get enough sleep, and sleep when the baby sleeps, can help prevent other psychiatric disorders in the postpartum.
> - Postpartum depression is important to get treatment for, not only for the mother's well-being, but also for optimal infant development.
> - Postpartum psychosis, in which a mother of an infant experiences psychotic symptoms such as being out of touch with reality, mood swings, and confusion, is considered a medical emergency and warrants going to the ER.
> - The postpartum is often a period of stress for new mothers and families, and all the more so during the pandemic. Rising distress during the pandemic may increase rates of both postpartum depression and postpartum anxiety.
> - Pregnant and postpartum women who acquire COVID-19 infection are at risk of developing Long COVID, which could potentially exacerbate or even cause postpartum depression and anxiety symptoms.
> - Pregnant women are at higher risk of developing severe complications from COVID-19 infection. The COVID-19 vaccine is safe in pregnancy, and it can prevent severe COVID-19 infection and Long COVID. Furthermore, getting the vaccine in pregnancy or postpartum can pass protective antibodies to the baby *in utero* or through breastfeeding.

References

Afshar, Y., Gaw, S.L., Flaherman, V.J. et al. (2020). Clinical presentation of coronavirus disease 2019 (COVID-19) in pregnant and recently pregnant people. *Obstetrics and Gynecology* 136: 1117–1125. https://doi.org/10.1097/AOG.0000000000004178.

American College of Obstetrics and Gynecologists (2023). Treatment and management of mental health conditions during pregnancy and postpartum: ACOG clinical practice guideline no. 5. *Obstetrics & Gynecology* 141: 1262–1288. https://doi.org/10.1097/AOG.0000000000005202.

Ceban, F., Kulzhabayeva, D., Rodrigues, N.B. et al. (2023). COVID-19 vaccination for the prevention and treatment of long COVID: a systematic review and meta-analysis. *Brain, Behavior, and Immunity.* https://doi.org/10.1016/j.bbi.2023.03.022.

Centers for Disease Control and Prevention (n.d.). Depression during and after pregnancy. https://www.cdc.gov/reproductivehealth/features/maternal-depression/index.html (accessed 16 July 2024).

Friedman, S.H. (2020). COVID is not what women expected when they were expecting [WWW Document]. https://www.kevinmd.com/2020/07/covid-is-not-women-expected-when-they-were-expecting.html (accessed 16 July 2024).

Friedman, S.H. and Resnick, P.J. (2009). Postpartum depression: an update. *Women's Health* 5: 287–295. https://doi.org/10.2217/WHE.09.3.

Friedman, S.H., Yang, S.N., Parsons, S., and Amin, J. (2011). Maternal mental health in the neonatal intensive care unit. *NeoReviews* 12: e85–e93. https://doi.org/10.1542/neo.12-2-e85.

Friedman, S.H., Prakash, C., and Nagle-Yang, S. (2019). Postpartum psychosis: protecting mother and infant. *Current Psychiatry* 18: 12–21.

Gorgui, J., Tchuente, V., Pages, N. et al. (2023). The impact of prenatal maternal mental health during the COVID-19 pandemic on birth outcomes: two nested case-control studies within the CONCEPTION cohort. *Canadian Journal of Public Health* 114: 755–773. https://doi.org/10.17269/s41997-023-00814-0.

Hessami, K., Romanelli, C., Chiurazzi, M., and Cozzolino, M. (2022). COVID-19 pandemic and maternal mental health: a systematic review and meta-analysis. *Journal of Maternal-Fetal and Neonatal Medicine.* https://doi.org/10.1080/14767058.2020.1843155.

Kandemir, H., Bülbül, G.A., Kirtiş, E. et al. (2023). Evaluation of long-COVID symptoms in women infected with SARS-CoV-2 during pregnancy. *International Journal of Gynecology & Obstetrics.* https://doi.org/10.1002/ijgo.14972.

Lin, C., Chen, B., Yang, Y. et al. (2023). Association between depressive symptoms in the postpartum period and COVID-19: a meta-analysis. *Journal of Affective Disorders* 320: 247–253. https://doi.org/10.1016/j.jad.2022.09.129.

Mahaffey, B.L., Levinson, A., Preis, H., and Lobel, M. (2022). Elevated risk for obsessive–compulsive symptoms in women pregnant during the COVID-19 pandemic. *Archives of Women's Mental Health* 25: 367–376. https://doi.org/10.1007/s00737-021-01157-w.

de Medeiros, K.S., Sarmento, A.C.A., Costa, A.P.F. et al. (2022). Consequences and implications of the coronavirus disease (COVID-19) on pregnancy and newborns: a comprehensive systematic review and meta-analysis. *International Journal of Gynecology & Obstetrics.* https://doi.org/10.1002/ijgo.14015.

Mitchell, A.R., Gordon, H., Lindquist, A. et al. (2023). Prevalence of perinatal depression in low-and middle-income countries a systematic review and meta-analysis supplemental content. *JAMA Psychiatry* 80: 425–431. https://doi.org/10.1001/jamapsychiatry.2023.0069.

Prasad, S., Kalafat, E., Blakeway, H. et al. (2022). Systematic review and meta-analysis of the effectiveness and perinatal outcomes of COVID-19 vaccination in pregnancy. *Nature Communications* 13: https://doi.org/10.1038/s41467-022-30052-w.

Provenzi, L., Grumi, S., Altieri, L. et al. (2023). Prenatal maternal stress during the COVID-19 pandemic and infant regulatory capacity at 3 months: a longitudinal study. *Development and Psychopathology* 35: 35–43. https://doi.org/10.1017/S0954579421000766.

Rokicki, S., Steenland, M.W., Geiger, C.K. et al. (2022). Trends in postpartum mental health care before and during COVID-19. *Health Services Research* 57: 1342–1347. https://doi.org/10.1111/1475-6773.14051.

Simbar, M., Nazarpour, S., and Sheidaei, A. (2023). Evaluation of pregnancy outcomes in mothers with COVID-19 infection: a systematic review and meta-analysis. *Journal of Obstetrics and Gynaecology.* https://doi.org/10.1080/01443615.2022.2162867.

Smith, E.R., Oakley, E., Grandner, G.W. et al. (2023). Clinical risk factors of adverse outcomes among women with COVID-19 in the pregnancy and postpartum period: a sequential, prospective meta-analysis. *American Journal of Obstetrics and Gynecology.* https://doi.org/10.1016/j.ajog.2022.08.038.

Turan, O., Hakim, A., Dashraath, P. et al. (2020). Clinical characteristics, prognostic factors, and maternal and neonatal outcomes of SARS-CoV-2 infection among hospitalized pregnant women: a systematic review. *International Journal of Gynecology & Obstetrics* 151: 7–16. https://doi.org/10.1002/ijgo.13329.

Villar da Motta, A.S., Ma, Y., Sardeli, A.V., and Velasque, L. (2023). Type of delivery and perinatal outcomes in pregnant women diagnosed with COVID-19: a systematic review and meta-analysis. *European Journal of Obstetrics, Gynecology, and Reproductive Biology.* https://doi.org/10.1016/j.ejogrb.2023.11.019.

Zambrano, L.D., Ellington, S., Strid, P. et al. (2020). Update: characteristics of symptomatic women of reproductive age with laboratory-confirmed SARS-CoV-2 infection by pregnancy status – United States, January 22–October 3, 2020. *MMWR. Morbidity and Mortality Weekly Report* 69 (44): 1641–1647.

Zhang, X., Wang, C., Zuo, X. et al. (2023). Study characteristical and regional influences on postpartum depression before vs. during the COVID-19 pandemic: a systematic review and meta-analysis. *Frontiers in Public Health* 11: https://doi.org/10.3389/FPUBH.2023.1102618/FULL.

11

The Impact of COVID-19 Infection on Child and Adolescent Mental Health

Joshua D. Feder

Department of Psychiatry, University of California at San Diego School of Medicine, La Jolla, CA, 92093, USA

Introduction

What are the effects of COVID-19 infection on child and adolescent mental health? In this chapter we will cover how COVID-19 infection can affect the mental health of children and teens at different ages. We want to answer the following questions:

1) How do children and teens experience the COVID-19 infection physiologically and psychologically? We will describe four experiences of children at different ages.
2) What are the neuropsychiatric problems related to, or triggered by COVID-19, and how can we treat these problems?
3) How does COVID-19 infection affect existing psychiatric problems?
4) How do social determinants of health, such as race, culture, socioeconomic status, and climate change impact the psychiatric problems of children and teens associated with COVID-19 infection?
5) How do we find neuropsychiatric problems in children and teens associated with COVID-19 infection?
6) What can we say to children and teens about neuropsychiatric problems associated with COVID-19 infection?

Managing Mental Illness After COVID-19 Infection, First Edition. Edited by Stephanie A. Collier.
© 2025 John Wiley & Sons, Inc. Published 2025 by John Wiley & Sons, Inc.

How Do Children and Teens Experience the COVID-19 Infection Physiologically and Psychologically?

Sometimes it is easier to think about multidimensional problems by using examples. We will begin by describing the lives of four people of different ages who are affected by COVID-19.

- Audra – an 18-month-old girl who was cared for by her grandmother.
- Emiliano – a 9-year-old boy with asthma.
- Raven – an autistic 12-year-old who chose their own name.
- Maeve – a 17-year-old young woman.

Infancy and Early Childhood

Audra was attending day care in March 2020 when the pandemic arrived. Her maternal grandmother Patricia, who was her primary caregiver, worked as a nurse at a local hospital. One week after the start of the lockdown, Patricia fell ill and died of COVID-19, *leaving Audra in the care of a foster family.*

While people generally think of COVID-19 as more dangerous for older adults, it is frequently severe in infants and young children, causing respiratory distress and secondary pneumonia. High fevers can result in seizures and neurological damage. When the illness persists, there is prolonged disruption in parent-child interaction. This could be due to hospitalization or merely the ongoing frequent interruptions of communication due to coughing, malaise, and other symptoms. As discussed in Chapter 10, for many, the COVID-19 pandemic has affected the caregiver-infant bond. Researchers (Gulati and Veliz 2023) found that the pandemic had a negative impact on the mother-infant bond, perhaps due to stress, depression, and anxiety in mothers during that time. This early impact on the infant may have important effects on emotional functioning throughout the child's lifetime and needs to be considered and addressed as the child develops.

Instead of the usual energetic dashing about of a typical toddler, Audra is fatigued. She is not experiencing the near-constant movement that teaches her how her body moves and acts on the world. Audra is profoundly sad in the absence of her grandmother. She is barely eating and is heard whimpering throughout the night. She is now listless and hardly engaging in the back-and-forth interactions with her foster family, which at this age are often centered on knowing who she is and what she wants. Now there is no "No!"

School Age

Emiliano is a nine-year-old boy with asthma. With the onset of the pandemic, his school shut down. Emiliano was nevertheless infected during an ad hoc *play group arranged by several families who were "isolating together."*

School-aged children are relatively spared from the potentially devastating effects of COVID-19 in older adults and infants. However, those with asthma or other preexisting medical conditions such as diabetes are at higher risk for severe physiological symptoms, as are children with preexisting neuropsychiatric conditions, such as attention deficit hyperactivity disorder (ADHD), anxiety disorders, autism, and others. The reason for the higher risk of severe COVID-19 symptoms with neuropsychiatric conditions is not clear. However, we know that COVID-19 has neurological effects on the brain, which is integrated into every physiological system. As these children already have neurological challenges, the added burden of the virus may make it even more difficult for their central nervous systems (CNS) to work with and help manage other body systems. For instance, gastrointestinal (GI) symptoms, which are common in children with ADHD, anxiety disorders, and autism, are also common in COVID-19 and may be more severe in these children. This makes sense, as the gastrointestinal system is highly enervated.

Emiliano is having great difficulty breathing. Although his asthma medications help somewhat, in between bouts he is anticipating having more trouble breathing. He develops rapid and shallow breathing, tingling in his fingers and nose, tunnel vision, and fear of impending death, symptoms which are concerning for a panic attack. Emiliano is terrified of separating from his mother, who herself needs to work to support the family.

Puberty

Raven is a proud autistic 12-year-old who chose their own name. They were very active in the school student council, persistently lobbying for equitable treatment of all students, most recently improving the inclusion of all students in their theater productions.

Pubertal children are also generally less prone to severe symptoms of COVID-19 unless there are other co-occurring medical conditions, including neuropsychiatric conditions, similar to school-age children. The impact of pubertal changes on mood, including irritability, depression, anxiety, and fatigue, and of body changes, such as gangly growth and a temporary increase in clumsiness, may add to the discomfort associated with viral infections such as COVID-19.

Raven has been experimenting with dressing in various ways to reflect their exploration of gender identity. But since this has relied on peer feedback, the temporary school closure left them without the interaction they needed. Although Raven's school has now reopened, they want to stick to safe rules for preventing COVID-19 infection. They feel obligated to wear a mask and to maintain social distance from other students, which leaves them feeling even more isolated.

Adolescence

Maeve, a 17-year-old high school senior, was active in the math club and played competitive lacrosse. At the beginning of the pandemic, Maeve started online clubs, kept up with her work, and delivered meals to the sick and isolated.

Teens are often asymptomatic carriers of COVID-19. Their risks have more to do with their increased mobility in society and their increased likelihood of spreading the infection to more vulnerable people and populations. Co-occurring conditions can nevertheless render adolescents more vulnerable to severe forms of the illness, and in particular, teens with postural orthostatic tachycardia syndrome (POTS) may be even more prone to dizziness and fainting.

Maeve has returned home from her second year of college. She dwells on her losses, including a lack of senior year activities in high school and having to spend her first year of college online. She was glad to finally go away to college, but now her all-night studying has triggered hypomanic episodes. She has periods of rapid speech and euphoric mood that alternate with crying and non-suicidal cutting of her thighs.

Organs Affected by COVID-19

Several organ systems are affected by COVID-19. There are a few unique considerations in children and adolescents.

Brain

COVID-19 can infect the central nervous system, which is made up of the brain and spinal cord. When the brain is infected, it can affect many skills – mathematics, reading, and even understanding the emotions of other people. Infection can impact both academic and social functioning. Teens aiming for better grades may become frustrated or may suffer from more misunderstandings with friends, family, and others.

Lungs

Most people think of COVID-19 as a disease primarily of the lungs, much like influenza. However, COVID-19 infection is actually more like respiratory syncytial virus (RSV) in that it is more likely to destroy lung tissue, which may take months or even longer to recover. COVID-19 infection may leave the person with a reduced capacity for air exchange. While most children and teens seem to fare well and return to sports and other activities relatively soon, some may lose their previous level of ability, which can be discouraging. This then places them at a greater risk for developing depression. They may also discontinue their previous activities.

Gastrointestinal (GI) System

COVID-19 can affect digestion and may result in cramping, diarrhea, and other pain and discomfort. In children, GI discomfort can lead to distraction from studies, poor sleep, and embarrassment surrounding their toileting needs. It may also be associated with the onset or worsening of irritable bowel syndrome (IBS) or Crohn's disease. GI symptoms can cause significant distress in children and teens. It may become part of a vicious cycle of anxiety and discomfort, in which the child or teen fears the discomfort and then becomes even more sensitive to it.

Heart

More data is accumulating to suggest that COVID-19 infection can have acute and ongoing impacts on the heart. Infection can lead to reduced heart efficiency or, at its worst, dangerous cardiomyopathy, which can affect the heart's ability to pump blood effectively. In children and teens who are often driven to be active, there may be a greater risk for cardiac damage when they return to physical activities too soon. Parents may be in the unenviable position of wanting their children, recovering from COVID-19 infection, to get back to school and activities. At the same time, they may be alarmed when their full-throttle children are unable or unwilling to understand the importance of parental admonitions to take it slowly when going back to physical activity.

Fatigue

While COVID-19 infection is often less severe in children and teens than in other age groups, many children and teens experience a profound and extended period of fatigue, which renders them unable to focus once they return to school. This may have a negative impact on their grades and their academic trajectory. It may also result in more social isolation due to their lack of energy to connect with their friends. The mid-teen years are the peak of the natural drive for socialization, and therefore, the subject of so many movies and TV shows. When COVID-19 infection is accompanied by fatigue, it may rob teens of this typical and intense experience of passion for people and important causes. Fatigue can be particularly problematic for autistic children and teens, for whom we often try to facilitate social connections during this vulnerable developmental period.

Long COVID

Most research on Long COVID is in adults (see Chapter 8). Still, many youths continue to suffer from a combination of symptoms that persist after their COVID-19 infection is no longer present. This Long COVID syndrome can take a variety of forms, including mood symptoms, anxiety, fatigue, headache, insomnia, dizziness, and cognitive problems (Agnihotri et al. 2023). Additional

Long COVID symptoms include shortness of breath, joint pain, blood clots, heart palpitations, and gastrointestinal problems. A 2023 consensus panel (Melamed et al. 2023) with a range of experts including neuropsychiatry published by the American Academy of Physical Medicine and Rehabilitation (AAPM&R) concluded that Long COVID is not caused by mental illness but needs to be taken as a separate and serious condition. The United States Centers for Disease Control (CDC) reports that about 7% of US adults and 1.3% of children experience Long COVID (Adjaye-Gbewonyo et al. 2023). Still, the definition of Long COVID is not precise and researchers continue to study this phenomenon in order to find better ways to prevent it or treat it. A recent study in adults shows that treating the acute COVID-19 infection with Paxlovid may reduce the risk of Long COVID (Xie et al. 2023). One study found that serotonin levels are lower in adults with Long COVID, which may point to the use of serotonin-specific reuptake inhibitor (SSRI) type antidepressants for the treatment of Long COVID (Wong et al. 2023).

What Are the Neuropsychiatric Problems Related to COVID-19, and How Can We Treat These Problems?

In a study of mental health problems during the COVID-19 pandemic (Dimitrov et al. 2023), researchers found that youth without preexisting mental health problems had greater increases in "externalizing" symptoms, such as irritability and overactivity. Due to the impact of COVID-19 on the brain, the infection can bring on a wide range of neuropsychiatric conditions for the first time. These are reviewed below, roughly in order from most common to least common:

Thinking: Executive Function

You should expect your child or teen to have more trouble focusing and concentrating after COVID-19 infection. This can last for weeks to months beyond the end of the initial infection and can become worse when your child or teen has greater demands in their academic work (for example, at finals time), or when there are other stressors in their lives.

We would expect more diagnoses of ADHD during the pandemic. While it does seem that the demand for ADHD medications has increased as result of the pandemic (which contributes in part to the nationwide shortage of stimulants in the US), one study of the records of the Kaiser Permanente managed care system (Yedia et al. 2023) found that actual requests for behavioral screening evaluations for ADHD did not change during the pandemic. This may be due to the overall shortage of mental health services during this time.

Executive function is a big topic, but one way to think about it is how your brain organizes information to solve the problems of everyday life. The most basic requirement for this to happen is to have enough ability to pay attention to your surroundings and figure out what is important to focus on. Many parents are familiar with ADHD. In ADHD, children, teens, and even adults may have trouble focusing and concentrating – they may have difficulty reading and absorbing written information, or paying attention to the road while driving. They may also be easily distracted by things that are unimportant.

These problems create additional difficulties with other parts of executive function like problem-solving. Problem-solving involves identifying a problem, coming up with a plan to solve the problem, working out the steps in the plan, following through with the steps, and adjusting the plan when things inevitably unfold differently than expected. Each of these steps has an additional level of complexity, and problem-solving may fail at any stage. COVID-19 infection puts physiological stress on the brain that makes each of these steps more difficult. In some ways, a bout of COVID-19 is like having a "minor" head injury. Although the person is not knocked out, they may experience difficulty in many areas – from basic attention and reading, to a loss of their complex math skills, to their complex ability to read social cues from others. Cognitive problem-solving and social problem-solving become harder. This is frustrating for the child or teen and can lead to significant academic and social problems.

Managing Cognitive Problems Related to COVID-19 Infection

When a child or teen has trouble thinking and struggles with mathematics, reading, or writing during or after COVID-19 infection, the most important thing for parents, adults, and other caregivers to remember is to give the child time to recover without excessive demands. The child or teen is likely to feel frustrated or alarmed over their diminished cognitive abilities. It is important to balance support for rest with support for testing the level of recovery to avoid either unduly extending the period of inability or creating demands that are only discouraging. It is best to gently and periodically test these out together and monitor together both their ability to do or understand a bit more and their capacity to extend the amount of time they can concentrate before becoming fatigued. Over time, whether weeks or months, the child or teen usually recovers. Some children or teens will meet criteria for ADHD or for specific learning disorders. These may be approached in their usual manner, with an emphasis on non-pharmacological approaches and supports. This should be done while keeping in mind that the child or teen may improve or recover at a far more rapid rate than would be seen in situations where the problem was not due to COVID-19 as a cause or exacerbating agent.

Emotions: Limbic Function

One important region of the brain affected by COVID-19 infection is the limbic system. We can artificially divide the brain into "thinking" and "feeling" parts that communicate. One important structure is the amygdala, which plays a very large role in how we control our emotions. The amygdala can be overreactive, allowing very intense emotional reactions. Conversely, it may be underreactive, leading to inadequate responses to important situations, such as an inability to comfort a friend in pain. COVID-19 infection can change the reactivity of the amygdala in either direction, leading to a child or teen who is even more irritable than usual in some developmental stages, such as toddlerhood and early teens. Some children and teens become less reactive and seemingly less caring about others (like how older teens may treat their parents as they start to separate and individuate).

Irritability is a symptom seen in the context of the child, the family, and the circumstances around the family, which includes the COVID-19 pandemic. Researchers who studied the rise and fall of irritability in children and teens during the COVID-19 pandemic (Cheung et al. 2023) found that children who were younger tended to be more irritable, as well as youths whose parents were more anxious.

Parents may notice a change of emotional reactivity in one direction or the other due to the virus that may last for weeks or months that may lead to a negative impact on their relationships with family and friends. As parents, although it does not mean that an irritable teen will not get a talking-to after a mean-spirited remark, it does mean that parents might be more effective in guiding their teen if they don't take such remarks personally. It may be helpful to think that it is the virus (not your teen) that is talking. Your kind concern will probably be easier for them to hear, even though they may still respond in an abrasive manner.

Some parents wonder whether these changes in emotional reactivity can be helpful. The answer is yes, sometimes. Some children who are overactive and overreactive at baseline tend to become calm when they become ill with a typical head cold. This observation sometimes guides treatment. We sometimes try medications, such as guanfacine, that reduce the "fight or flight" part of the nervous system to treat anxiety, ADHD, and other problems. If the child tends to become calm when they are falling ill, it may be a sign that the medication is helpful. However, if the child becomes cranky when they are falling ill, we might avoid this medication strategy. With COVID-19 infection, we might also see children or teens become less reactive, similar to their response to any viral illness. This is probably rare, however, because the other problems of thinking (see *Thinking/ Executive Function* above) due to COVID-19 are likely to be quite frustrating or depressing. Similarly, if a child who is usually too calm and disconnected becomes more sensitive and aware of those around them, we might be inclined to welcome the change. Indeed, with some autistic children, it is in some ways easier to help a child who is irritable to become more connected and to engage in problem-solving than a child who is emotionally distant. However, if it happens that following COVID-19 infection, a child who was not very connected and engaged is more so now because they are more easily upset or annoyed, parents may benefit from good coaching. They will need to learn how to negotiate with the child in a productive manner that leads to the child's increased ability to problem-solve. This can help break the cycle of nonproductive arguing.

Managing Emotional Upset Related to COVID-19

The initial approach to managing COVID-19-related irritability and mood lability in children and teens is non-pharmacological. The next sections will lay out how parents and caregivers can first try to work with the child or teen to understand the reasons why the child or teen is upset and to address those reasons first. After this, the following sections will describe how to then use relationship-based approaches to help the person calm down and problem-solve to manage their upset.

Decoding Upset

It is often helpful to use the HALT mnemonic as a starting point: Hungry, Angry, Lonely, Tired. The feeling of hunger can cause upset, often termed "hangry." Like with any significant physiologically stressful event, children and teens who are in the throes of COVID-19 or in a recovery phase may be more sensitive to hunger (MacCormack and Lindquist 2019). The word hungry is also a reminder to consider other physical discomfort, such as constipation or pain.

Angry refers to any kind of frustration, often related to disappointment over expectations. For instance, if a teen is still recovering from COVID-19 infection, and she expects to be allowed to sleep in but needs to stop by school to pick up assignments, she may react with upset or anger. This could be due to the stress on her body from the virus itself – the fever, aches, and subtle changes in cell function – and the time it takes to recover. Parents may need to be more proactive in planning the school visit the day before. They can consider options such as having the teen go later in the day or receiving the information by phone. Generally, it is helpful to say the following out loud while planning: "We have a plan, but no plan works out exactly like we expect. So, let's see what happens and figure out what to do when the plan comes out differently than what we expect." Repeating this idea over time will build a sense of collaborative exploration that can diminish the tendency to react due to unmet expectations.

Lonely refers to a range of emotional reactions. During the pandemic, loneliness may stem from isolation from friends, but also sadness and grief related to the impact of COVID-19 on the life of a child or teen. The kinds of sadness will be detailed in the next section, but for our purposes here, it is important to know that emotional upset is often related to sadness. The best response to loneliness is typically to empathize with the child or teen while trying to avoid sounding patronizing. For instance, it is often better to say: "It sounds so hard to be so tired" rather than "You are tired because of the virus." The more empathic approach is less likely to be met with intense emotional reactions.

Tired refers to the profound fatigue that many children and teens experience with COVID-19 infection and its aftermath. While Tired comes last in the HALT mnemonic, it might be the most common reason for emotional upset in this setting. Any child or teen is prone to emotional upset when they are tired for any reason, and the presence or recent infection with COVID-19 can make this more intense. Rest really is the antidote to fatigue, but exercise is also important to improve stamina. Recent research confirmed what we thought, i.e. that children and teens exercised less during the pandemic (by about 17 minutes per day). They also increased screen time by about 84 minutes (a 52% increase) (Madigan 2023). Considering that we already recommend about 15–20 minutes of moderate to vigorous exercise daily for children and teens, this represents a loss equivalent to the entire daily recommended dose of exercise. Work with your child or teen to balance ample rest with periods of physical activity, gently working to gradually increase endurance over time. Good nutrition is also important here. Children and teens under the stress of the illness may crave simple sugars and carbohydrates, as well as fatty and salty foods. Try to help them balance their diet to include lean proteins, fruits and vegetables. Do not exclude fat since some fat is important for building cell membranes and other functions. Hydration is also important. Children and teens who are ill or recovering from COVID-19 might not feel thirsty, but they require more than their usual hydration to recover. Tell them to drink enough water until their urine runs clear (not yellow).

There are many additional reasons for upset beyond HALT, but this mnemonic is meant to help you start thinking about the reasons behind a child or teen's actions instead of reacting to them with punishments or other consequences. Other reasons a child or teen may be upset include:

- Sensory processing problems: light or sight, sound, touch, taste or flavor, smell, internal sensations of position in space, motion, and internal discomfort. A child may experience oversensitivity, undersensitivity, or a combination of sensations. One child might be too sensitive to light, another might be upset over the loss of the ability to taste foods, and a third child might be more sensitive to sound but not bothered by their own loud cries.

- Motor function and motor tone: Children and teens who have been infected with COVID-19 may have lower motor tone – that is, it is harder for them to do activities such as sitting up in a chair. For them, some activities seem to require a tremendous amount of energy and result in fatigue and irritability. Their coordination may also be impacted, with the child or teen more prone to stumbling or spilling, which contributes to frustration and upset.
- Communication: We all experience some communication misunderstandings in everyday life. However, children and teens with COVID-19 infection, or in recovery from the virus, may be more prone to misunderstand neutral or even positive statements as negative or even threatening, resulting in emotional upset. They may also have more trouble expressing their experiences and asking for what they need. It is important to remain calm and patient with the child or teen and either give them more space, or remain present and gently supportive. Parents and caregivers deserve support to help them stay calm, whether from good friends or professionals. One study found that a specially designed mindfulness app was helpful during the COVID-19 pandemic for parents and caregivers from communities with fewer resources, including access to care and parent coaching (Wei et al. 2023).
- Visual systems: We are visual animals. It is worth thinking about how we act when we are ill or under stress. We might, as with other forms of communication, misinterpret neutral facial expressions as negative or criticizing. This happens with children and teens who are fighting or recovering from COVID-19 infection. They may also experience bright light or busy visual settings, such as shopping centers, as distressing. The typical emotional reactivity related to the use of video games may also be worse, which may be at least partially related to cognitive difficulties. Calm care and reduced visual stimulation or complexity can help with upset related to visual system problems related to COVID-19 infection. That said, in a study of gaming habits of adolescent males, researchers identified a significant protective factor for mental health challenges and loneliness – using videogaming as a portal for social interaction (Maiyuran et al. 2023).
- Cognitive (thinking) difficulties: These are mentioned here for completeness. If a child or teen is emotionally upset, you might consider whether they are upset because the virus or recovery process is making it harder for them to think. See the section above on *Cognition* for more ideas on how to help your upset child or teen due to difficulties thinking after COVID-19 infection.

When working with a child or teen to understand and address their reasons for emotional upset, use a relationship-based strategy to help your child or teen feel better understood and to feel emotionally steady. This means staying present when your child or teen is upset and not ignoring them or using time-outs. Try to stay calm and listen to your child or teen. Empathize with them. It may take some time for your child or teen to settle down, and you may need to do this many times, and that's ok. Their experience of having you stay calm and present over many difficult moments will help them become more resilient over time. They will then be better able to tolerate difficult moments in the future.

Once your child or teen is calmer, you may be able to team up with them to better think about and address their reasons for being upset. These techniques can be used for all children and teens who are upset, but I am putting them here so that parents and caregivers will have them handy. Listen carefully to the child or teen's concerns and *join* their concerns, at least to the extent of offering authentic empathy: "That sounds so difficult." Work on ideas to try to improve the situation: "I wonder what you'd like to try to make this better." If you have an idea, offer it as a possibility, not an instruction: "Sometimes when people are tired and take a rest, they feel a lot better. You might want to try it. It's up to you." It is important to give your child or teen the option[1] of whether to take a suggestion because if they choose to do it (whether it is their idea or yours), they will have a sense that they are taking action (agency), and this builds their confidence that they can solve problems. If you direct them to try an idea, this often backfires. The child or teen becomes more dependent on you to tell them what to do. They may also defy you and refuse to try anything. In either situation they will not build self-confidence in problem-solving. Your job is to regroup and keep trying. Your gentle persistence in supporting your child or teen to work on problem-solving will pay off. Some things will work out, and some won't – but this in itself is an important lesson that will help your child or teen learn to persevere: "You win some and you lose some."

Sadness: Loss, Trauma, Grief, Guilt, Shame, Depression, and Other Mood Problems

COVID-19 has brought tremendous grief and loss to our lives, wherever in the world we live. We usually think of loss as having to do with the death of a family member or friend. Many children and teens have lost grandparents and other elders. They may have also lost parents, especially if their parents were unable to avoid exposure to the virus before the advent of vaccines. COVID-19 has disproportionally affected people engaged in services or jobs that require in-person work. For many, the loss of a parent or other caregiver happened during a time of trauma. In some places these losses were complicated by war or displacement due to other factors, creating a complex trauma where the child or teen experienced

---

1 Giving children or teens the power to try or not try ideas does not means suspending all rules and limits. There are times when they need to get up, times to shut down electronics, times to go to school, safety rules, etc. Give your child options to try ideas within these limits and boundaries. The limits and boundaries help them learn what they can and cannot do, and the freedom within those limits and boundaries gives them the space to build their emotional resilience and problem-solving skills.

overwhelming stress and had to endure it without the help of their parent or caregiver. Children may experience a range of symptoms in these situations (Ford et al. 2022), including the loss of control of their emotions or a regression in bodily functions (for example, loss of toilet training), as well as problems with attention and behavioral control. They may also feel negatively about themselves and experience difficulties connecting with other people. Children may experience other losses, too, such as missing sports or being at school. These losses can create deep sadness. Children of any age (even infants) can experience loss. Common symptoms include:

- Withdrawal from interacting
- Changes in appetite, up or down
- Poor concentration
- Changes in energy: sluggish fatigue or agitation
- Loss of emotional control, such as tantrums
- Loss of bodily control, such as toileting accidents

One study (Wergeland et al. 2023) found that the need to put off important events was the highest rated stressor for youth during the COVID-19 pandemic and that the severity of "internalizing symptoms," such as sadness and anxiety, was related to how well the child or teen was able to use active coping strategies.

Normal non-pathological reactions to loss (aka grief) usually diminish over weeks or months, and children and teens resume connecting with others, playing, and functioning well. One group (Ahmadi et al. 2023) developed a brief and effective treatment for use in psychiatric emergency settings for COVID-19-related grief. This intervention uses several "10-minute behavioral modules, over two consecutive days, on self-compassion, engagement, resilience, gratitude for traumatic/loss reminders with emotion regulation, distress tolerance, and safety planning skills."

However, some children and teens are impacted by loss in ways that are more damaging. For instance, a teen may experience intense guilt if they believe that they infected an elderly relative who then died. A child might believe they are bad because bad things happened, experiencing intense shame about who they are, a feeling that presents a challenge for parents and mental health professionals. While it may seem illogical for a child to feel this way, and perhaps it is illogical, it is nevertheless true: many children tend to blame themselves for the things that go wrong in their lives – whether it is a divorce, a death, or a lost game of Candy Land (a game of chance).

Beyond grief and loss, in some children and teens COVID-19 infection may be associated with the onset of an episode of depression. Depressive disorders occur when sadness or depressed mood interferes with the child's ability to function at school or home, often affecting a child's ability to interact with friends. Depression is more profound and persists longer than the few weeks or months of a grief reaction. It is often marked by a number of possible symptoms, many of which overlap with reactions to loss, including:

- Feeling negative about oneself, "I am bad, defective, etc.," the world, and the future
- Sleep can be disturbed – either sleeping less or sleeping more, waking up a lot, or having very deep sleep
- Loss of interest in favorite activities
- Changes in energy, including less energy and fatigue, or agitation and overactivity
- Poor concentration
- Changes in appetite, either increased or decreased
- Some children develop suicidal thinking.

If you are concerned about these symptoms in your child or teen, try to take them for an urgent mental health assessment.

Does COVID-19 infection itself cause depression? A recent report that looked at 53 studies (meta-analysis) covering a total of 40 807 children and teens in 12 countries found substantial increases in depression among youth related to COVID-19 infection, especially among girls and adolescents (Madigan et al. 2023). Depression is common in most families, and a family history of depression places a person at higher risk of depression. Stressful events routinely trigger depressive episodes (Richter-Levin and Xu 2018) – whether it is a divorce, a move, or a global pandemic with lockdown. Whether the viral infection itself can do this is a matter of conjecture, but since some depressive episodes occur in association with most viral illnesses (especially Epstein-Barr virus, the virus that causes mononucleosis), it is a fair bet that COVID-19 can do the same. There is evidence that COVID-19 is associated with increases in suicidal thinking in older children (ages 8–12) and in teenagers, especially teen girls (Korczak et al. 2022). A study by Schindel et al. (2023) found that up to 15% of youths screened positive for suicidality across a variety of clinics in the US. Suicide is the second leading cause of death for youth ages 10–24 in the US and the rates have been rising over the past two decades. For parents and caregivers, this means that all youths ages 12 and up, and those between the ages of 8 and 12 with any suspicion of depression or suicidality should be screened for suicidal thinking using developmentally appropriate screening methods (American Academy of Pediatrics 2023).

According to one study, the numbers of psychiatric hospitalizations for children and teens for overdose rose during the COVID-19 pandemic as well (Hsu et al. 2023). However, a review that looked at multiple research studies (Lee et al. 2023) found mixed results, with more studies showing a decrease in suicide attempts in youth during the pandemic. The researchers attributed this to greater availability of telehealth and awareness of mental health needs overall during the pandemic. Suicidality is typically associated with depression; however, in youth it is also commonly associated with bipolar illness, substance abuse, conduct disorder (when children have little regard for rules or for the rights of others), and in adjustment disorder (a strong reaction to a big life change). In a study comparing suicide attempts before and during the COVID-19 pandemic (Gracia et al. 2023), researchers found that before the pandemic, youths having a suicide attempt tended to have preexisting mental health problems and current adjustment disorders or conduct disorders. By contrast, youths seen for suicide attempts during the pandemic did not tend to have preexisting mental health problems, but they experienced recent depression or anxiety disorders.

Other mood conditions may also be related to COVID-19 infection. Prolonged grief disorder was recently added to the Diagnostic and Statistical Manual of Mental Disorders, Fifth Edition, Text Revision (DSM-5TR) (American Psychiatric Press 2022) to include people who have a form of grief that is not getting in the way of functioning the way that a depressive disorder does. However, it lasts far longer (years or decades), longer than typical grief. Children and teens with COVID-19- related losses may have now experienced several years of grief. Another mood disorder related to COVID-19 infection is bipolar disorder. Children and teens who experience depressive episodes at earlier ages or with greater severity are at far greater risk of developing bipolar disorder. Bipolar disorder is a collection of conditions where the person experiences depressive phases as well as manic or near-manic phases of increased energy, irritability, perhaps euphoria, and even psychosis. Once a child or teen has both depressive and manic (or near manic) episodes, the depression that appeared first is often thought of (in retrospect) as the initial phase of the bipolar condition, rather than a depression that turned into bipolar disorder. What is the COVID-19 connection? Similar to unipolar depression, the onset of bipolar disorder is often associated with a stressor. This may include the physiological stress of COVID-19, especially as the virus tends to affect the brain. It may be the trigger in a child or teen with a genetic vulnerability to developing bipolar disorder.

Treatment of Sadness, Grief, and Depression in Youth Related to COVID-19 Infection

As with other forms of sadness, the sadness that occurs with COVID-19 infection may respond to non-pharmacological treatments and, at times, also to medications. Use the relationship-based approach described in the previous section as a starting point, helping your child or teen feel calm and regulated. Then support them in a process of problem-solving that gives them maximum choices to try out ideas. Exercise, activity, social opportunities, and proper nutrition are important parts of any approach to depression. It is also critical to address sleep problems, which are often associated with emotional disturbances, especially depression, during the COVID-19 pandemic (Gauthier-Gagné et al. 2023). Many families are aware of sleep hygiene measures (avoid lying in bed awake, get up at the same time every morning [even on weekends], avoid electronics in the evening, etc.) However, parents need to remember to specifically problem-solve and plan with their child or teen on how to implement these ideas to really change their sleep patterns.

Specific therapies, such as cognitive behavioral therapy (CBT), play therapy, and insight-oriented therapy, are often helpful. Therapists may need to address concerns specific to the COVID-19 situation, such as feelings of sadness and loss over difficulties with thinking, or shame or guilt related to the impact of the virus on loved ones. When symptoms are severe, and particularly when they are persistent or include suicidal thinking, it is important to consider the use of antidepressant medications. These should be prescribed by professionals who know the important limitations and side effects of these medications in their use with children. For the most part, only a few medications, such as fluoxetine and sertraline, have good research of efficacy in children and teens for depression. Some children and teens can become hypomanic or manic on antidepressants, and although antidepressants may be lifesaving when they reduce suicidal thinking, about 1% of children and teens report new suicidal thinking while taking antidepressant medications. Family members and clinicians should therefore watch for this rare but important side effect.

Anxiety and related disorders: These include generalized anxiety disorder (GAD), separation anxiety disorder, specific phobias (including agoraphobia), obsessive-compulsive disorder (OCD), and post-traumatic stress disorder (PTSD).

COVID-19 is an infection that affects the body and has specific effects on the brain. It is an unpleasant experience at the least, and devastating at its worst. So, it is no surprise that children can be worried about COVID-19: afraid of getting it, afraid of others getting it, afraid of the death it may bring, and afraid of other losses too. These worries can spread to other fears, including a generalized fear of the world, of the existence of other illnesses, of making friends (who might get sick), and of any change. When these worries affect a child or teen's functioning for many months, they might have a generalized anxiety disorder (GAD).

Separation anxiety disorder is also understandable in the context of COVID-19. A child (or teen) may become ill and frightened to be separated from family members. This is particularly poignant given the experiences of many families during the height of the pandemic when they (or relatives) might be ill and separated from family to try to stop the spread of the virus. Even now, it is common for families to isolate members who are infected, or suspected to be at risk, of COVID-19 infection. Children or teens may be at risk for separation anxiety disorder due to other prior experiences of illness or loss, or it may be their preexisting style of relating with their parents or other caregivers. The stress of the illness itself, and its impact on the brain, make emotional regulation more difficult and can compound the anxiety. Although the large meta-analysis (Madigan et al. 2023) found only a mild increase in the numbers of children and teens experiencing all anxiety disorders associated with COVID-19, certainly the children who had anxiety disorders triggered by COVID-19 suffered substantially.

Some children, teens, and adults develop specific phobias related to COVID-19, such as fear of enclosed spaces (a type of claustrophobia), fear of going out of doors (agoraphobia), and fear of being with schoolmates (a special kind of school phobia).

All these anxiety conditions are treatable with therapy (including CBT, play therapy, and insight-oriented therapy) and can be tailored to the context of COVID-19, with the goal or reducing the anxiety to a point where the child or teen is comfortable enough to resume everyday levels of function. See Box 1 for more on teletherapy. If needed, medications such as fluoxetine, sertraline, and other SSRI medications have the best evidence for efficacy for anxiety disorders in children and teens. In general, these medications are more effective for anxiety than they are for depression. Even so, the neurologic impact of a COVID-19 infection may make treatment more difficult because the child or teen is having more trouble thinking and managing their emotions.

Another condition that is sometimes considered different from the other anxiety disorders is OCD. OCD in children and teens is characterized by obsessions (for example, about germs) and compulsions (for example, too much handwashing). Children in particular often have less insight into the irrational nature of their obsessions and compulsions. But let's back up a bit. While it makes sense that if a child is fated to have OCD, and if there is COVID-19 around, the child

---

Box 11.1   Teletherapy

- Some children and teens do really well with online therapy.
- Some children and teens do not pay attention during online therapy.
- Sometimes seeing the home is very helpful – the layout, the toys, the tech.
- Privacy is important in online therapy: Who is in the room? Who can hear?
- Boundaries are important in online therapy: appropriate clothing, appropriate home setting.

might have their obsessions and compulsions focus on COVID-19. But can COVID-19 cause OCD? That is not clear, although like for other neuropsychiatric conditions, it may be that COVID-19 makes it harder for a child or teen who is prone to OCD to avoid falling into the repetitive patterns of thinking that are associated with brain changes in OCD. What about treating OCD if it is related to COVID-19? Treatment of OCD is in some ways quite different than treatment of other anxiety disorders. The goal in OCD treatment is not so much to reduce anxiety, but to tolerate anxiety. If we try to stop a person from worrying about, say, germs that cause COVID-19, we are really trying to convince them that there is no risk at all. But this is impossible, as there is always risk. Efforts to eliminate the anxiety do not work very well. But if we learn to accept some risk, we are more able to join the world without the obsessions or doing the compulsions. The other difference in OCD treatment with children and teens is that if the child or teen does not have the insight that their obsession or compulsion is irrational, we need to use more family-oriented approaches to treatment. These may teach parents and other caregivers how to help the child resist compulsions and combat obsessions and to have the strength not to try to reassure the child and inadvertently increase their worries. Medication is often very helpful in the treatment of OCD. When SSRI medications are used for OCD, the dosages that are effective are generally higher than those used for other anxiety disorders or depression.

We mentioned complex trauma in the section on loss. However, we also need to remember that the experience of COVID-19 for children and teens, from the illness itself (when it is severe) to the impact on their families in terms of health, finances, and even where they live, on school and community, and the images on social media, can be overwhelming and frankly toxic to the child or teen's emotional health. Children and teens can have acute stress reactions with any combination of irritability, agitation, withdrawal, sadness, and behavioral acting out. The virus itself can make the child or teen more neurologically vulnerable to these stress reactions. And when the reaction lasts a long time, or perhaps comes on later (maybe after a heroic initial period of cooperation and hard work during the initial period of disaster), we call this PTSD. Symptoms of PTSD include a combination of some or all of the following symptoms: intrusive symptoms (for example, nightmares, flashbacks); avoiding things connected to the trauma; changes in thinking or mood; change in energy level or reactivity. The full definition is in the DSM-5TR, but the point is that PTSD has a lot of symptoms, it can be difficult to treat, and if the person has been recently infected with COVID-19, like with other neuropsychiatric conditions, treatment may be more difficult because the child or teen's brain has to work a lot harder to think about new ideas for understanding the trauma in a more productive way. Specific therapies for PTSD include:

- Trauma-focused cognitive behavioral therapy (TF-CBT)
- Developmental relationship-based play therapy such as DIR-Floortime (which is the Developmental, Individual-differences, and Relationship-based model)
- Child-parent psychotherapy (CPP)
- Parent-child interaction therapy (PCIT)

Medication for PTSD in children and teens is less reliably helpful. However, many medications can be tried, such as central alpha agonists (guanfacine, prazosin) for general upset and to reduce nightmares, and SSRIs such as fluoxetine for associated anxiety and sadness.

Substance Use

Children and teens who are under stress are at a higher risk for using substances to feel better. Some youths use marijuana and/or alcohol, others use nicotine, and fewer use other drugs of abuse. It is important to note that children and teens who smoke or vape have more problems with respiratory function to begin with, which places them at higher risk of severe respiratory symptoms if they become infected with COVID-19 (Bhatia et al. 2021).

There are no data that link COVID-19 infection with the beginning of new substance use disorders in teens. In fact, the overall rates of alcohol use in teens decreased from 29.2% to 22.7% between 2019 and 2021 and from 21.7% to 15.8% for marijuana use during the same period. However, the use of inhalants increased, perhaps due to the isolation from other substances of abuse (Hoots et al. 2023). Still, among teens who used substances, about 35% used more than one drug of abuse during the pandemic. This makes the treatment of substance use disorders more challenging in those who are using.

The stress of the COVID-19 pandemic, with its isolation and disruption of typical social development, and its associated anxiety, depression, and trauma, all combine to add to the risk that some youth will start earlier or use more substances than they otherwise might have if they did not have access to substances. Substance use usually gives brief relief followed by worsening of distress, which leads to more substance use and interferes with efforts to address the distress more directly. Treatment of substance use problems in youth, whether or not related to COVID-19, is usually more effective when there is a family-based approach that includes motivational interviewing (helping the child or teen weigh the risks and benefits of using substances and eventually planning to reduce or stop using), psychotherapy, and sometimes the off-label use of medications such as bupropion (an antidepressant) to reduce cravings. If the substance use is severe or persistent, more intensive treatment will be needed, such as intensive outpatient, partial hospital, or perhaps residential treatment.

Eating Disorders

Eating disorders in children and teens, such as anorexia nervosa (AN), increased in the first wave of the COVID-19 pandemic (Dimitropoulos 2023). These cases seem to be different from pre-pandemic cases in that they were less severe and less likely to be complicated by additional psychiatric conditions (Bracké et al. 2023). Pandemic-related cases of AN also had less restoration of weight, which might be due to less effective treatment due to the restrictions imposed by the pandemic.

Treatment of eating disorders in youth often uses in-person family therapy and group therapies. It is therefore possible that treatment does not work as well if therapy is conducted online. Some people with eating disorders, especially AN, require lifesaving in-patient treatment, even during a pandemic. Still, another study (Vaccarro et al. 2023) compared cases of AN of similar severity before and during the COVID-19 pandemic and found that the cases of AN during the pandemic resolved more quickly. It appears that AN during the pandemic is just a different kind of AN.

Obesity is another problem related to the COVID-19 pandemic, likely related to the more sedentary lifestyles of children and teens, who were less able to participate in physical exercise and other activities (Nicodemo et al. 2021).

What can parents and caregivers do? Here are some resources that might help you understand and address eating disorders in your child or teen:

- Lock, J. and Le Grange, D. (2015). *Help Your Teenager Beat an Eating Disorder*, 2e. New York, NY: Guilford Press.
- National Institutes of Health on eating disorders, with resources for families: http://www.tinyurl.com/chytfe93

Delirium, Psychosis, and Catatonia

When children or teens become ill, they sometimes experience rapid changes in their mood and thinking. They may be thinking fine one minute, then a short time later, they are unaware of where they are, or perhaps who they are, and they may become agitated. This is called delirium and can reflect a dangerous level of physical illness that requires prompt medical assessment.

By contrast, childhood psychoses tend to be rare, but also gradual in their development. Children with psychosis may experience hallucinations (usually auditory, or hearing voices that say mean or cruel things) or delusions. Delusions are fixed, false beliefs, like believing that the government has implanted spies in their kidneys to track their urine for secret messages. While the onset of a psychotic condition is often a surprise, in retrospect there are usually signs that it was coming, often including such things as social withdrawal, a decline in grades, and low-level paranoia. Some psychoses are triggered by outside events, most commonly substance use.

Marijuana doubles the risk, and amphetamines and cocaine are also associated with psychosis. But what about COVID-19? Psychotic episodes can come in association with an acute illness. While the data on COVID-19 are limited, it may be reasonable to assume that rare cases of psychosis might be triggered by the virus. This could be due to the stress of the illness psychologically, or the stress of the illness on the body, particularly with its propensity to go to the brain and reduce the ability of the person to maintain rational thoughts. For more on psychosis as a result of COVID-19 infection, see Chapter 7. Thankfully, it does not appear that the COVID-19 pandemic increased hospitalizations in youth for psychosis (Bruges-Boude et al. 2023). Treatment of psychosis is largely the same, regardless of the trigger: try to reduce the offending triggers (substances, illness, stress) and treat the hallucinations and delusions with supportive therapy and medication.

During the height of the pandemic, Raven had a rapid onset of apparent upset. They were pacing about, unable to say what was wrong, and at times lashing out with their arms in a way that was unfocused. They knocked over lamps and even caught their mother with a painful blow to her arm. An astute doctor diagnosed Raven with catatonia and helped bring the problem under control with lorazepam. Another medication, aripiprazole, was slowly reduced and discontinued since it may have contributed to the problem. The lorazepam was then gradually reduced over many months.

Catatonia can appear as either a stiff, wooden, mute condition, or as a form of incoherent agitation. Rates of catatonia in youth rose with the pandemic (Munez et al. 2023). It is not surprising that catatonia rates increased in youth with intellectual disabilities, a population more prone to catatonia (some researchers believe that autism is closely related to catatonia). Interestingly, there is also an association of catatonia with vaccine-related cardiomyopathy. This might be related to problematic increases in catecholamine hormones, such as dopamine and adrenaline, that can cause muscle cell malfunction. Treatment of catatonia often requires high dosages of lorazepam or other benzodiazepines, or in life-threatening malignant catatonia, electroconvulsive therapy (ECT). Despite fears surrounding ECT, it is very effective for catatonia and has far fewer side effects than many psychotropic medications. However, it can be difficult to obtain, especially for minors.

How Does COVID-19 Affect the Treatment of Preexisting Psychiatric Problems?

The treatment of psychiatric conditions in children and teens is complex. Parents and caregivers, as well as clinicians, can see more comprehensive guides (Feder et al. 2023). While we have discussed the treatment of many of these conditions while talking about neuropsychiatric conditions associated with or caused by COVID-19, here we will talk briefly about treatment from the opposite perspective, that is, how having COVID-19 might affect ongoing treatment of pre-existing neuropsychiatric conditions.

In general, the addition of COVID-19 to any preexisting neuropsychiatric condition in a child or teen will make that condition more complicated and/or harder to treat. This is in part due to the stress that the person is experiencing, which makes it harder for them to stay calm, regulated, and able to think. Fatigue and other symptoms rob the child or teen of their ability to participate in treatment. Additionally, COVID-19 infection on the brain itself makes any psychiatric condition harder to treat. One study (Karlovich et al. 2023) found that youths with preexisting OCD and ADHD were more likely to require admission to a psychiatric hospital for attempting suicide during the pandemic. Therapy as well as medication may have less impact when the child or teen also has COVID-19 or is recovering from the infection. We need to be more supportive, more patient, and sometimes more assertive with our treatments in these situations.

For example, the addition of COVID-19 infection to anxiety disorders often colors those conditions at the same time that it makes them harder to treat. A child with agoraphobia (fear of going out of the house) may now have a reason for avoiding ever leaving the house, i.e. fear of COVID-19 infection or of spreading COVID-19 infection. OCD may take the form of obsessions about COVID-19 exposure. Separation anxiety may have a theme of fear that a parent might become ill with COVID-19. The general treatment will remain the same, with specific adjustments for these COVID-19-related aspects. However, as noted above, therapy may require more time and work, and medications may be less effective. This kind of problem is true for all neuropsychiatric conditions, including but not limited to depression, bipolar disorder, ADHD, eating disorders, autism, substance use, and psychosis.

The loss of in-person schooling created an added burden on students with preexisting psychiatric conditions (Hu and Yamamoto 2023), with 72% reporting more difficulties learning and 83% reporting increased distractibility. The authors found differential impacts of online learning based on diagnostic categories:

> *For subjects with ASD, the common complaint of online school was losing school-based accommodations and structure. For subjects with mood disorders, the common complaint was having less social interaction. For subjects with ADHD, the common complaint was that online school is boring. For subjects with anxiety, the common complaints were being self-conscious about seeing themselves on screen and being stressed academically.*

Another study from Brazil had similar findings, adding that a loss of in-person schooling also impacted sleep, appetite, and emotional behavior (Silva Filho et al. 2023). One might expect that for autistic students the pandemic might have had negative effects due to the loss of in-person social communication supports and care. One study (Cho et al. 2023) found that while there was great variability, most autistic youth did not have a substantial change in their overall level of function over the course of the pandemic. This may be related to the recent finding that the most popular and traditional forms of autism support (traditional Applied Behavioral Analysis) did not have a measurable effect size before the pandemic, in contrast with forms of support that use developmental relationship-based methods, which are only recently growing in availability to families (Sandbank et al. 2020).

How Do Social Determinants such as Race, Culture, Socioeconomic Status, and Climate Change Impact the Psychiatric Problems in Children and Teens Associated with COVID-19 Infection?

While one study found similar rates of depression and anxiety associated with the COVID-19 pandemic in low- and middle-income vs high-income countries (Harrison 2023), families who suffer racial discrimination tended to have a greater burden of mental health challenges during the COVID-19 pandemic (Abdallah 2023). In a separate study, while all racial groups experienced higher rates of depression and anxiety during the COVID-19 pandemic, Asian and Latino youth had higher depression scores relative to other racial groups, reflecting racial injustices depicted in the media for those groups (Nguyen et al. 2023). Karlovich and colleagues found increased rates of psychiatric hospital admissions for suicide attempts in Hispanic and lesbian, gay, bisexual, transgender, and questioning (or queer) (LBBTQ+) youth during the COVID-19 pandemic that remained elevated after the peak of the pandemic and the availability of vaccines (Karlovich et al. 2023). Children and adolescents from minoritized communities also suffered more food insecurity during the pandemic, impacting their health and contributing to their higher levels of distress and risk for mental health problems (Center on Budget and Policy Priorities 2023).

While all families grappled with significant challenges during the COVID-19 pandemic, those from minoritized backgrounds bore a heavier burden of neuropsychiatric effects due to a combination of social determinants of health. People with jobs that allowed remote work could more effectively isolate, contrasting with those compelled to work in public spaces, exposing them and their families to higher infection risks. Apart from specific sectors such as medical, political, and law enforcement professions, a large proportion of those working outside the home belonged to lower socioeconomic strata, with a disproportionate representation of people of color. Minoritized populations faced barriers to healthcare access, including remote medical care and therapy, and encountered fewer online learning opportunities for students. Furthermore, these communities were more likely to live in locations susceptible to severe climate events, compounding their experiences of loss and trauma due to the interplay of these factors.

How Do We Find Neuropsychiatric Problems in Children and Teens Associated with COVID-19 Infection?

When should you worry about your child or teen? Prior to the COVID-19 pandemic, studies showed that about one in five children and teens had a diagnosable neuropsychiatric condition, or, a problem with thinking or emotions that was getting in the way of their functioning (whether at home, at school, or in the community). Since the pandemic, more youth are at risk for these problems (Murthy 2021). All youth ages 8–18 should be screened periodically for anxiety and depression, and all youth ages 12 and up should also be screened for suicidality, whether at regular medical checkups, in school and sports settings, or at home (American Academy of Pediatrics 2023). While some parents may be concerned about upsetting their child by doing these screenings, research shows the opposite. For instance, in one study youths reported having relief from feeling suicidal when they are asked about it (Dazzi et al. 2014). Here is an excellent surgeon general's report on youth and mental health after the pandemic, as well as some screening tests that your primary care healthcare professional can use with your child or teen to see whether they might have a neuropsychiatric problem:

- Protecting Youth Mental Health: The U.S. Surgeon General's Advisory https://www.hhs.gov/sites/default/files/surgeon-general-youth-mental-health-advisory.pdf
- Patient-Reported Outcomes Measurement Information System (PROMIS measures) http://www.tinyurl.com/yuy3yr9f
- Pediatric Symptom Checklist-17 (PSC-17) http://www.tinyurl.com/8km26brm

In general, if your child has anxiety, sadness, learning problems, social difficulties, and especially if your child is talking about suicide, call your primary care clinician. If your country has a national mental health crisis line (such as 988 in the US), you can call this number as well. In general, try to arrange to have your child assessed as soon as possible if you're concerned about neuropsychiatric problems. As there are many kinds of neuropsychiatric problems, including eating disorders, autism, psychosis, and substance use, it is important to seek assessment for any difficulty your child is having that interferes with their function at home, school, or in the community. If you are concerned about trauma in your teen as a result of the pandemic, it helps to know about a screening test for COVID-19-related-PTSD in teens that primary health or mental health clinicians can use to assess your child:

- University of California Los Angeles (UCLA) COVID trauma screen: https://istss.org/getattachment/Clinical-Resources/Assessing-Trauma/UCLA-Posttraumatic-Stress-Disorder-Reaction-Index/UCLA-Brief-COVID-19-Screening-Form-English-4-13-20.pdf

   Also be on the lookout for subtle effects of Long COVID symptoms, such as ongoing fatigue, sadness, anxiety, poor school performance, or more reliance on substances.

What Can We Say to Children and Teens About Neuropsychiatric Problems Associated with COVID-19 Infection?

It is difficult to talk with children and teens about COVID-19. There are so many unknowns – Will it come back worse? When is the next pandemic coming? Will we be prepared? There are also many controversies: Should we mask? Get Vaccinated[2]? Close the schools again? No one has all the right answers. As a parent, caregiver, or teacher, it is important to be truthful, but also kind, when you talk with children or teens about difficult topics. Whether speaking about disaster, war, or the COVID-19 pandemic, there are several principles of Trauma Informed Care. Use these as a guide to help children and teens navigate the pandemic, the neuropsychiatric problems associated with COVID-19 infection, and any other traumatic events in their lives.

- *Safety*: Children and teens cannot stay calm, and they are unable to effectively solve problems and face difficulties when they do not feel safe. Although we can never guarantee safety, we can do our best to help children and teens to feel safe. We should tell them that. But we also have to balance safety with living meaningful lives, as life entails some risk. What do you say to a child or teen? Use "we" language, such as: "We will figure this out together, we will stay part of the world, and we will be careful enough."
- *Provide choices when possible*: As noted above in the section on emotions, children and teens need to make choices in order to become able to solve problems on their own. They should not depend on us to tell them, and we do not want

---

2 While I recognize the controversy surrounding vaccination, as a medical professional who has read the medical literature to date, I recommend vaccinations for children and teens, including COVID-19, influenza, and RSV.

them to defy our repeated requests. If you are talking about an assessment, and you have options, provide them with choices: "Do you want to work first on sadness or on sleeping better?"

- *Work together*: Just like we should not make all decisions for our children and teens, we should not leave them to make all choices. Support their decision-making, and help them work through the pros and cons: "What do you like about this plan for catching up at school? What don't you like about it? Let's make a plan that works for both of us."

- *Be trustworthy*: Sometimes we use ideas about heaven or say, "It's all the way it's supposed to be" to help children and teens cope better with loss. Unfortunately, these ideas do not help children and teens figure out what they can do to cope better. It is more helpful to be direct. Say "He died," and talk about what this means. However, you do not need to give unnecessary and frightening details that could cause harm. This can be especially difficult when people die by suicide. Depending on the developmental level of the child, you might tell them the person died, or you might tell them the person died by suicide. However, you might not talk about the details of how they died. Note that we no longer say "committed suicide" since this inaccurately implies that suicide is more of a choice than part of an illness, and this may create shame in addition to the sorrow that a life was lost to illness. Asking a child or teen about whether they want to die, or whether they have thoughts about killing themselves, does not create the idea in their minds. Rather, asking about these thoughts makes it seven times more likely that they will tell you about their thoughts about killing themselves. Although suicide might be one of the most important topics here, there are many other day-to-day examples of trustworthiness. Establishing trustworthiness helps your child or teen know that you will do your best to feed them, clothe them, house them, and listen to them.

- *Empower*: Ultimately, we hope to help children and teens build resilience. This is their ability to stay calm enough to respond in helpful ways to the difficulties of life without becoming overwhelmed or disabled by these difficulties. I like to say, "We will get through this together." While no one can guarantee any outcomes, we can pledge to stay with our children and teens. Paradoxically, this pledge tends to empower children and teens, enabling them to think critically and take action to face their problems and challenges.

Conclusion

The enduring repercussions of the COVID-19 pandemic on the mental well-being of children and teens are evident, and our journey is ongoing as we adapt to the virus's changes. This adaptation is reflected in the alternative life choices made by our children and teens in response to the pandemic. We see the aftermath of infection in both the neuropsychiatric and physical effects of the virus. It remains crucial to continue to pay attention to the effects of infection, try to prevent reinfections, and manage the psychological and social impacts of COVID-19. As we navigate ongoing challenges, including new global disasters that have emerged since the pandemic's onset, my hope is that a deeper understanding of the effects of COVID-19 infection on children and teens will equip us with the skills to manage the next disasters. Importantly, I hope we can approach these challenges with space for love and joy in our lives.

Learning Points

- COVID-19 infection can profoundly impact the mental health of children and teens, leading to immediate difficulties with thinking and learning.
- Infection can cause or exacerbate numerous mental health conditions, including depression, anxiety, and eating disorders.
- The effects of the infection on the brain may take months for recovery, requiring patience.
- Mental health conditions arising from COVID-19 infection may differ from those unrelated to the virus, requiring distinct approaches to treatment.
- Preexisting mental health conditions are exacerbated and become more challenging to treat in the presence of COVID-19 infection.
- The broader effects of the pandemic, including the infection itself, shape the development of children and teens in ways that need to be considered throughout their lives.

References

Abdallah, M. (2023). The impact of racial discrimination on mental health outcomes of children and adolescents with psychiatric disorders during the COVID-19 pandemic. *Journal of the American Academy of Child & Adolescent Psychiatry* 62 (10): https://doi.org/10.1016/j.jaac.2023.07.669.

Adjaye-Gbewonyo, D., Vahratian, A., Perrine, C.G., and Bertolli, J. (2023). Long COVID in adults: United States, 2022. NCHS Data Brief No. 480 September 2023. https://www.cdc.gov/nchs/data/databriefs/db480.pdf (accessed 16 July 2024).

Agnihotri, O., Champagne-Aves, N., Sivachidambaram, M. et al. (2023). A scoping review of neuropsychiatric sequelae of long COVID-19 in children and adolescents. *Journal of the American Academy of Child & Adolescent Psychiatry* 62 (10): https://doi.org/10.1016/j.jaac.2023.09.021.

Ahmadi, N., Pynoos, R., and Berkowitz, S. (2023). Unmasking and addressing COVID-19-related grief reactions among suicidal youth: pilot evidence for an enhanced psychiatry emergency room safety preventive intervention. *Journal of the American Academy of Child & Adolescent Psychiatry* 62 (10): https://doi.org/10.1016/j.jaac.2023.09.468.

American Academy of Pediatrics. (2023). Suicide: blueprint for youth suicide prevention. https://www.aap.org/en/patient-care/blueprint-for-youth-suicide-prevention (accessed 16 July 2024).

American Psychiatric Association (2022). *Diagnostic and Statistical Manual of Mental Disorders*, Fifthe Text Revision (DSM-5-TR). American Psychiatric Association Publishing https://www.psychiatry.org/psychiatrists/practice/dsm.

Bhatia, G., Chatterjee, B., and Dhawan, A. (2021). Adolescents, drugs, and COVID-19: special challenges during the pandemic. *Indian Journal of Psychological Medicine* 43 (2): 95–99. https://doi.org/10.1177/0253717621988998.

Bracké, K., Steegers, C., Van der Harst, T. et al. (2023). The implications of the COVID-19 pandemic on eating disorder features and comorbid psychopathology among adolescents with anorexia nervosa and matched controls: a comparative cohort design study. https://doi.org/10.1016/j.jaac.2023.09.043.

Bruges-Boude, A., Lynch, S., and Leong, A.W. (2023). Impact of the COVID-19 pandemic on admissions for psychosis in a pediatric population from an urban area of the United States before and during the COVID-19 pandemic. *Journal of the American Academy of Child & Adolescent Psychiatry* 62 (10): https://doi.org/10.1016/j.jaac.2023.09.305.

Center on Budget and Policy Priorities (2023). Tracking the COVID-19 economy's effects on food, housing, and employment hardships. https://www.cbpp.org/research/poverty-and-inequality/tracking-the-covid-19-recessions-effects-on-food-housing-and (accessed 16 July 2024).

Cheung, T., Korczak, D., Tombeau Cost, K., and Anagnostou, E. (2023). Change matters: using latent growth curve model to study the trajectory of irritability in children and youth throughout the COVID-19 pandemic. *Journal of the American Academy of Child & Adolescent Psychiatry* 62 (10): https://doi.org/10.1016/j.jaac.2023.09.206.

Cho, Y.J., Kim, E., Kim, H. et al. (2023). Resilience amid adversity: unraveling the impact of COVID-19 on individuals with ASD. *Journal of the American Academy of Child & Adolescent Psychiatry* 62 (10): https://doi.org/10.1016/j.jaac.2023.09.414.

Dazzi, T., Gribble, R., Wessely, S., and Fear, N.T. (2014). Does asking about suicide and related behaviours induce suicidal ideation? What is the evidence? *Psychological Medicine* 44 (16): 3361–3363. https://doi.org/10.1017/S0033291714001299. Epub 2014 Jul 7. PMID: 24998511.

Dimitropoulos, G. (2023). Changes in the incidence of new-onset anorexia nervosa and atypical anorexia nervosa among youth during the COVID-19 pandemic in

Canada. *Journal of the American Academy of Child & Adolescent Psychiatry* 62 (10): https://doi.org/10.1016/j.jaac.2023.07.646.

Dimitrov, L.V., Bolton, C., Danielson, M.L. et al. (2023). Impact of the COVID-19 pandemic on mental health in a general pediatric sample. *Journal of the American Academy of Child & Adolescent Psychiatry* 62 (10): https://doi.org/10.1016/ j.jaac.2023.09.373.

Feder, J., Tien, E., and Puzantian, T. (2023). *Child Medication Fact Book for Psychiatric Practice*, 2e. Newburyport: Carlat Publishing.

Ford, J., Spinazzola, J., Van der Kolk, K., and Chan, G. (2022). Toward an empirically based Developmental Trauma Disorder diagnosis and semi-structured interview for children: The DTD field trial replication. *Acta Psychiatrica Scandinavica* 145 (6): 628–639. http://www.tinyurl.com/4t5zkpwj.

Gauthier-Gagné, G., Somerville, G., Saha, S., and Gruber, R. (2023). Objective sleep difficulties are associated with emotional responses during the COVID-19 pandemic among typically developing adolescents. *Journal of the American Academy of Child & Adolescent Psychiatry* 62 (10): https://doi.org/10.1016/ j.jaac.2023.09.250.

Gracia-Liso, R., Portella, M.J., Puntí-Vidal, J. et al. (2023). COVID-19 pandemic has changed the psychiatric profile of adolescents attempting suicide. *International Journal of Environmental Research and Public Health* 20 (4): https://doi.org/ 10.1016/j.jaac.2023.09.161.

Gulati, A. and Veliz, S. (2023). Impact of the COVID-19 pandemic on maternal mental health and its relation to mother-infant bonding. *Journal of the American Academy of Child & Adolescent Psychiatry* 62 (10): https://doi.org/10.1016/ j.jaac.2023.09.458.

Harrison, L. (2023). The indirect effects of COVID-19 on child and adolescent mental health in low- and middle-income countries. *Journal of the American Academy of Child & Adolescent Psychiatry* 62 (10): https://doi.org/10.1016/j.jaac.2023.07.647.

Hoots, B.E., Li, J., Hertz, M.F. et al. (2023). Alcohol and other substance use before and during the COVID-19 pandemic among high school students – youth risk behavior survey, United States, 2021. *Morbidity and Mortality Weekly Report (MMWR) Supplements* 72 (1): 84–92. http://dx.doi.org/10.15585/mmwr.su7201a10.

Hsu, C., Angal, C., Alavi, M. et al. (2023). Increase in overdose-related suicide and psychiatric hospitalization in youth presenting to the emergency department for suicidality during the COVID-19 pandemic. *Journal of the American Academy of Child & Adolescent Psychiatry* 62 (10): https://doi.org/10.1016/j.jaac.2023.09.072.

Hu, W. and Yamamoto, H. (2023). The impact of school changes such as online learning and return to in-person learning during the COVID-19 pandemic on children and adolescents with psychiatric disorders. *Journal of the American Academy of Child & Adolescent Psychiatry* 62 (10): https://doi.org/10.1016/ j.jaac.2023.07.671.

Karlovich, G., Kalluru, J., and Ghobrial-Sedky, K. (2023). Youth suicide gestures and attempts throughout the COVID-19 pandemic in a tertiary hospital, Cooper University Hospital in Camden, NJ. *Journal of the American Academy of Child & Adolescent Psychiatry* 62 (10): https://doi.org/10.1016/j.jaac.2023.09.279.

Korczak, D.J., Madigan, S., and Vaillancourt, T. (2022). Data divide – disentangling the role of the COVID-19 pandemic on child mental health and well-being. *JAMA Pediatrics* 176 (7): 635–636. https://doi.org/10.1001/jamapediatrics. 2022.0791.

Lee, G., Zou, N., Durand, D. et al. (2023). A systematic review on changes in suicide attempts in pediatric population after the start of the COVID-19 pandemic, Journal of the American Academy of Child & Adolescent Psychiatry. 62 (10): https://doi. org/10.1016/j.jaac.2023.09.492.

MacCormack, J.K. and Lindquist, K.A. (2019). Feeling hangry? When hunger is conceptualized as emotion. *Emotion* 19 (2): 301–319. https://doi.org/10.1037/ emo0000422.

Madigan, S. (2023). Global changes in risk factors for child and adolescent mental distress through the lens of meta-analytic research. *Journal of the American Academy of Child & Adolescent Psychiatry* 62 (10): https://doi.org/10.1016/ j.jaac.2023.07.644.

Madigan, S., Racine, N., and Vaillancourt, T. (2023). Changes in depression and anxiety among children and adolescents from before to during the COVID-19 pandemic: a systematic review and meta-analysis. *JAMA Pediatrics* 177 (6): 567–581. https://doi.org/10.1001/jamapediatrics.2023.0846.

Maiyuran, H., Abdallah, M., Nakamura, C.M. et al. (2023). The impact of social isolation on adolescent psychiatric patients during the COVID-19 pandemic. *Journal of the American Academy of Child & Adolescent Psychiatry* 61 (10): https://doi.org/10.1016/j.jaac.2023.07.670.

Melamed, E., Rydberg, L., Ambrose, A.F. et al. (2023). Multidisciplinary collaborative consensus guidance statement on the assessment and treatment of neurologic sequelae in patients with post-acute sequelae of SARS-CoV-2 infection (PASC). *PM&R: The Journal of Injury, Function, and Rehabilitation* 15 (5): 640–662. https://doi.org/10.1002/pmrj.12976.

Munez, J., Walia, G.S., Winch, A., and Grados, M.A. (2023). A time-series analysis of risk factors for catatonia in youth during the COVID-19 pandemic. *Journal of the American Academy of Child & Adolescent Psychiatry* 62 (105): https://doi. org/10.1016/j.jaac.2023.09.310.

Murthy, V. (2021). *Protecting Youth Mental Health: The U.S.* Surgeon General's Advisory. https://www.hhs.gov/sites/default/files/surgeon-general-youth-mental-health-advisory.pdf.

Nguyen, J., Lee, J., and Hite, A. (2023). The impacts of the COVID-19 pandemic on symptoms of child and adolescent psychiatric patients by race. *Journal of the*

American Academy of Child & Adolescent Psychiatry 62 (10): https://doi.org/10.1016/j.jaac.2023.07.673.

Nicodemo, M., Spreghini, M.R., Manco, M. et al. (2021). Childhood obesity and COVID-19 lockdown: remarks on eating habits of patients enrolled in a food-education program. *Nutrients* 13 (2): 383. https://doi.org/10.3390/nu13020383.

Richter-Levin, G. and Xu, L. (2018). How could stress lead to major depressive disorder? *IBRO Reports* 22 (4): 38–43. https://doi.org/10.1016/j.ibror.2018.04.001. Erratum in: IBRO Rep. 2020 Dec 10;9:324. PMID: 30155523; PMCID: PMC6111061.

Sandbank, M., Bottema-Beutel, K., Crowley, S. et al. (2020). Project AIM: autism intervention meta-analysis for studies of young children. *Psychological Bulletin* 146 (1): 1–29.

Schindel, B.J., Gornik, A.E., Ngur, M.R. et al. (2023). The impact of the COVID-19 pandemic on suicide risk screenings within pediatric neurodevelopmental and related clinics. *Journal of the American Academy of Child & Adolescent Psychiatry* 62 (105): https://doi.org/10.1016/j.jaac.2023.09.445.

Silva Filho, O., Gonçalves Camacho, K., Fernandes Nehab, M. et al. (2023). Children and adolescents' behavior and learning during the Covid-19 pandemic in Brazil: caregivers' perceptions. *Journal of the American Academy of Child & Adolescent Psychiatry* 62 (10): https://doi.org/10.1016/j.jaac.2023.09.231.

Vaccarro, D.H., Zhang, Z., Wang, Y. et al. (2023). Characteristics of adolescent anorexia nervosa before and during the COVID-19 pandemic. *Journal of the American Academy of Child & Adolescent Psychiatry* 62 (10): https://doi.org/10.1016/j.jaac.2023.09.052.

Wei, C., Floyd, J., Mazzaferro, M., and Duarte, C.S. (2023). The COVID-19 parents coping intervention study: pilot testing an mHealth mindfulness program. *Journal of the American Academy of Child & Adolescent Psychiatry* 62 (10): https://doi.org/10.1016/j.jaac.2023.09.387.

Wergeland, G., Mowatt Haugland, B.S., Sørebø Danielsen, Y., and Hysing, M. (2023). Coping strategies, stress responses, and internalizing symptoms in a clinical sample youth aged 13-19 during COVID-19. *Journal of the American Academy of Child & Adolescent Psychiatry* 62 (10): https://doi.org/10.1016/j.jaac.2023.09.243.

Wong, A.C., Devason, A.S., Umana, I.C. et al. (2023). Serotonin reduction in post-acute sequelae of viral infection. *Cell* 186 (22): 4851–4867. https://doi.org/10.1016/j.cell.2023.09.013.

Xie, Y., Choi, T., and Al-Aly, Z. (2023). Association of treatment with nirmatrelvir and the risk of post-COVID-19 condition. *JAMA Internal Medicine* 183 (6): 554–564. https://doi.org/10.1001/jamainternalmed.2023.0743.

Yedia, M., Serizawa, R., Harris, B. et al. (2023). Trends in ADHD screening requests before and during the COVID-19 pandemic. *Journal of the American Academy of Child & Adolescent Psychiatry* 62 (10): https://doi.org/10.1016/j.jaac.2023.09.167.

12

Reference Tables

Table 12.1 Commonly prescribed psychotropic medication for children (<18 years).

Medication	Condition	Minimum age for approval
Fluoxetine	Major depressive disorder (MDD) Obsessive-compulsive disorder (OCD) Social anxiety disorder Panic disorder	8 years and older for MDD 7 years and older for OCD and social anxiety disorder 10 years and older for panic disorder
Sertraline	Major depressive disorder Obsessive-compulsive disorder Panic disorder Social anxiety disorder	6 years and older
Escitalopram	Major depressive disorder Generalized anxiety disorder (GAD)	12 years and older
Duloxetine	Major depressive disorder Generalized anxiety disorder	7 years and older
Aripiprazole	Bipolar disorder Schizophrenia	10 years and older for bipolar disorder 13 years and older for schizophrenia
Risperidone	Bipolar disorder Schizophrenia	10 years and older for bipolar disorder 13 years and older for schizophrenia
Quetiapine	Bipolar disorder Schizophrenia	10 years and older for bipolar disorder 13 years and older for schizophrenia

(Continued)

Table 12.1 (Continued)

Medication	Condition	Minimum age for approval
Olanzapine	Bipolar disorder Schizophrenia	13 years and older
Lithium	Bipolar disorder	12 years and older
Valproate	Bipolar disorder	10 years and older

Source: Adapted from Lorberg et al. (2019), pp. 6–7.

Table 12.2 Potential interactions between psychiatric medications and common COVID-19 treatments.

Psychiatric drug class	Examples	Potential interactions with nirmatrelvir/ritonavir (paxlovid)
Antidepressants	Selective serotonin reuptake inhibitors (SSRIs), serotonin-norepinephrine reuptake inhibitors (SNRIs), tricyclic antidepressants (TCAs), bupropion, mirtazapine trazodone	• Can take with citalopram, fluoxetine, fluvoxamine, paroxetine, sertraline • Decreases bupropion levels • Increases desvenlafaxine, mirtazapine and trazodone levels
Antipsychotics	Clozapine, haloperidol, olanzapine, pimozide, quetiapine, risperidone	• Olanzapine is preferred • Increases levels of haloperidol and quetiapine • Contraindicated with clozapine, lurasidone, and pimozide
Anxiolytics	Benzodiazepines	• Avoid combining with midazolam or triazolam • Increases alprazolam, clonazepam, diazepam, and chlordiazepoxide
Mood stabilizers	Carbamazepine, lamotrigine, lithium, valproate	• Contraindicated in people taking carbamazepine • Reduces lamotrigine concentration • No interaction with lithium • May lower valproate

Source: Adapted from Boppana et al. (2023).

Table 12.3 Common medications for the treatment of agitation.

Medication	Dose range
Benzodiazepines	
Lorazepam	0.5–1 mg by mouth, intramuscular, or intravenous
Diazepam	5–10 mg by mouth, intramuscular, or intravenous
Antipsychotics	
Haloperidol	2–10 mg by mouth, intramuscular, or intravenous (0.5–2 mg in older adults)
Risperidone	1–2 mg by mouth (0.25–2 mg in older adults)
Olanzapine	10–20 mg by mouth or intramuscular (2.5–10 mg in older adults)
Other agents	
Clonidine	0.1 mg by mouth
Diphenhydramine	25–50 mg by mouth, intramuscular, or intravenous
Gabapentin	100–200 mg by mouth

Table 12.4 Commonly used benzodiazepines.

Drug	Half-life (hr)	Onset	Significant metabolites
Lorazepam	10–20	Intermediate	No
Diazepam	20–100	Fast	Yes
Alprazolam	12–15	Fast	Yes
Clonazepam	30–40	Intermediate	Yes
Temazepam	10–20	Intermediate	No

Source: Peng et al. (2022) and Management of Substance Use Disorders Work Group (2021), p. 32.

Table 12.5 Starting and stopping an antidepressant.

Starting dose	Start with the usual starting dose in depression. May start with half the usual starting dose in anxiety.
Titration	Can increase dose every two to four weeks until symptoms are in remission or you have reached the maximum dose. (Fluoxetine is an exception: wait four weeks between dose changes due to its long half-life.)
Tapering off	Most antidepressants require gradual taper with the exception of fluoxetine, which can be stopped. Gradually lower the dose every two to four weeks.

Table 12.6 Benzodiazepine prescribing information.

Starting dose	Start with the usual starting dose.
Titration	Can increase every 3–14 days until symptom control is achieved.
Maximum dose	Variable; aim for the lowest effective dose.
Tapering off	Depends on frequency/length of treatment. Taper can last from a minimum of two weeks to six months or longer.

Table 12.7 Antipsychotic side effects.

- Movement issues like tremors, stiffness, agitation
- Tardive dyskinesia
- Sedation/sleepiness
- Drooling
- Neuroleptic malignant syndrome
- Dizziness and blood pressure drop when standing
- Myocarditis
- Weight gain
- Dry mouth
- Constipation
- Urinary retention
- Increased risk of arrhythmia, sudden cardiac death
- Blurred vision

Source: Adapted from World Health Organization (2016), p. 42.

Table 12.8 SSRI/SNRI side effects.

- Dry mouth
- Heart rhythm changes
- Suicidal thoughts
- Weight gain
- Greater risk of bleeding
- Sexual dysfunction
- Feeling nervous or anxious
- Sleepiness
- Headache
- Nausea, vomiting, or diarrhea
- Insomnia

Source: NHS (2021a) and World Health Organization (2016), p. 29.

Table 12.9   Valproate side effects.

Common

  Weight gain

  Nausea

  Diarrhea

  Tremor

  Lethargy

  Sedation

  Dizziness

  Ataxia

Uncommon

  Polycystic ovary syndrome (PCOS)

  Rash

  Hair loss

Rare

  Hepatic insufficiency

  Thrombocytopenia

  Pancreatitis

  Severe cutaneous reactions

Source: NHS (2021b) and World Health Organization (2016), p. 43.

Table 12.10   Carbamazepine side effects.

Common

  Nausea, vomiting

  Dizziness

  Nystagmus

  Sedation

  Blurred vision, double vision

  Ataxia

Uncommon

  Hyponatremia

  Rash

  Confusion

  Leucopenia

(Continued)

Table 12.10   (Continued)

Rare

Severe cutaneous reactions

Agranulocytosis

Aplastic anemia

Atrioventricular block

Hepatitis

Renal dysfunction

Hypersensitivity to anticonvulsants

Source: Mayo Clinic (2024a) and World Health Organization (2016), p. 43.

Table 12.11   Lithium side effects.

Common

Nausea, vomiting

Diarrhea

Hypothyroidism

Dizziness

Tremor

Dry mouth

Increased thirst

Uncommon

Fainting

Muscle weakness

Diabetes insipidus

Water retention

Rare

Seizures

Cardiac arrhythmia

Blurred vision

Renal dysfunction

Coma

Source: Heyda et al. (2024), Mayo Clinic (2024b) and World Health Organization (2016), p. 43.

Table 12.12 Common COVID-19 medications and associated psychiatric side effects.

Medication	Psychiatric side effects
Corticosteroids	Mood swings
	Agitation
	Insomnia
	Psychosis
Hydroxychloroquine and Chloroquine	Mood changes
	Anxiety
	Psychosis
Interferons	Concentration difficulty
	Depression
	Irritability

Source: Adapted from Bilbul et al. (2020).

References

Bilbul, M., Paparone, P., Kim, A.M. et al. (2020). Psychopharmacology of COVID-19. *Psychosomatics* 61 (5): 411–427. https://doi.org/10.1016/j.psym.2020.05.006.

Boppana, U., Leonard, T.S., Jolayemi, A. et al. (2023). Drug-drug interactions between COVID-19 treatments and psychotropic medications: an updated study. *Cureus* 15 (12): e50469. https://doi.org/10.7759/cureus.50469.

Heyda, S.A., Avula, A., and Swoboda, H.D. (2024). Lithium toxicity. In: *StatPearls (Internet)*. Treasure Island, FL: StatPearls Publishing.

Lorberg, B., Davico, C., Martsenkovskyi, D., and Vitiello, B. (2019). Principles in using psychotropic medication in children and adolescents. In: *IACAPAP e-Textbook of Child and Adolescent Mental Health* (ed. J.M. Rey and A. Martin), 6–7. Geneva: International Association for Child and Adolescent Psychiatry and Allied Professions.

Management of Substance Use Disorders Work Group (2021). *VA/DoD Clinical Practice Guideline for the Management of Substance Use Disorders*, 32. Washington, DC: Department of Veterans Affairs and Department of Defense.

Mayo Clinic (2024a). Carbamazepine (oral route). https://www.mayoclinic.org/drugs-supplements/carbamazepine-oral-route/side-effects/drg-20062739?p=1 (accessed 16 July 2024).

Mayo Clinic (2024b). Lithium (oral route). https://www.mayoclinic.org/drugs-supplements/lithium-oral-route/side-effects/drg-20064603 (accessed 16 July 2024).

NHS (2021a). Side effects – antidepressants. https://www.nhs.uk/mental-health/talking-therapies-medicine-treatments/medicines-and-psychiatry/antidepressants/side-effects (accessed 16 July 2024).

NHS (2021b). Valproic acid. https://www.nhs.uk/medicines/valproic-acid (accessed 16 July 2024).

Peng, L., Morford, K.L., and Levander, X.A. (2022). Benzodiazepines and related sedatives. *Medical Clinics of North America* 106 (1): 113–129. https://doi.org/10.1016/j.mcna.2021.08.012.

World Health Organization (2016). mhGAP Intervention guide for mental, neurological and substance use disorders in non-specialized health settings: mental health Gap Action Programme (mhGAP). Version 2.0. 29–43.

Index

a

acceptance and commitment therapy (ACT) 43–45, 75, 97
acetaminophen 61
acquired immune response 70
ACT *see* acceptance and commitment therapy (ACT)
acute confusion 12
acute onset 57
acute respiratory distress syndrome (ARDS) 54, 178
acute stress reactions/acute stress responses 89–90
Addison's disease 176
adverse childhood experiences (ACE) 125
Age-Friendly Health Systems (AFHS) Initiative of the Institute for Healthcare Improvement (IHI) 56
agoraphobia 21, 234
alprazolam 119
American Academy of Physical Medicine and Rehabilitation (AAPM&R) 224
Ampligen 157
amygdala 87, 172, 174
angiotensin-converting enzyme-2 (ACE2) receptor 142
angular gyrus 39
anorexia nervosa (AN) 238
anterior cingulate gyrus 39
antianxiety medications 186
anticoagulant 155
antidepressants 74, 186

doses 253
medications 10
anti-inflammatory drugs 12, 77
anti-inflammatory proteins 37
anti-platelet agents 149
antipsychotic medications 10, 130, 185–186
antipsychotics 36, 54, 61, 80, 185
antisocial personality disorder 176
antiviral drugs 12
anxiety 85, 171
assisting a person with anxiety 102–106
brain structures 86
with COVID-19 and chronic health conditions 95–96
disorders 85
GAD 92–93
OCD 93, 105
panic disorder 93–94
social anxiety disorder 93
specific phobias 91–92
disproportionate impact, of COVID-19 89
experiences of 94–95
neurobiology of 85–88
stress responses, to trauma and loss
acute stress reactions 89–90
grief 90
prolonged grief disorder 90–91
PTSD 90
symptoms 16
treatment of
environmental modifications 101
lifestyle modifications 98

Printed and bound by CPI Group (UK) Ltd, Croydon, CR0 4YY

04/11/2024

14585585-0001